THE CONSTITUTION IN WARTIME

Beyond Alarmism and Complacency

Mark Tushnet, editor

Duke University Press

Durham & London 2005

© 2005 Duke University Press

All rights reserved

Printed in the United States of America on acid-free paper ∞

Typeset in Carter & Cone Galliard by Keystone Typesetting, Inc.

Library of Congress Cataloging-in-Publication Data and republication

acknowledgments appear on the last printed page of this book.

THE CONSTITUTION IN WARTIME

CONSTITUTIONAL CONFLICTS

A Series with the Institute of Bill of Rights Law
at the College of William & Mary

Series editors: Neal Devins and Mark Graber

To the memory of John Hart Ely

CONTENTS

Introduction

——◆◆◆——

Mark Tushnet

Most recent public discussion of the U.S. Constitution and war—both the war on terrorism and the war with Iraq—has been dominated by two voices: alarmists who see in every action taken by the Bush administration a portent of gross restrictions on the civil liberties of all Americans, and administration shills who see in those actions entirely reasonable, perhaps even too moderate, accommodations of civil liberties to the new realities of national security. Books with titles like *Lost Liberties: Ashcroft and the Assault on Personal Freedom*[1] and *The War on Our Freedoms: Civil Liberties in an Age of Terrorism*[2] are countered by books with titles like *Treason: Liberal Treachery from the Cold War to the War on Terrorism*[3] and *Useful Idiots: How Liberals Got It Wrong in the Cold War and Still Blame America First*.[4]

Alarmists and shills may perform valuable political services, rallying the (domestic) troops already on their sides. And indeed, the competition between shrill voices might actually benefit the nation. Often political leaders might prefer that their initiatives—and their oversights—be ignored, but alarmists and shills bring public attention to the leaders' actions. Even as they degrade public discourse, the alarmists and the shills might promote better policy outcomes by forcing political leaders to address issues they might prefer to duck.

Yet whatever their contributions to the policy-making process, alarmists and shills contribute rather little to public understanding of the real constitutional issues raised by war. As September 11, 2001, recedes in time, scholars are beginning to speak in more modulated tones. Some may be nervous about the Bush administration's actions, but do not speak in the outraged tones of the alarmists. Some may be nervous because the polarization of public discourse may lead the public to believe, erroneously, that anything not hypercritical of the Bush administration's actions amounts to an endorsement of its positions.

This book presents initial reflections in what might be called this second generation of more temperate responses to the Bush administration's declaring a war on terrorism. Written from a variety of perspectives in law and political science, the essays share several characteristics that distinguish them from the first set of responses to the policies adopted and advocated after the September 11 attacks.

The first responses were rather obvious reflections of their authors' *prior* policy preferences. Civil libertarians who did not trust Attorney General John Ashcroft before September 11 treated the administration's policies and proposals as just another example of its insensitivity to questions of civil liberties. Administration supporters, in turn, tended to have thought — before September 11 — that national policy with respect to crime generally and the threat of terrorism specifically placed too much value on civil liberties and too little on deterrence and punishment. In addition, the first responses were markedly short on analysis. A smattering of references to the past, particularly to the internment of Japanese-Americans during the Second World War, came close to exhausting the examination of history. Loose statements about the need to balance liberty and security, and about the president's role in shaping public debate for good or ill, came close to exhausting the examination of politics.

The second generation of scholarship on war and the Constitution, as represented in this collection, differs in several ways. For one thing, the effects of prior positions are, if not entirely absent, damped down. People with civil libertarian inclinations remain suspicious of the Bush administration's initiatives, but they take seriously the possibility that prior tradeoffs between liberty and security should be reconsidered. People already suspicious of the extent to which constitutional law protected civil liberties remain inclined to accept more security-oriented policies, but they acknowledge the possibility that those policies do indeed pose threats to civil liberties properly understood.

In addition, second-generation scholarship brings the insights of existing studies of constitutionalism and policy making to bear on the development of policy during wartime. One way to put this point is that second-generation scholarship treats constitutional policy making during wartime as an *example* of constitutional policy making generally, not as an exception to it. The aim is to deal with questions about constitutionalism during wartime in just the way one deals with questions about constitutionalism in other circumstances. (The exception here, of course, is precisely those studies taking up the claim by some political theorists that emergency situations are discontinuous from ordinary political life — and even here, the discussion is cast in terms of political theory, not immediate policy preferences.) So, for example, second-generation scholars rely on Madisonian ideas about "ambition countering ambition" to examine the way in which the president and Congress interact in making constitutional policy during wartime. Or they invoke rational choice theories or behavioral law and economics, to account for the ways in which policy emerges from the preferences of representatives and, ultimately, the people who elect them.

The historical sensibility of second-generation scholars is deeper, too. On the surface level, those scholars have expanded their attention from a few selected examples to the wider scope of American history. For example, the picture of civil liberties during the Second World War that emerges when one examines all relevant decisions from 1941 to 1945 (and after) is decidedly more complex than the picture one gets when internment is the only policy brought into view. Some second-generation scholars attempt to discern broad patterns of response to the constitutional issues posed by war, using current conditions to raise questions about the precise nature of the constitutionalism that runs through American history. Here the work fits into a literature on the political traditions and character of the American people.

Finally, second-generation scholarship uses the occurrence of war to reflect on the political theory of liberal constitutionalism. The most obvious examples are studies that take up the question, Is war an *exception* to the Constitution, or an example of when adhering to the Constitution is particularly important? The thesis that war is an exception to constitutionalism is jarring, particularly because of its association with the German (and Nazi) political theorist Carl Schmitt, but second-generation studies at least take the thesis seriously. On a different level, second-generation studies examine the implications of integrating war into ordinary constitutional theory.

The essays in this book touch on nearly all the themes in second-generation scholarship that I have identified. They fall into two main categories, the first addressing constitutional questions about war and civil liberties (and incidentally about the effectiveness of courts as defenders of civil liberties in wartime), the second addressing questions about war and the allocation of power between the president and Congress.

Part I sets the stage with three essays. Mark Brandon introduces many of the book's themes, setting them in the context of reflections on national character, patriotism, and political theory. Brandon asks, for example, Is law silent during wartime? And he uses the political theory he describes to question the way in which the national government is structured to address wartime conditions. War can strain republican government in many ways — by requiring secrecy, for example, and by enhancing the power of military officials who are ordinarily under tight civilian control. Brandon stresses the weakness of Congress more than the authors of other essays in this collection do. Brandon's deepest claim is that wartime conditions — which he emphasizes might characterize far more of the history of the United States than we might initially think — push a nation toward a statism that is, Brandon argues, inconsistent with constitutionalism itself.

I examine two questions in my contribution to part I. First, pursuing in some greater detail questions raised by Brandon, I ask, In what sense are we in wartime circumstances today? Second, assuming that wartime conditions are likely to generate extraordinary policy responses, how should those responses be accommodated in the way we think about the Constitution? Are they constitutional because the Constitution provides room for extraordinary policy responses in extraordinary conditions, or are they extralegal, neither constitutional nor unconstitutional? And if the latter, what does it mean to say that policies are extralegal? Eric Posner and Adrian Vermeule place the arguments of the alarmists and the shills in an analytic framework, blending public choice theory and behavioral law and economics. They pry out the assumptions that underlie the claims of the alarmists, in particular, and express skepticism about whether those assumptions are fair representations of social and political reality.

Part II deals with war and civil liberties. The alarmists' position is clear: war almost inevitably leads to the adoption of policies that undermine civil liberties in pursuit of a domestic security that can never be purchased by violations of basic rights, and the Bush administration's policies illustrate this danger. The shills' position is clear as well: war almost inevitably leads overly cautious politicians to refrain from taking the steps necessary to ensure domestic security, although astute leaders will avoid inappropriate concerns about civil liberties and adopt the policies that are needed to defend the nation, and fortunately George W. Bush is such a leader. The essays in part II try to avoid direct confrontation with the policies adopted by the Bush administration, to reflect upon the more general claims made about war and civil liberties.

Each essay reaches conclusions specific to its particular focus, but one overarching message emerges from them all: The story of war and civil liberties is more complicated than either the alarmists or the shills tell us. Mark Graber argues that wartime conditions have sometimes produced *increases* in civil rights and civil liberties, particularly when the war is fought on ideological premises that dictate advances in civil rights and civil liberties, not their limitation. The notion that law is silent during wartime, I argue, rests on observations better explained by two interlinked problems: decision makers act with imperfect information, and they do so within bureaucracies that generate bureaucratic pathologies not unique to wartime.

Part III turns to the allocation of power in wartime. Again, alarmists and shills often agree that power flows to the executive branch during wartime. Crisis in general may well expand the power of the national government as a whole, although it is worth emphasizing—as the essays in part II suggest—that expanded national power can be used to advance civil liberties as well as restrict them. A national government with greater power might use this power to curb the power of *private* organizations that might discriminate against dissenters and others.[5]

Like the essays in part II, those in part III are informed by historical practice. Indeed, one of their general themes, it might be said, is that understanding historical practice provides a better way of understanding the relations between Congress and the president in wartime than does any other technique of constitutional interpretation. The authors show that neither the text nor the original understanding of the distribution of power between the president and Congress in wartime is clear. They also emphasize how much of our constitutional law of separation of powers in wartime has emerged not from the courts, but from the interactions between the political branches. We have a great deal of (complicated) practice, without much of a theory that can give us a grasp on the problems, or even some sense of how to think about the significance of constitutional development outside the courts. The constitutional law of separation of powers in wartime and the politics of separation of powers are so intimately intertwined, the essays suggest, that we should think of this aspect of constitutional law *as* the product of politics rather than of any sort of distinctively legal analysis.

William Treanor's essay opens part III by examining the treatment of warmaking power *outside* the courts, in the interpretations offered by Congress and the presidency, and in the interactions between those institutions. Politics, Treanor suggests, places limits on the structural transformations that wartime can produce. Power may flow toward the executive during wartime, but the flow need not be inevitable nor strikingly large. Politics, not some deep force involving military operations, drives the flow of power within the national government.

Richard Pildes and Samuel Issacharoff bring the courts into the picture, but to the same end. They provide a careful legal analysis of judicial decisions in the past to show that courts have typically placed heavy weight on the degree to which Congress has approved executive actions in assessing the constitutionality of presidential initiatives. Departing from the general practice in these essays, Pildes and Issacharoff apply their analysis to recent controversies, and show that the courts have applied the same principles. The picture they paint, then, is not one of power flowing to the executive over congressional objection, but one of agreement between the branches on how to allocate power during wartime — an agreement that is contingent upon the persistence of wartime conditions and, of course, on political compromises between the president and Congress.

Peter Spiro's essay introduces yet another player in the political process — the international legal community. He argues that international actors, and international law, have begun to exert constraints on domestic policy making, again through what is probably best understood as a political process.

We conclude in part IV with essays that expand our focus even more broadly. David Luban pursues a contrast touched on in some of the other essays: the tension between using the model of war and using the model of law to respond to terrorism. Luban argues that the two models are fundamentally incompatible, and that the Bush administration's effort to "mix and match" elements of each model is more threatening, as a matter of legal theory, than either model on its own. We conclude with a provocative essay by Sotirios Barber and James Fleming, who start with what seems at the outset to be a vigorous attack on the very legitimacy of the Bush administration because of the way in which it took office, through what the authors believe to be a lawless decision by the Supreme Court. Then, in what might seem a surprising turn, Barber and Fleming suggest that the Supreme Court's decision might be defended as a way of preserving the nation's unity. They then pursue that thought in a discussion of whether the Bush administration's actions in the war on terrorism might be defensible in exactly the same way — as lawless but justified by the very idea that the United States is, and must remain, a nation. This essay returns us to the theme of sovereignty introduced by Mark Brandon, thereby demonstrating how the issues that each essay focuses on are only aspects of more general concerns about constitutionalism in wartime.

NOTES

1 Cynthia Brown, ed., 2003.
2 Richard C. Leone, ed., 2003.
3 Ann Coulter, 2003.
4 Mona Charen, 2003.
5 The Supreme Court's vigorous enforcement of the rights of Jehovah's Witnesses during the Second World War was provoked by incidents of widespread *unofficial* attacks on Witnesses after the Court upheld the power of state governments to require them to pledge their allegiance to the flag. See West Virginia Board of Education v. Barnette, 319 U.S. 624 (1943), overruling Minersville School District v. Gobitis, 310 U.S. 586 (1940). For the attacks on the Witnesses, see, e.g., Shawn Francis Peters, *Judging Jehovah's Witnesses: Religious Persecution and the Dawn of the Rights Revolution* (2002).

PART I

WAR AND THE AMERICAN CONSTITUTIONAL ORDER

Mark E. Brandon

HISTORY OF AMERICAN MILITARY CONFLICT

The United States is a regime founded on military conflict. This is to say more than that the United States relied on a war of secession to gain independence from Britain. It is to say also that the United States has resorted frequently in its history to military force. From the Revolution to the present, armed forces of the United States have participated in eighty-four distinct, significant engagements.[1] Of these, six were declared wars, ten were undeclared wars, and the rest were significant actions (including campaigns against Indians). In aggregate, these wars and actions have occurred in 182 of the 228 years since 1776 (80 percent of the life of the nation). In the last quarter of the eighteenth century, there were twelve years in which the United States *did not* use its military according to my classification (or 48 percent of that period); in the nineteenth century, there were twenty-eight such years (28 percent); in the twentieth century, there were but six such years (6 percent); so far in the twenty-first century, there have been no such years. Thus, the United States has been at war or engaged in significant military action for most of its corporate life. Military action has been such a substantial part of the history of the nation that it is not unfair to characterize the United States as a warrior state.

I should be clear about my meaning. The warrior state is not necessarily a martial state. Hence, the term need not connote a regime that glorifies war or the military, nor one in which the military controls the administration of state, nor one that comprehensively organizes and regulates society for predominantly militarist purposes, akin to Sparta in ancient Peloponnesus. In fact, it is one of the distinctive aspects of the American experience that the nation's military actions have tended neither to arise from nor to provoke a crisis; that is, the nation has typically used military force under conditions in which (1) the survival of the order is not at risk and (2) the order can simultaneously fight and maintain a domestic life that appears to be "normal." Nor need we question in each instance the validity of the nation's motives or its reasons for action. In using the term "warrior state," therefore, I have in mind merely a regime for which the use of military force is a regular aspect of the nation's life. My aim is to reflect on the possible constitutional implications of a warrior state, no matter how well intended it might be.

CONSTITUTIONAL IMPLICATIONS

We may roughly characterize a constitutionalist order as one that includes (1) institutions authorized by and accountable to the people (both in the making of the order and in the regular operation of government); (2) some notion of limited government (whether by the designation of purposes for governmental action, the specification of rights, or the allocation of authority among institutions); and (3) rule of law (which connotes the regularization of processes by which public norms are made and applied). Neither war nor the military that wages it is inherently anti-constitutionalist. In fact, Alexander Hamilton offered a military justification for ratifying the proposed Constitution of the United States. He bemoaned "the imbecility of our government" under the Articles of Confederation. Hamilton obsessed that the country was facing "impending anarchy." As military weakness was at the heart of this crisis, he said, defense was the linchpin of the solution. Moreover, he insisted, the power of defense was illimitable. War, or the power to wage it, was a comprehensive "unconfined authority" on which the success and survival of the extended commercial republic depended.[2]

But as even Hamilton sometimes conceded, strength alone was an insufficient justification for the Constitution. Put differently, if war (or the military) can create or conserve conditions for making or maintaining a constitutionalist politics, it cannot establish constitutional authority.[3] The reason rests in the distinction between power and authority. Hamilton comprehended something of this distinction when he posited that the proposed Constitution was an "experiment" in whether it were possible "to establish good government through reflection and choice," instead of through "accident and force."[4] In a constitutionalist order, then, the exercise of power must be authorized, justified, and constrained. Power alone is inadequate. Clinton Rossiter pushed the point further. "[T]he complex system of government of the democratic, constitutional state," he wrote, "is essentially designed to function under normal, peaceful conditions. . . . 'Democracy is a child of peace and cannot live apart from its mother[.]' . . . 'War is a contradiction of all that democracy implies. War is not and cannot be democratic.'"[5]

There is, therefore, an ineluctable and potentially dangerous tension between military force and constitutional government. This tension makes for a vexing dilemma. Although raising and deploying armed forces may be indispensable for sustaining a secure environment for constitutionalist politics, creating a safe place and constructing safe roles for military institutions are among the most troublesome challenges of a constitutionalist order. Continual military engagement can pose special dangers, because it can create and perpetuate conditions that are uncongenial to constitutionalism. In this essay, I consider five areas in which such conditions might hold — national ethos, rights, republican government, the allocation of institutional authority, and sovereignty — and I suggest why a constitutionalist might worry that the conditions are present in the American order.

National Ethos

Doubtless the warrior state is inconsistent with the self-image of most Americans and with the standard proclamations of their public officials. Even in time of war, most politicians insist that the history, purpose, and ethos of the nation are peaceful.[6] It is not mysterious that Americans would want to see themselves in this way. The normative precepts of constitutionalism presuppose a degree of peace — sufficient to sustain reflection and choice — in the regular affairs of the order; if Americans aim to be constitutionalist, therefore, it makes sense that they should see their motives as peaceful. Still, how to reconcile their aspiration with the nation's behavior?

One way to do so is to construct the world in terms of "us" and "them" or, somewhat differently, in terms of "friend" and "enemy."[7] There are many ways of dividing the world on these terms—national, ideological, economic, religious, racial, and others. Often the conflict is viewed as implicating competing ways of life. But whatever the content of a particular classification, it can be useful, not simply as a description of the world or of competing aspirations, but also because it protects against the disabling or disorienting effects of psychic dissonance. If we have acted in warlike ways, it is because "others" have been responsible. Those others have been— are—dangerous. They have provoked us. They have threatened us. Or worst, they have physically attacked us. If we respond militarily, our behavior is not inconsistent with, but rather attempts to preserve, the ethos of peace that genuinely defines us.

The psychic incentives for this logic have contributed also to a kind of moralism in American foreign policy. This disposition is not confined to the kind of morality represented by the internationalist diplomatic agendas of Presidents Wilson and Carter. Hence, it is not coextensive with what Robert Osgood characterizes as a pure form of "idealism" (whose psychological antonym is "egoism").[8] The moralist disposition I have in mind extends to a more primal (and conflictual) moralism whose constituent elements are good and evil. In the American context, this form of moralism surely has cultural roots in Puritanism, which posited the existence of a covenantal relationship between political community and God. For American Puritans, evil was in them—in all of us—as fallen creatures. Their struggle, simultaneously humble and arrogant, was to make themselves worthy of the beneficence that the Maker of the Universe had generously bestowed on them, if not on others.[9]

By the second half of the twentieth century, of course, Americans were not saddled with doubt about their worthiness. We can see the lightened load in Jimmy Carter's repeated invocations of the goodness and decency of the American people. It is not that the concept of evil was unimportant to Mr. Carter, certainly not for the individual who might be tempted to sin; but most of President Carter's public moralism focused on the aspiration to goodness, without attempting to balance it with references to evil.[10] In the context of foreign policy, then, Mr. Carter could unashamedly pronounce: "It is a new world that calls for a new American foreign policy—a policy based on constant decency in its values and on optimism in our historical vision."[11] Part of President Reagan's rhetorical talent was his ability to re-store allusions to evil without calling into question the basic goodness of America. Hence, he could insist that the United States had realized the Puritan aspiration to "a shining city on a hill" and could depict the Soviet Union as an "evil empire."[12] George W. Bush has retained the simple struc-ture of Mr. Reagan's moral rhetoric but adapted invocations of evil to contemporary events.[13]

Allusion to evil is politically potent because it reflects a particular psycho-logical form: the patriotic personality. Osgood describes the form in this way:

> A citizen's dependence upon his nation assumes a distinct intimacy because he confers upon the object of his allegiance the attributes of a person so closely identified with his own personality that he virtually acquires a second self, in whose behalf he can feel friendly, hostile, gen-erous, selfish, confident, afraid, proud, or humiliated almost as poi-gnantly as he would feel these emotions for himself in his relations with other individuals. However, the conscience of this vicarious personality, unlike the private conscience, is relieved by the sanction of patriotism, so that a citizen can manage with a sense of complete moral consistency to combine lofty altruism toward his own nation with extreme egoism to-ward other nations and thereby actively support a standard of ethics in foreign relations which he would not dream of tolerating in his private dealings.[14]

In short, the patriotic personality conjoins the two elements of Osgood's antinomy — idealism and egoism — without fully integrating them. The dis-tinction between friend and enemy reinforces and stabilizes the segregated elements of this personality.

The bifurcation of political personality is useful. It promotes the cohesion and attachment necessary for sustaining a voluntary political order com-mitted to resolving conflict through reflection and choice. At the same time, it can both justify an aggressive posture toward others and diffuse the psy-chic dissonance of this posture (as against the image of peacefulness) by rationalizing aggression as self-defense. What, then, makes the personality and the ethos that reflects it problematic from a constitutionalist stand-point? The primary danger is that it is almost perfectly rational even as it is segregated. That is, it may create a too-perfect enclosure, converting attachment to *patria* into an article of faith and rendering the peaceful self-image essentially nonfalsifiable. This combination can effectively make the citizenry incapable of judging possible deviations from the image of peacefulness. Those citizens who presume to judge will risk being labeled "the enemy," or at least complicit with the enemy.[15] What follows is that even if the peaceful self-image is a desirable aspiration and even if it is an accurate description of some (or most) events, the image will cease to be useful for constitutionalist purposes, because it will lose the capacity to constrain or direct action. In short, it will justify almost any behavior, and no one will be the wiser. Ironically, therefore, although a form of nationalism can be useful for creating and maintaining constitutionalist institutions, a comprehensively nationalist ethos can weaken the constitutionalist character of those institutions.

Rights

Conventional wisdom posits that in time of war, rights tend to give way to power. Rossiter, for example, argues that any state, even a constitutional state, will resist its own physical destruction and will do so by any means at its disposal, even anti-constitutionalist means. Hence in time of war, "[c]ivil liberties, free enterprise, constitutionalism, and government by debate and compromise" give way to needs of state.[16] So framed, this is an empirical claim. I shall argue that it is overstated. Still, there is enough evidence supporting it that in a nation at war the status of rights — whether civil liberties, personal liberties, or rights to property or of enterprise — might be worrisome from the standpoint of constitutionalism. This worry aside for now, one question is this: To the extent that the empirical claim is accurate, what might justify it?

From within American constitutional discourse, there are two prominent ways of approaching the question. The first is to invoke the ancient precept *Inter arma silent leges* (in time of war the law is silent) as principle's pragmatic concession to necessity. This is certainly the approach of Thomas Jefferson's letter to J. B. Colvin: "A strict observance of the written laws is doubtless one of the high duties of a good citizen, but it is not the highest. The laws of necessity, of self-preservation, of saving our country when in danger, are of higher obligation."[17] Some version of the precept seems to lie behind Abraham Lincoln's suspension of provisions of the Constitution during the Civil War.[18] The precept also underwrites the Supreme Court's ratification of Lincoln's seizure of commercial ships despite the absence of a declaration of war[19] and the Court's strained strategy of institutional self-preservation in *Texas v. White*.[20] And *silent leges* lurks beneath Justice Jackson's dissent in *Korematsu v. United States*: "I would not lead people to rely on this Court for a review that seems to me wholly delusive. . . . If the people ever let command of the war power fall into irresponsible and unscrupulous hands, the courts wield no power equal to its restraint."[21]

At first glance, the precept of *silent leges* seems an extreme solution to a constitutional problem, especially when we consider how frequently the United States finds itself at war. Perhaps, for example, it presumes too quickly that war generically threatens the survival of the order. Some wars might — the Revolution, the Civil War, and the Second World War maybe — but most seem not to do so. Perhaps, too, the precept underestimates the capacity of judges to distinguish and stand against unnecessary restrictions on liberty in times of military mobilization. Does not the precept, moreover, make judges complicitous in extra-constitutional actions, requiring them to look the other way (or give legal cover) when political or military actors claim necessity?

If these are vices, the precept might nonetheless have its virtues. For one, it concedes without dissembling the brutish hold that survival has on even a constitutionalist order. For another, it sensibly acknowledges that judges are not competent to domesticate all problems, that even law properly has its limits. And it might keep off the books a principle of decision that "lies about like a loaded weapon ready for the hand of any authority that can bring forward a plausible claim of an urgent need."[22] These virtues aside, there might be ways to tame the precept while conceding its dangerousness. Following Rossiter's lead,[23] perhaps we could craft conditions for the safe use of the precept. For example: (1) The suspension of ordinary norms and processes would be permissible only in conditions of genuine crisis, threatening the survival of the order. (2) The suspension may be invoked only in an express and formal manner, by an authoritative body other than the agent wielding extra-constitutional power. (3) The suspension should be confined to those means that are strictly necessary to addressing the present crisis. (4) The suspension must expressly be temporary, limited to the duration of the crisis, revocable at any time by the authorizing body, but only by the authorizing body and never by the delegate of extra-constitutional power.

Despite these virtues and mitigations, the Court has opted for an alternative approach to the status and operation of rights in time of military conflict. Specifically, it has invoked a more modern precept, that the scope or content of a right depends on the weight of the governmental interest asserted for a policy that potentially restricts or diminishes the right. In short, interests of state are balanced against those of individuals, groups, or (sometimes) the collective body of citizens.[24] This balancing approach is distinguishable from *silent leges* in its willingness to adjudicate explicitly the "legality" of governmental policy: Military conflict or war implicates weighty interests that might well justify the truncation of rights. In *Korematsu v. United States*, for example, the Court held that war was a special context for civil liberty: "[H]ardships are part of war, and war is an aggregation of hardships. . . . [W]hen under conditions of modern warfare our shores are threatened by hostile forces, the power to protect must be commensurate with the threatened danger."[25]

Among the virtues of this approach is that it comports with how the Court treats rights in ordinary times. Because the analytic methods are common, the Court projects an image of judicial competence, diminishes the sense that the Court is "copping out," and secures the apparent reach of rule of law. These in turn have the ancillary (or purposeful) benefits of promoting the authority of the Court and, in relevant cases, supplying a legitimating stamp on governmental action. It is also the case that the standards the Court employs — rationality, intermediate scrutiny, strict scrutiny, clear and present danger, and others — can provide a degree of flexibility and subtlety in adjudicating competing interests. These permit the Court to make fine judgments about the nature of the military conflict, the severity of the danger to interests of state, and the character of the claimed right.

It is precisely these virtues, however, that can make balancing dangerous. As Justice Black indicated in *Korematsu*, military action on behalf of the nation will frequently look substantial and exigent, as weighed against the parochial claims of mere individuals. This appearance would seem to be all the more powerful when the action involves war, especially a serious war resting on a plausible claim of self-defense. It is conceivable, therefore, that balancing could be subtly corrosive of rights precisely because it is so familiar. Gone is the sense of judicial humility in the face of issues of defense and foreign policy. Gone is the extraordinary character of *silent leges*. When judges, through balancing, uphold a governmental policy, they make it look ordinary. Ironically, this result might be more subversive of rights than outright suspension (assuming that suspension would be followed by renormalization).

It would be a mistake, however, to make too much of these worries, for American constitutional history presents another irony: apart from the abolition of slavery and the enfranchisement of black men and eventually all women, the greatest expansion of civil and political liberty in the United States occurred in the most recent half century, a period that is an unbroken chain of wars and significant military actions. This circumstance commends restraint in presuming a general or unavoidable antagonism between war and liberty.

Even the Supreme Court has not turned a blind eye toward claimants of rights in time of war. That fact is significant. It may be that the rate at which it has done so, and the manner, are partly a function of "docket control." One way in which the Court can control its docket is to render decisions — especially libertarian decisions — after hostilities have subsided. It may also be that the Court has rarely enforced rights in cases that have required an expenditure of substantial institutional capital. Certainly, some of the Court's failures to enforce rights have been spectacular. But the aggregate record is decidedly mixed, and the Court has sometimes made more of rights than one might expect in light of the conventional wisdom.

Nonetheless, it is worth asking questions about what the Court has and has not done with respect to rights. For example, even in cases in which the Court has overturned a governmental policy, to what extent has government already gotten what it wanted by the time the Court has decided? Which intrusions into liberty are never litigated, and which legal presumptions lie behind public or institutional acquiescence in such policies? Which particular groups — not simply aliens or conscientious objectors generically — are disfavored in litigation? More specifically, which rights, and whose, are (not) protected, under what circumstances, and why?

Even stories of success, from the standpoint of rights, are not fully exempt from the gravitational force of national security. W. E. B. Du Bois argued, for example, that *Brown v. Board of Education* "would have been [im]possible without the world pressure of communism. . . . It was simply impossible for the United States to continue to lead a 'Free World' with race segregation kept legal over a third of its territory."[26] Lucas Powe notes that the United States' brief *amicus curiae* in *Brown* explicitly invoked the relation between civil rights for blacks at home and the struggle against communism abroad. If this invocation were not decisive, Powe writes, it "could not fail to impress Cold Warrior patriots sitting on the Court."[27]

Brown aside, however, it does seem that concern for national security has contributed to the diminution of rights, not simply for identifiable groups but for everyone. Certainly, it has inured Americans to certain intrusions on person or liberty — for example, searches or surveillance in public areas — that would have been unthinkable a generation ago. Many of these intrusions are never litigated; or, if they are, they do not make it onto the Supreme Court's docket.

Operation of Republican Government

The third front on which the constitutional inquiry is important relates to the daily operation of republican government. James Madison claimed famously that the basic logic of the incipient American order was republican. That is, its aim was self-government, its structure one in which government "derives all its powers directly or indirectly from the great body of the people."[28] Under such a system not only are the people entitled to rule themselves, but they exert a low-tension force that directs and constrains the personnel who populate formal institutions of government. There are many ways of contriving a system of self-government; but however contrived, military conflict can strain it.

The first source of strain is the level of secrecy required for both tactics and strategy in the prosecution of military actions. Plainly, some sorts of secrecy are justified in this context. At the same time secrecy poses several problems for republican government. One is that it restricts the flow of information — certainly to the public but sometimes even to governmental officials — that might be useful for framing public policy (including the desirability of pursuing particular military actions). Another is that secrecy bleeds. That is, it expands beyond the realm necessary for sustaining successful military operations. Still another is that in a regime in which military secrecy proliferates, civilian control of the military succeeds only to the extent that civilian personnel are conscientious and trustworthy. James Madison criticized the first condition: "Enlightened statesmen will not always be at the helm."[29] Thomas Jefferson criticized the second: "[F]ree government is founded in jealousy not confidence; it is jealousy and not confidence which prescribes limited constitutions, to bind down those whom we are obliged to trust with power."[30] Jefferson assumed that the people themselves could be relied upon to check unscrupulous politicians. In practice, of course, there are many reasons this assumption might not hold. One is that the people often lack sufficient information to serve as a rational check, especially in time of war. Another is that even if they know enough, people can sometimes be sufficiently inflamed against an external enemy to create internal enemies as well, essentially devouring not only potential friends but even themselves.

The final problem for republican government in time of military conflict is that civilian government sometimes effectively delegates responsibility over plainly domestic matters to military authorities. This was undoubtedly the case with the exclusion and internment of persons of Japanese descent in the Second World War. It was also the case with the executive proclamation of martial law in Hawaii after the bombing of Pearl Harbor, a status that was maintained long after the emergency precipitating the imposition had passed.[31] Even if government does not formally delegate authority to the military, civilian institutions can sometimes act, for purposes of both policy and administration, as extensions of the military; or civilian institutions can be susceptible to the influence of a militarist orientation in formulating or administering public policy.[32]

In his farewell address, President Eisenhower warned that the danger was not simply from the military but from "the conjunction of an immense military establishment and a large arms industry."[33] The rise of this conjunction, he said, was a rational response to "a hostile ideology, global in scope, atheistic in character, ruthless in purpose, and insidious in method." Hence, "we can no longer risk emergency improvisation of national defense; we have been compelled to create a permanent armaments industry of vast proportions." Eisenhower insisted, however, that this very instrument for the country's defense was itself a threat. "We must guard against the acquisition of unwarranted influence, whether sought or unsought, by the military-industrial complex. The potential for the disastrous rise of misplaced power exists and will persist."[34]

Allocation of Institutional Authority

The fourth way in which the military experience of the United States bears upon the capacity to sustain a constitutionalist order is that militarism can gradually alter working notions of institutional authority. That is, military engagement can alter the allocation of power or responsibility among institutions of government. I have in mind, specifically, the accretion of power in the executive branch.

The problem of institutional relations — the location and limitation of powers to direct foreign affairs, regulate the military, and wage war — is a murky area of constitutional law. Part of the murkiness is traceable to the text of the Constitution, which divides particular powers between Congress and the executive. I shall avoid the tedium of ticking off particular powers. Suffice it to say that Congress's powers in Article I are numerous and specific, while the president's powers in Article II are few and general.

Although the record of the debates of the Constitutional Convention is sketchy, there is reason to believe that the Constitution's delegations and obligations were motivated in part by a desire among some framers to reject the British monarchical model of war and foreign affairs in favor of a republican model. That is, primary responsibility for the commitment and regulation of troops in combat was to belong to Congress.[35] One reason rested on the assumption that Congress represented a wider range of people and interests than the executive and possessed a greater capacity for deliberative decision.[36]

Practice and experience, however, soon rendered archaic this vision of the centrality of a deliberative Congress. Instead, they vindicated an alternative model envisioned by at least one founder that the way to maintain and constrain a republican system is to "contriv[e] the interior structure of the government, [so] that its several constituent parts may, by their mutual relations, be the means of keeping each other in their proper places. . . . Ambition must be made to counteract ambition. The interest of the man must be connected with the constitutional rights of the place."[37] The difficulty with this general prescription for institutional conflict is that it begs for resolution in particular cases. For one thing, it might be constitutionally desirable, when possible, to resolve conflicts in a principled manner. For another, it might be desirable, as a matter of pragmatic self-interest, to have a device for circumscribing Madison's model of institutional warfare in times of military conflict. Enter the Supreme Court.

Chief Justice Marshall insisted that "[t]he province of the court is, solely, to decide on the rights of individuals," and not to inquire into "[q]uestions in their nature political."[38] Despite this limitation, the Court has sometimes found ways to insert itself into disputes over the scope of institutional authority in time of military conflict. The institutional contexts in which cases might arise tend to be threefold (here I cannot improve upon Justice Jackson's formulation in his concurrence in *Youngstown Sheet & Tube v. Sawyer*): (1) the executive might act pursuant to an express or implied delegation of authority by Congress (supporting "the strongest of presumptions" in favor of the executive); (2) the executive might act in the face of congressional silence (implicating a "zone of twilight" or uncertainty); and (3) the executive might act in the face of an express or implied congressional prohibition (where the president's authority is "at its lowest ebb").[39]

Put briefly, the story of American constitutional politics with respect to institutional relations in the context of military conflict has been one of steady erosion of Congress's power to prevent, confine, or even direct military action and of steady accretion of executive discretion and control. The reasons for these trends are complex. They include the president's direct authority to command the military, the president's dominant role in foreign affairs, and the increasing importance of the United States — politically, economically, culturally, and militarily — throughout the world. They include also Congress's general inability or unwillingness to check executive prerogatives, whether by express prohibition or through control of the purse. The sources of Congress's weakness range from a desire not to look unpatriotic when the president commands the political stage, to a fear of appearing less than supportive of American troops who stand in harm's way, to the obvious disabilities afflicting institutions that must coordinate collectively.

We may add to these considerations that Congress's primary power with respect to particular conflicts is merely to declare war, not to wage it. Congress may terminate appropriations necessary for waging war, but doing so is almost always politically untenable. Moreover, although Congress has the power to make rules for regulating the armed forces, the more direct "street-level" control that flows from the executive's authority as commander in chief often supersedes general rules of regulation. Even a motivated Congress can find it difficult to enforce rules against a president who sees the world differently from Congress. Considerations of policy, too, have historically reinforced executive prerogative free from congressional control: "self-defense" (entailing authority to deploy troops to defend against aggression); "neutrality" (authority to deploy troops in foreign venues to protect American citizens and property, so long as the troops are neutral toward factions competing in the venue); and "collective security" (authority to intervene pursuant to international agreements or treaties to promote the joint security of signatory nations).[40] Beyond these considerations is the historical deference paid to the president in foreign affairs, an area that bears such a close kinship to military action.[41] Although Congress's powers over war and foreign affairs are numerous, the logic of the Constitution's allocation of power and the historical deference that the executive has enjoyed in foreign affairs tend to favor the president. They do, that is, unless Congress can rely on another institution to shore up its position.

At one time, it appeared that the Court might be willing to do so and hence to uphold the sometimes populist positions of Madison and Jefferson against the centralist position of Alexander Hamilton.[42] In *Little v. Barreme*,[43] for example, the Court, through Chief Justice Marshall, held that the secretary of the navy could not exceed the bounds of express congressional authorization in seizing certain ships on the high seas.

Despite this beginning, the Court has shied from insinuating itself into inter-institutional disputes over control of military action. Even when the Court has stepped in — because avoidance was difficult or because there were political incentives or legal reasons to intercede — it has supported executive authority more often than not. This has frequently been true even when interests of property or personal liberty — Marshall's "rights of individuals" — were at stake. Hence in the *Prize Cases*, the Court affirmed the condemnation of merchant vessels seized pursuant to President Lincoln's order to blockade Confederate ports in 1861, although Congress had not declared war. The Court boldly declared that the president had authority *jure belli* (by right of war) to order a blockade of ports of seceding states, "which neutrals are bound to regard." This declaration was problematic not merely because it threatened the notions of delegated and reserved powers that were central parts of the logic of the Constitution, but because it obliterated institutional devices for checking the president's power. For the Court held that the question of whether the president was acting within the proper scope of his authority "is a question to be decided *by him*, and this Court must be governed by the decisions and actions of the political department of the Government to which this power was entrusted. . . . The proclamation of blockade is itself official and conclusive evidence to the Court that a state of war existed which demanded and authorized a recourse to such a measure, under the circumstances peculiar to the case."[44] Eight decades later, similar though not identical reasoning would lead the Court to ratify the exclusion and internment of ethnic Japanese in *Hirabayashi*[45] and *Korematsu*.[46]

In the *Steel Seizure Case*,[47] however, the Court pulled back. The United Steel Workers had called a strike that would have shut down much of the country's production of steel. In a preemptive move, to preserve production generally and, moreover, to continue production of munitions for the war in Korea, President Truman ordered the seizure of targeted mills and the continuation of production under the secretary of commerce, who appointed the presidents of affected firms to continue day-to-day management. The president notified Congress and said he would comply with congressional will in the matter. Congress offered no formal reply.

Although the Court struck down the president's order, its members could not agree on why. Among the Justices' opinions, Jackson's concurrence revealed the subtlest understanding of the implications of the case and the sources of constitutional principle for resolving it. What the case called for, he said, was a conceptual framework capable of explaining and justifying the contextually contingent allocation of institutional power. The relevant context in *Youngstown* was military conflict. I have already noted his tripartite scheme for resolving disputes between executive and Congress. Agreeing with Black that Truman's order was "incompatible with the . . . implied will of Congress," Jackson urged not that the order was ipso facto unconstitutional, but that the Court should "scrutinize [it] with caution" to determine whether it was unconstitutional. Two of the president's claims are relevant here: (1) that Article I designates the president as commander in chief, which implies general powers over war, and (2) that the president possesses "inherent powers" derived from "the customs and claims of preceding administrations."[48]

Against the first claim, Jackson responded in four ways. First, the Constitution delegated the power to declare war "only to Congress." Second, although a state of war can exist (and presumably might justify executive action) without formal declaration, an expansive understanding of war powers did not follow from that fact. "[N]o doctrine . . . would seem to me more sinister and alarming than that a President whose conduct of foreign affairs is so largely uncontrolled, and is often unknown, can vastly enlarge his mastery over the internal affairs of the country by his own commitment of the Nation's armed forces to some foreign venture." Third, "the title Commander-in-Chief *of the Army and Navy* [does not] constitute him also Commander-in-Chief of the country." Fourth, whatever the president's authority to employ armed forces "against the outside world for the security of our society," authority is absent "when it is turned inward, not because of rebellion but because of a lawful economic struggle between industry and labor." "No penance would ever expiate the sin against free government of holding that a President can escape control of executive powers by law through assuming his military role."[49]

Against the second claim, Jackson dismissed what he called its "unarticulated assumption": "that necessity knows no law." We might doubt the wisdom of vesting emergency powers anywhere, he said, but "emergency powers are consistent with free government only when their control is lodged elsewhere than in the Executive who exercises them." In our experience, the safest repository is the legislature. Does such a location make national government vulnerable to incompetence in dealing with emergencies? Jackson said no: "Congress may and has granted extraordinary authorities which lie dormant in normal times but may be called into play by the Executive in war or upon proclamation of a national emergency."[50]

Jackson's concurrence is the most substantial, forthright, unapologetic, and well-reasoned commitment by a member of the Court, not to mention by the Court as a collective body, to side with Congress against the accretion of executive power in the military context in the twentieth century. It is open to question, however, how influential it has been in affecting the behavior of national institutions. One reason for my skepticism grows out of a point that Jackson himself observed: "We may say that power to legislate for emergencies belongs in the hands of Congress, but only Congress itself can prevent power from slipping through its fingers."[51]

Congress has been a less than vigorous defender of its own authority. The

War Powers Resolution[52] is not an exception to this observation, for it reveals more about Congress's weakness than its power. Certainly, it has been ignored or flouted far more frequently than followed. Even when presidents have adhered to its technical requirements, they have sometimes done so without conceding the existence of a constitutional obligation.[53] In fact, some in the White House, including presidents, have posited that the resolution is an unconstitutional intrusion on the executive's authority over the military and foreign affairs.[54] There are several reasons executive resistance has been possible. First, the resolution's very existence is an implicit concession to the toothlessness of Congress's constitutional authority to declare war. Second, Congress has repeatedly lacked the will to use its institutional clout to enforce the resolution. Third, the resolution's language and logic virtually invite niggling legalism by the executive. Hence, presidents have interpreted the War Powers Resolution as granting implicit permission to engage in covert operations or conduct military operations that can be completed within the resolution's sixty-day limitation.[55] At least one president conducted covert foreign operations, despite specific express prohibitions by Congress.[56] The principal effect of the resolution has been simply to shift the political risk that comes from the possible failure of an undeclared war.[57] Perhaps such a shift was the predominant motivation of many members from the beginning. If so, it merely underscores the chronic weakness of Congress in this area.

Sovereignty

The fifth area in which we might point to troubling trends in the American order concerns not institutional relations directly but the authority of the order itself. Let me frame this as a proposition: The persistent American reliance on war and military action has affected the regime's view of its own authority; specifically, it has weakened a constitutionalist conception of authority and strengthened a statist conception that is ultimately antagonistic to constitutionalism.

The sovereignty of the people is at the heart of American constitutionalism. Some scholars contest this claim,[58] but it is sufficiently well established that I offer it here as a fact. The reason for the place of popular sovereignty is partly an accident of history and partly a function of the logic of constitutionalism. The historical accident grew out of the fact that the English conception of authority was grounded in sovereignty. When part of British North America separated from Britain, declared itself the United States, and eventually constructed new political institutions, it retained the concept of sovereignty but jettisoned the English conception. In crafting a replacement, the Americans drew on their extensive and long-standing experience with self-government — even self-constitution.

This accident of history is relevant to the logic of constitutionalism. I have argued elsewhere that all political regimes — even constitutionalist regimes — "arise to some degree from illegality." Illegality is one way we recognize a regime as distinct from its predecessors or its successors. The Constitution of the United States, for example, was illegal from the standpoint of both the Articles of Confederation and the specific instructions that Congress gave the Constitutional Convention. This sort of illegality invites a basic question: When a new constitution appears on the scene, and a new regime lays claim to it, why should anyone pay it any mind, let alone obey? This question of authority is important, because if the regime aims to be constitutionalist, the founding cannot be simply a brute fact. It must be justified. Here's how. The new order will try to explain itself (because this, among other things, is what a constitutionalist order must do). Typically, it will do so by reference to the manner in which it came to exist. Hence the constitutionalist preoccupation with origins. The story of the founding becomes the device for self-justification. And it becomes part of the logic of the new regime.[59]

In the United States, the self-told story has typically been one of popular creation. Two general approaches have been notable. One is antifederalist. Framed simply, the antifederalist approach posits that the Constitution, and hence the order that traces its authority to the Constitution, were authorized by the people of antecedent states. The other approach is federalist. In this context, federalism presumes that the Constitution's (and the order's) authority derives from the people not of states but of the nation as a whole. It is not my purpose here to explore the analytic details or implications of these approaches. I note simply that whichever approach one employs, each invokes the people as the source for constitutional authority. This is a useful notion. It comports with widely held conceptions of the ultimate rule of recognition; it promotes the idea that the people are the proper beneficiary of governmental action; and it serves as a check against governmental excess or folly.

The Court in some contexts, however, has called into question the relevance of popular sovereignty to war and foreign affairs. A forthright and influential articulation of this position is Justice Sutherland's opinion of the Court in *United States v. Curtiss-Wright Export Corp.*[60] It held that constitutional constraints on executive authority were qualitatively different as between "foreign or external affairs" and "domestic or internal affairs."[61] Thus, Congress would have been constitutionally prohibited from delegating power to the president to make criminal law had the context been domestic; but constitutional limitations do not apply in the same way in the context of foreign affairs. Why might this be so? Sutherland offered two rationales.

One was a variation on the story of the creation of American constitutional order, a variation that combined antifederalist and federalist tropes but essentially read the people out of one aspect of constitutional politics: "[T]he primary purpose of the Constitution was to carve from the general mass of legislative powers then possessed by the states such portions as it was thought desirable to vest in the Federal government. . . . That this doctrine applies only to powers that the states had, is self-evident. And since the states severally never possessed international powers, such powers could not have been carved from the mass of state powers but obviously were transmitted to the United States from some other source."[62] What source? "The Union," wrote Sutherland, "existed before the Constitution." Before ratification, "it is clear that the Union . . . was the sole possessor of external sovereignty, and in the Union it remained without change save in so far as the Constitution qualified its exercise."[63]

The second rationale, buttressing the first, was "the law of nations." "As a member of the family of nations, the right and power of the United States [in the fields of war and foreign affairs] are equal to the right and power of the other members of the international family. Otherwise, the United States is not completely sovereign." Consequently, "the investment of the Federal government with the powers of external sovereignty did not depend upon the affirmative grants of the Constitution." If these powers "had never been mentioned in the Constitution, [they] would have vested in the Federal government as necessary concomitants of nationality."[64]

The problems that Sutherland's statist conception of sovereignty posed for constitutionalism were heightened by four additional aspects of his analysis, each of which pertains to considerations we have previously considered: executive exclusivity, secrecy, the blending of military action with foreign affairs, and the blending of both to matters of domestic concern.

Sutherland anthropomorphized the national government in the person of the president. The primary effect of this impersonation was not to rank the authority of competing institutions, but to focus authority exclusively in the executive: "The President alone has the power to speak or listen as a representative of the nation." Hence, "we are here dealing [with] . . . the very delicate, plenary and exclusive power of the President as the sole organ of the Federal government in the field of international relations — a power which does not require as a basis for its exercise an act of Congress."[65] Let's put aside the fact that this formulation is inconsistent with a fair reading of the constitutional text, even in the context of war or foreign affairs. Under Sutherland's theory, not only has the state become the president, but the president has become sovereign.

The danger of such a concentration is exacerbated by Sutherland's willingness to tolerate a high level of secrecy in the conduct of foreign affairs. "[The President], not Congress, has the better opportunity of knowing the conditions which prevail in foreign countries, and especially is this true in time of war. He has his confidential sources of information. He has his agents in the form of diplomatic, consular and other officials. Secrecy in respect of information gathered by them may be highly necessary, and the premature disclosure of it productive of harmful results."[66] The difficulty here is not that secrecy of some sorts is categorically impermissible, especially in foreign affairs. But because secrecy is problematic, its management requires sensitivity and special institutional checks against abuse. When authority is vested exclusively in the executive, most useful institutional checks are unavailing.

Still, a constitutionalist might not worry deeply about these tendencies as long as they are confined to limited aspects of the conduct of diplomacy with other nations. Sutherland did not so limit his theory. For one thing, he held that the need for executive control and secrecy is "especially" acute "in time of war."[67] Again, I do not claim that secrecy per se is illicit. Some secrecy is necessary for the successful prosecution of military actions. Sutherland's theory, however, makes the executive the exclusive repository of information "especially . . . in time of war" and perhaps also during any sort of military action that can plausibly be linked to national security or the national interest. This position undermines institutional checks that not only are desirable for a healthy constitutional system (if we believe Madison) but also are established by the Constitution itself.

This is not the only way in which Sutherland's theory of presidential power reaches beyond foreign affairs, strictly understood. For it also extends to domestic matters. Sutherland himself left open this possibility, notwithstanding his opening embrace of the distinction between internal and external affairs. The president, he held, requires "a degree of discretion and freedom from statutory restriction which would not be admissible were domestic affairs alone involved."[68] Thus, only when matters are strictly domestic should executive discretion be constrained by the Constitution or statute. When domestic affairs touch matters of international or military concern, however, they cease to subject presidential power to conventional limits. When might such a connection be present? Perhaps often, especially given the incessancy of militarism in American experience and ethos.

The Antifederalist John DeWitt claimed that the proposed Constitution of the United States was "nothing less than a hasty stride to Universal Empire in this Western World."[69] He was wrong, of course. The Constitution was not a hasty step. Nor need it (nor the government it authorized) have been imperial in the sense DeWitt intended.[70] But as Felix Frankfurter noted in the *Steel Seizure Case*, "The accretion of dangerous power does not come in a day. It does come, however slowly, from the generative force of unchecked disregard of the restrictions that fence in even the most disinterested assertion of authority."[71]

I am suspicious of apocalyptic visions and prophecies of doom. Still, I sense reasons for disquiet over the health of constitutionalism in the United States. My focus here has been only on one aspect of the American order: the history and practice of militarism. The ethos that has ignored it, the institutional spinelessness that has permitted it, and the judicial doctrines that have justified it threaten to enfeeble constitutionalism in America.

Significant Military Conflicts of the United States

1775–1783: Revolutionary War
1775–1783: campaigns against the British (declared)
1775–1783: dispersal of pro-British Iroquois (Indian campaign)

1791: Miami (under Little Turtle) defeat Gen. Arthur St. Clair (Indian campaign)

1794: United States defeats Miami, Shawnee, et al. in Battle of Fallen Timbers (Indian campaign)

1794: militias suppress Whiskey Rebellion in western Pennsylvania

1798–1801: quasi-war with France (undeclared)

1801–1805: First Barbary War (undeclared)

1806–1810: anti-piracy patrols in Gulf of Mexico

1810–1814: seizure of Spanish territories in West Florida

1811: Gen. William Henry Harrison defeats northwestern tribes at Tippecanoe (Indian campaign)

1812–1815: War of 1812 (declared)

1814: Gen. Andrew Jackson defeats Creek tribes at Horseshoe Bend (Indian campaign)

1814–1830s: anti-piracy patrols and raids in the Caribbean

1815: Second Barbary War (undeclared)

1816–1818: First Seminole War (Indian campaign)

1818: USS *Ontario* seizes control of Oregon Territory

1820–1861: African slave-trade patrols

1832: Black Hawk War to expel the Sauk and Fox from Illinois (Indian campaign)

1835–1842: campaigns (including Second Seminole War) against southeastern tribes (Indian campaign)

1846–1848: Mexican War (declared)

1847: Pueblo revolt suppressed (Indian campaign)

1853–1854: Commodore Perry's demonstrations and invasions to "open" Japan

1854: bombardment and burning of Greytown, Nicaragua

1861–1865: Civil War (undeclared)

1861–1865: "pacification" of the Navajo (Indian campaign)

1863–1864: retaliation, demonstration, and compulsion against Japan

1872: defeat of the Modoc in Oregon (Indian campaign)

1876: Sitting Bull and Crazy Horse defeat Custer at Little Big Horn (Indian campaign)

1877: Nez Perce (under Chief Joseph) defeated (Indian campaign)

1890: end of armed Indian hostilities at Wounded Knee (Indian campaign)

1898: Spanish-American War (declared)

1899–1902: Philippine insurrection campaign

1900–1901: China relief expedition, after outbreak of Boxer Rebellion

1902–1934: Latin American campaigns

1902: U.S. forces prevent Colombia from putting down an insurrection (instigated by United States) in Isthmus of Panama

1903–1914: occupation of Isthmus of Panama after Colombia refuses to ratify treaty granting to United States a right of way in Panama

1906–1909: Cuban pacification

1909: U.S. Marine Corps deployed to Nicaragua to destabilize presidency of José Santos Zelaya

1912–1925: first Nicaraguan campaign

1912–1941: demonstrations, patrols, and landing parties in China, after Japanese invasion (including intensified landings and bombardments in response to factional hostilities, 1922–1927)

1914: seizure and bombardment of Veracruz

1914–1917: Mexican border campaign after *Dolphin* affair and Pancho Villa's raids

1915–1934: Haitian campaign

1916–1924: U.S. Marines' occupation of Dominican Republic

1917–1918: First World War (declared)

1917–1922: occupation of Cuba

1918–1919: series of skirmishes with Mexican bandits and troops

1918–1920: Allied occupation

1918–1920: U.S. troops police Panama

1918–1922: occupation of Vladivostok, Soviet Russia, after Bolshevik Revolution

1920–1922: U.S. Marine Corps occupation to protect U.S. property

1926–1933: second Nicaraguan campaign

1941–1945: Second World War (declared)

1945–1949: troops occupy parts of China to support nationalists against Japanese, then against communists

1948–1949: Berlin airlift

1950–present: Korean Conflict

1950–1953: Korean War (undeclared)

1950–1955: U.S. Seventh Fleet protects Formosa from attack by communists

1953–present: U.S. forces police Demilitarized Zone

1958: U.S. Marine Corps deployed to Lebanon

1961: invasion of Cuba at Bay of Pigs

1962: Cuban missile crisis

1962–1975: Vietnam War and aftermath

1962–1973: military operations in Vietnam (undeclared)

1962–1975: support for government of Laos

1965: intervention in Dominican Republic's civil war

1967: intervention to support government of Congo against a revolt

1970: incursion into Cambodia

1975: evacuation from Vietnam and Cambodia

1975: U.S. forces retake USS *Mayaguez*

1982: participation in multinational force and observers in the Sinai

1982: participation in multinational force in Lebanon

1983: invasion of Grenada

1983–1989: exercises to support Honduras against Nicaragua

1986: air strikes against Libya

1987–1988: naval forces protect shipping lanes in Persian Gulf after Iran-Iraq War

1988–1989: invasion of Panama and seizure of General Noriega (Operation Just Cause)

1989–present: military personnel support "war on drugs" in Andean nations

1990–present: Persian Gulf War against Iraq

1990–1991: military operations (Operations Desert Shield / Desert Storm) (undeclared)

1992–present: postwar policing of Iraq

1992–1993: intervention in Somalia (Operation Restore Hope)

1992–1995: multinational interventions in the Balkans (Operations Sharp Guard / Deny Flight / Deliberate Force) (undeclared)

1993: missile attack on Baghdad, Iraq

1993–1994: intervention in Haiti (Operation Uphold Democracy)

1999: bombing of Kosovo and Federal Republic of Yugoslavia (Operation Allied Force)

2001–present: war against terrorism

2001–present: invasion of Afghanistan (Operation Infinite Justice) (undeclared)

2002–present: mobilization for and invasion of Iraq (Operation Iraqi Freedom) (undeclared)

2003–present: U.S. Marine Corps deployment to Philippines

Sources: Ellen C. Collier, "Instances of Use of United States Forces Abroad, 1798–1993," http://www.history.navy.mil/wars/foabroad.htm (Washington: Congressional Research Service, Library of Congress, 7 October 1993) (visited 24 June 2002); Robert D. Kaplan, "Supremacy by Stealth: Ten Rules for Managing the World," *Atlantic Monthly*, July–August 2003, 66–83; Louis Fisher, *Presidential War Power* (Lawrence: University Press of Kansas, 1995); "U.S. Combat Force of 1,700 Is Headed to the Philippines," *New York Times*, 21 February 2003.

NOTES

1 See appendix to this chapter.

2 The Federalist Nos. 15, 22, 23 (Alexander Hamilton).

3 Mark E. Brandon, *Free in the World: American Slavery and Constitutional Failure* (1998), 206–7.

4 The Federalist No. 1 (Alexander Hamilton).

5 Clinton L. Rossiter, *Constitutional Dictatorship: Crisis Government in the Modern Democracies* (1948), 5.

6 Note, for example, George W. Bush, "State of the Union Address" (28 January 2003), http://www.whitehouse.gov/news/releases/2003/01/20030128-19.html (visited 29 January 2003).

7 On the distinction between friend and enemy, see Carl Schmitt, *The Concept of the Political* (George Schwab trans., 1976), 25–37, 45–53.

8 Robert Endicott Osgood, *Ideals and Self-Interest in America's Foreign Relations: The Great Transformation of the Twentieth Century* (1953), 4.

9 See, for example, Edmund S. Morgan, *The Puritan Dilemma: The Story of John Winthrop* (1958), 69–83.

10 For an early example of Mr. Carter's moralism, see Carter, *Why Not the Best?* (1975), 9–11, 154.

11 "Address on Foreign Affairs" (22 May 1977), in Carter, *Keeping Faith: Memoirs of a President* (1982), 141.

12 Ronald Reagan, *An American Life* (1990), 568–71.

13 See George W. Bush, "Address to the Nation" (11 September 2001), http://
www.whitehouse.gov/news/releases/2001/09/20010911–16.html (visited 19
July 2002); "Address to Joint Session of Congress" (20 September 2001), http://
www.whitehouse.gov/news/releases/2001/09/20010920–8.html (visited 19
July 2002); "Remarks by the President" (16 September 2001), http://www
.whitehouse.gov/news/releases/2001/09/20010916–2.html (visited 19 July
2002); "State of the Union Address" (29 January 2002), http://www.white
house.gov/news/releases/2002/01/20020129–11.html (visited 8 November
2002); "Remarks at National Day of Prayer and Remembrance" (14 September
2001), http://www.whitehouse.gov/news/releases/2001/09/20010914–2.html
(visited 19 July 2002).

14 Osgood, *Ideals and Self-Interest*, 11.

15 Attorney General John Ashcroft has flirted with such characterizations. See, for
example, Ashcroft, "Testimony before the Senate Committee on the Judiciary"
(6 December 2001), http://www.usdoj.gov/ag/speeches/2001/1206transcrip
senatejudiciarycommittee.htm (visited 24 February 2003); "Prepared Remarks to
the International Association of Chiefs of Police Conference" (7 October 2002),
http://www.usdoj.gov/ag/speeches/2002/100702chiefsofpolicemn1.htm (visited 24 February 2003).

16 Rossiter, *Constitutional Dictatorship*, 5, 11–12.

17 Thomas Jefferson, "Letter to J. B. Colvin" (20 September 1810), in Lipscomb
ed., *The Writings of Thomas Jefferson* (1903), vol. xii, 418.

18 See Abraham Lincoln, "Message to Congress in Special Session" (4 July 1861),
in Roy P. Basler ed., *The Collected Works of Abraham Lincoln*, v. 4 (1953), 429–31.

19 The Prize Cases, 67 U.S. 635 (1863).

20 74 U.S. 700 (1869).

21 323 U.S. 214 (1944), at 248 (Jackson, J., dissenting).

22 *Id.* at 246.

23 Rossiter, *Constitutional Dictatorship*, 297–306.

24 Chief Justice Rehnquist conflates the doctrine of *silent leges* with that of balancing. See William H. Rehnquist, *All the Laws but One: Civil Liberties in Wartime* (1998), 224. I believe that this conflation is mistaken.

25 *Korematsu*, 323 U.S. at 219 (Black, J., for the Court).

26 Du Bois, *The Autobiography of W. E. B. Du Bois* (1968), 333.

27 Lucas A. Powe Jr., *The Warren Court and American Politics* (2000), 34–36.

28 The Federalist No. 39 (James Madison).

29 The Federalist No. 10 (James Madison).

30 Thomas Jefferson, "The Kentucky Resolutions of 1798," in Henry Steele Com-
mager and Milton Cantor, eds., *Documents of American History*, vol. 1 (1988),
178–84.

31 See Edward S. Corwin, *The President: Office and Powers, 1787–1957* (1957), 253; Rossiter, *Constitutional Dictatorship*, 284–85.

32 See generally Dana Priest, *The Mission: Waging War and Keeping Peace with America's Military* (2003).

33 Geoffrey Perret, *Eisenhower* (1999), 599.

34 Tom Wicker, *Dwight D. Eisenhower* (2002), 132.

35 See James Madison, *Notes of Debates in the Federal Convention of 1787* (1987), 45–46, 448, 476.

36 See Louis Fisher, *Presidential War Power* (1995), 1–11.

37 The Federalist No. 51 (James Madison).

38 Marbury v. Madison, 5 U.S. 137, 169–70 (1803).

39 343 U.S. 579, 635–38 (1952).

40 John E. Nowak and Ronald D. Rotunda, *Constitutional Law*, 6th ed. (2000), 253–55.

41 *Id.* at 229–30.

42 *Id.* at 252–55.

43 6 U.S. 170 (1804).

44 The Prize Cases, 67 U.S. at 670.

45 320 U.S. 81 (1943).

46 323 U.S. 214 (1944).

47 Youngstown Sheet & Tube v. Sawyer, 343 U.S. 579 (1952).

48 *Id.* at 634–35, 637–38.

49 *Id.* at 641–46.

50 *Id.* at 646–53.

51 *Id.* at 654.

52 50 U.S.C. §§ 1541–48 (passed 7 November 1973, over presidential veto).

53 See Walter F. Murphy, James E. Fleming, and Sotirios A. Barber, *American Constitutional Interpretation*, 2nd ed. (1995), 460.

54 See Fisher, *Presidential War Power*, 131–61.

55 Harold Hongju Koh, *The National Security Constitution: Sharing Power after the Iran-Contra Affair* (1990), 39–40.

56 The president was Reagan. The prohibitions were contained in the Boland Amendments, which were riders to annual appropriations from 1982 to 1986.

57 Accord, John Hart Ely, *War and Responsibility: Constitutional Lessons of Vietnam and Its Aftermath* (1993), 54.

58 See, for example, Ronald Dworkin, *Taking Rights Seriously* (1977, 1978); Murphy, Fleming, and Barber, *American Constitutional Interpretation*, 45–47.

59 Brandon, *Free in the World*, 186–89. See also Bruce Ackerman, *We the People: Transformations* (1998), 49–53.

60 299 U.S. 304 (1936).

61 *Id.* at 315. Sutherland would later extend the logic of his opinion in *Curtiss-Wright* to a decision holding that mere executive agreements — embodied in diplomatic correspondence and not subject to ratification by the Senate — were constitutionally binding. United States v. Belmont, 301 U.S. 324 (1937).

62 *Curtiss-Wright*, 299 U.S. at 316.

63 *Id.* at 317.

64 *Id.* at 318.

65 *Id.* at 319–20.

66 *Id.* at 320.

67 *Id.*

68 *Id.*

69 John DeWitt, "Essay III" (5 November 1787), in Ralph Ketchum ed., *The Anti-Federalist Papers and the Constitutional Convention Debates* (1986), 313.

70 But see The Federalist Nos. 1, 6, 13, 22, 23, 28 (Alexander Hamilton).

71 *Youngstown Sheet & Tube*, 343 U.S. at 594 (Frankfurter, J., concurring).

EMERGENCIES AND THE IDEA OF CONSTITUTIONALISM

Mark Tushnet

How should war be incorporated into American constitutionalism? I believe that there are three basic positions. The first is that the Constitution's *general* standards should be applied in wartime, and the nation's involvement in war might be relevant to determining whether those standards are satisfied.[1] So, for example, race-based classifications are subject to strict scrutiny, and can survive constitutional challenge only if they are narrowly tailored to advance compelling government interests. Suppose a government adopted a race-based classification in wartime and defended it on the ground that the classification advanced an interest in winning the war. That interest is clearly more "compelling" than other interests sometimes offered in defense of race-based classifications, and — on at least some understandings of the relevant tests — the more compelling an interest is, the less narrowly tailored the classification must be. A race-based classification that would be unconstitutional during peacetime might be constitutional during wartime, not because the constitutional standards differ, but because their rational application leads to different results.

The second position is that the constitutional rules applicable during wartime are categorically different from those applicable during peacetime.[2] Perhaps a race-based classification employed during wartime need satisfy only rational basis review, for example. We can describe this view as acknowledging that the Constitution applies during wartime, but as contending as well that the Constitution is bifurcated into one set of provisions applicable during wartime and another applicable during peacetime.

The differences between the first and the second positions may well be rather small. The first position requires decision makers to think that war is relevant to the application of universal standards, while the second allows them to think that war triggers the application of a distinctive set of standards. But nothing in the conceptual scheme rules out the possibility that with respect to any particular constitutional problem, the substantive standard to be applied under the second approach will lead to the same outcome that application of the universal standard, taking war into account, would lead to under the first approach.

The third approach is different. It treats war as presenting the possibility of justifying a widespread suspension of legality. This approach is most closely associated with the legal theorist Carl Schmitt, whose work, discredited for a generation because of the role it played in rationalizing the Nazi regime, has attracted a great deal of recent attention.

This chapter outlines the three approaches, and concludes by arguing that American constitutionalists should take the third one seriously, so as to avoid providing law-based justifications for actions that while perhaps understandable in pragmatic and perhaps even in non-pragmatic moral terms, undermine the values expressed in the rule-of-law tradition.

THE FIRST TWO APPROACHES

Addressing Congress in December 1862, Abraham Lincoln said, "The dogmas of the quiet past are inadequate for the stormy present. The occasion is piled high with difficulty, and we must rise to the occasion. As our case is new, so we must think anew, and act anew. We must disenthrall ourselves, and then we shall save our country."[3] Lincoln elegantly put what has become a standard point about legal and constitutional analysis: Circumstances alter cases. That is, the constitutional doctrines developed in connection with commercial advertising or even political speech in ordinary times may not be appropriate in other circumstances.

The Case For

Writing in the context of an economic rather than a military crisis, Justice Harlan Fiske Stone argued that constitutional law did not need to be displaced, but only properly interpreted, to deal effectively with the crisis. As he put it, "Emergency does not create power, [but] emergency may furnish the occasion for the exercise of power."[4] And just as emergency may create the occasion for the exercise of power, emergency may provide a justification for actions that would, absent the emergency, be unjustified intrusions on civil liberties. As Justice Holmes put it, "When a nation is at war many things that might be said in time of peace are such a hindrance to its effort that their utterance will not be endured so long as men fight and that no court could regard them as protected by any constitutional right."[5] Holmes might be read as expressing a resigned acceptance of the inevitable, but it is better to read him as asserting that what counts as a violation of free expression in peacetime is just different from what might count as a violation of free speech in wartime.[6]

According to the first approach, this must be right. Its proponents believe that at the most abstract level, a nation's commitment to principles of free expression persists undiminished no matter what the circumstances. The question is whether the scope of the particular civil liberty at issue is properly defined with reference to wartime conditions.

Here we can distinguish between two general approaches to the definition of constitutional rights, a balancing approach and a categorical approach. Plainly, wartime conditions are relevant when constitutional rights are defined by balancing competing interests. Balancing approaches, though, raise in acute form the concern that wartime will distort the law. Judges no less than other government officials are susceptible to the pressures of events. Justice Robert Jackson made some astute observations about the war power that are applicable as well to the definition of constitutional rights with reference to wartime conditions: "[T]his vague, undefined and indefinable 'war power' . . . is usually invoked in haste and excitement when calm legislative consideration of constitutional limitation is difficult. It is executed in a time of patriotic fervor that makes moderation unpopular. And, worst of all, it is interpreted by judges under the influence of the same passions and pressures."[7] Judges, one might fear, will undervalue some elements in the balance and overvalue others, and so define constitutional rights in a way that on reflection should be troubling.

Categorical approaches are designed to offset this tendency by screening out of consideration the features of the circumstances that are likely to induce misjudgment. And under some conditions they may succeed in doing so, when the categorical rules address decision makers who might not appreciate the importance of considerations that the decision makers might think peripheral to their more central tasks. Consider, for example, a categorical rule against torture by police officers. Judges might think that in the abstract they can imagine situations in which torture might be a valuable investigative technique. Judges might think that they must communicate rules effectively to police officers. They might also think that any verbal formulation of the (limited) circumstances in which torture might be acceptable is too likely to be misinterpreted in ways that would lead the officers to engage in torture more often than they should. The judges could then conclude that they should announce a categorical rule against torture despite their awareness that such a rule does not correspond to their own sense of what is acceptable.

Categorical approaches make most sense, then, when the judges are designing rules for others to follow. Unfortunately, they do so in the form of precedents, that is, in the form of rules that they themselves are to follow. It takes a mind-set that is, I think, quite difficult to achieve for a person to rule out of consideration for himself or herself in the future something that the person today thinks plainly relevant to decision. The difficulty in the context of defining constitutional rights in wartime is obvious. The circumstances of war are something like an elephant in the living room. Judges might agree that a categorical rule is desirable, but say that the rules simply differ in wartime. That is, they would take the category *war* as relevant to defining the applicable rule, and screen out *other* considerations. Alternatively, the judges might *try* to screen out the wartime circumstances in their formulation of the rule. But try as they might, judges are quite unlikely to be able to ignore the elephant's presence. True, they might not explicitly mention the elephant in defining the categorical rule they invoke, but one can rightly be skeptical about any claim that the elephant played no part as the judges thought about what the rule should be.

What this means, though, is that one will be hard pressed to say, in any other than an advocate's voice, that civil liberties are violated in wartime. Judges will test government actions against the Constitution. They may often find that the actions do not violate the Constitution, either because the judges place the wartime circumstances in the balance as they define constitutional rights or because they formulate categorical rules that take the fact of war as relevant to triggering one or another rule. It is not, then, that law is silent in wartime. Rather, it is that sometimes it speaks in tones that advocates of particular positions do not like. But after all, how is that different from any other time?

The Case Against

Suppose we took the original constitution as the sole guide for determining whether the exercise of emergency powers is permitted. *Blaisdell* — the case saying that emergency does not create power — itself illustrates the primary difficulty with this course. The case involved a state law suspending the obligation of debtors to pay their debts during a period of national economic distress. As the dissenters in *Blaisdell* pointed out, this was precisely the kind of law that the constitutional ban on state laws impairing the obligation of contracts was directed at: in writing the ban, the drafters of the Constitution had in mind Rhode Island statutes suspending the obligation of debtors to repay their debts during a period of local (and, to a degree, national) economic distress.[8]

The general point is clear. Constitution drafters anticipate some emergencies, but they fail to anticipate all the ones that future decision makers will believe they must deal with. Facing a constitution seeming not to authorize or, worse, to prohibit actions that policy makers deem necessary for responding to the perceived emergency, decision makers, including courts, will feel pressure to "interpret" the constitution so as to allow the actions.

Perhaps there is nothing wrong with this sort of creative interpretation. After all, as John Marshall wrote in one of his great opinions, "we must never forget, that it is *a constitution* we are expounding," one that is "to be adapted to the various *crises* of human affairs."[9] One might worry, though. What is one to make of a decision upholding a policy because it was a permissible response to crisis? I think there are two possibilities. The Whiggish one is that the exaggerated perception of crisis will discredit the decision as a precedent. The other, more worrisome, is that later policy makers, including courts, will say, "Well, the action taken then didn't violate the constitution even though there wasn't such a severe threat to social order, so the action under consideration today certainly won't violate the constitution because we face a more severe threat, and the courts upheld the earlier policy in the face of a less substantial one."[10]

The worrisome possibility deals with the *consequences* of treating the action in question as lawful. Courts may well succumb to the understandable pressure to reconcile the inevitable with the Constitution; judges as members of the governing élites will feel the same need for emergency powers that other members of those élites do,[11] and judges as judges will feel some need to make what seems necessary be lawful as well. But in explaining why the current circumstances fit within constitutional provisions designed for other circumstances, judges may make the exceptional the normal. As David Dyzenhaus has put the point in a related context, "one cannot, as Carl Schmitt rightly argued, confine the exception. If it is introduced into legal order and treated as such, it will spread."[12] The temporary will be made permanent, threatening civil liberties well beyond the period of the emergency.[13]

Posner and Vermeule properly question this consequentialist challenge to the rationalization of emergency powers. The consequentialist challenge rests on two assumptions. The first, which they concede might be correct, is that conditions change after the emergency has passed. The second, which they question, is that judges will be unable to distinguish between the earlier circumstances, which justified the suspension of legality, and the present ones, which do not. Posner and Vermeule note that proponents of the consequentialist fear do not identify the psychological mechanism by which a precedent is extended beyond the point to which its reason extends. Yet the consequentialist concern might be different. Posner and Vermeule in their response follow the typical consequentialist in assuming that emergencies end, and they question the consequentialist's fear that action taken during an emergency will become a precedent for actions taken during normal times. But perhaps the consequentialist's concern is that the (purported) emergency will never end.

Early statements by the Bush administration about the war on terrorism were to the effect that the war was one of indefinite duration. And indeed, it is worth noting that statements about the existence of a war on terrorism go back quite a long way. President Ronald Reagan's first inaugural address, delivered as the Iranian hostage crisis was ending, said that the United States would use "the will and courage of free men and women" as a "weapon" against "those who practice terrorism and prey upon their neighbors."[14] The 1996 revision of the federal habeas corpus statute goes by the acronym AEDPA, for "Anti-Terrorism Effective Death Penalty Act."

The already long duration of the "war on terrorism" suggests that we ought not think of it as a war in the sense that the Second World War was a war. It is, perhaps, more like a condition than a war — more like the war on cancer, the war on poverty, or, most pertinently, the war on crime. Suspending legality during a time-limited war is one thing. Suspending it during a more or less permanent condition is quite another. The latter is the end of the rule of law itself.

To the extent that the war on terrorism is a condition rather than a more traditional war, it seems clear that the proper response for legal analysis is to think through what the more or less permanent balance between liberty and security should be.[15] Put another way, war as a condition is a *normal* state of affairs, not an emergency in which extraordinary measures might be appropriate. And the normal constitutional rules ought to apply in normal conditions — although, again, what the normal rules are might take into account the conditions that the nation is experiencing.

EMERGENCY AS THE OCCASION FOR EXTRALEGAL DECISIONS

The case for treating emergency as the occasion for the suspension of legality rests on a set of judgments.[16] First, the suspension of legality is (almost) inevitable. Second, attempting to identify — in law — the circumstances under which legality can be suspended is futile. And, third, attempting to do so is pernicious as well, because it undermines the important values captured in the rule-of-law tradition.

Why is the suspension of legality almost inevitable? Constitution designers cannot anticipate all the forms of emergency that will arise and prompt governing élites to expand their power,[17] perhaps beyond the limits that the constitution designers imposed. At best, constitution designers will use the crises they have experienced to develop some general criteria identifying crises, but even such modeling will inevitably fall short. What, if anything, can constitutional law contribute to thinking about the role of law in emergencies?

We could follow the first or second approaches discussed earlier, leaving the regulation of emergency powers to the initial constitution. Or we could place legal restraints — in the constitution — on triggering emergency powers and on the powers that can be used in emergencies. And finally, we could acknowledge that executive officials will exercise extra-constitutional emergency powers. I use the term *extra*-constitutional to introduce a third term, distinct from *legal* or *illegal*. Extra-constitutional powers are neither legal — a person exercising them is immune from sanction pursuant to law — nor illegal — a well-functioning legal system does not require the invocation of sanctions (public or private) against a person exercising them. Rather, extra-constitutional powers are "reviewed" — and disciplined — not by law but by a mobilized citizenry. Having dealt with the first course already, I take up the others here.

Constraining Emergency Powers by Constitutionalizing Them

Constitution writers can acknowledge that emergencies will arise by attempting to anticipate them and regulate the responses that emergencies elicit. The U.S. Constitution, for example, contains a provision on emergencies: "The Privilege of the Writ of Habeas Corpus shall not be suspended, unless when in Cases of Rebellion or Invasion the public Safety shall require it."[18] This identifies the *occasions* on which the protection afforded by the writ of habeas corpus can be suspended — rebellion or invasion — and provides a *criterion* for determining when the writ can be suspended — public safety.[19]

The Suspension Clause provides an example as well of some problems associated with seeking to constrain emergency powers by addressing them in a constitution.[20] The primary difficulty is the fundamental one, that constitution writers cannot anticipate all the occasions on which governing élites will think that it is good policy to invoke emergency powers, nor can they specify in detail all the criteria regulating such invocations. For example, was the attack on the World Trade Center towers an "invasion" within the meaning of the Suspension Clause? If so, is the *threat* of an invasion, in the form of some similar attack, ground for suspending the writ?

That emergencies with unanticipated characteristics arise means that such emergencies will place pressure on whatever constitutional provisions there are. If the attack on the World Trade Center towers was not exactly an invasion of the sort the framers had in mind, still, governing élites may think, it is enough like such an invasion to mean that the Constitution permits suspension of the writ. And if that attack is enough like a (true) invasion, so the threat of another attack might be enough like a (true) invasion. And so forth.[21]

The general point is obvious: Constitutional provisions that purport to regulate the invocation of emergency powers will be subject to pressure on precisely those occasions when the provisions seem not to address the situation facing policy makers, which are also precisely the occasions when restrictions on the invocation of emergency powers would seem most important. Including emergency powers provisions in a constitution might well be futile, because those powers will be exercised no matter what the constitution says.

One might think, as Oren Gross does, that we can avoid these difficulties by imposing only procedural obligations on officials who suspend legality. They must, Gross says, "openly and publicly acknowledge the nature of their actions."[22] They are then subject to retrospective evaluation, criticism, and perhaps sanction. Yet Gross's approach cannot avoid *some* substantive elements, because those elements serve as the triggers for invocation of his approach. Consider the official who says (to himself or herself, of course), "The nature of the present emergency is such that an open and public acknowledgement that I am departing from legality would undermine the effectiveness of the action that must be taken." Gross's approach simultaneously licenses the official to do so and — by definition, not by the social reaction he anticipates — condemns the official for doing so.

Louis Michael Seidman has forcefully made the general point here. One cannot use law to determine when legality should be suspended.[23] Suppose we think that suspension of legality is dangerous and ought not be done except when circumstances most urgently require it. We list the circumstances that in our present judgment would justify the suspension of legality, and the procedures to be used to determine when those circumstances exist (or, in Gross's approach, simply specify procedures that must be used whenever an official seeks to suspend legality). Along comes an emergency. Perhaps it has characteristics that can, with a lawyer's ingenuity, be found on the list. All well and good. But suppose the emergency is new, that the specified procedures are ill suited to determining whether *this* is an emergency, or that the official believes that invoking the procedures will vitiate the action being taken. In all these cases, the government can contend, the emergency is so pressing that it requires suspension of the legality expressed in the list of criteria for determining whether legality should be suspended, and the procedures for doing so. There is, I think, no response to this argument available to those who believe that suspension of legality is sometimes defensible.

But there is a further point. Governments operating after the invocation of emergency powers provisions are sometimes called *regimes of exception*.[24] That term properly recalls the proposition stated by Carl Schmitt, that the person who has the power to invoke the exception is the true sovereign in a nation.[25] Further, Schmitt argued that the (liberal) rule of law could not— either conceptually or practically—limit a nation's response to perceived emergencies. Schmitt initially distinguished between an absolute form of emergency rule, in which the invocation and use of emergency powers were completely unconstrained, and a rule-of-law form, in which the law identified the occasions for invoking emergency power, the criteria for doing so, and the precise types of action that emergency power justifies.[26] A year later Schmitt rejected this distinction, arguing that only the first form of emergency power is available because emergencies are situations in which a nation's very existence is perceived to be at stake, and the rule of law cannot constrain a nation's efforts to survive. This third approach, Schmitt understood, cannot be cabined by legality itself. Officials may suspend legality whenever they think it appropriate, that power being inherent in the offices they hold. The public's recourse lies in the future, not in controls imposed in the short run.

It is important to emphasize the breadth of the foregoing argument. As Carl Schmitt understood, the invocation of emergency powers is continuous with, not distinct from, quotidian politics, which are *always* open to the arguments for suspension of legality that I have outlined. It would be pretty if the reality were otherwise, but the possibility that ordinary politics can be transformed into the suspension of legality needs to be acknowledged, if only so we can understand what politics is.

As I have emphasized, regimes of exception *will* arise; the only real question is how to locate them in relation to the nation's constitution. Or, put another way, was Schmitt right the first time, in holding out the possibility of a constrained system of emergency powers, or the second, in insisting that only the absolute form of emergency rule was possible? Consider one aspect of emergency powers under Schmitt's first view. Constitutional provisions dealing with emergency powers place regimes of exception *within* the constitutional order. Constitutional provisions dealing with emergency powers provide a language of justification for the invocation of emergency powers, even though the precise language used in the constitution may be inapt for the occasions on which emergency powers are invoked. The provisions provide executive officials with a fig leaf of legal justification for the expansive use of sheer power. What appears to be emergency power limited by the rule of law is actually unlimited emergency power. As a matter of social self-understanding, it is better to see the thing as it is, not as one might wish it to be. Doing so *might* make it possible to arrive at more accurate retrospective evaluations. But no matter what, we are better off understanding how our constitutional system works — in emergencies and, according to Schmitt, therefore in normal times as well — than we are in misunderstanding it.

Emergency Powers *outside* the Constitution

David Dyzenhaus argues that judges can domesticate emergency powers by subjecting their exercise to the ordinary requirements of the rule of law. In the view of other authors — who take the position that Schmitt initially did — well-designed emergency powers provisions can avoid the difficulties that have arisen with existing ones. The second option is, as Seidman has shown, not really available. And, the first may overestimate the ability of judges to resist the pressures that lead other public officials to suspend legality.

Dyzenhaus hints at another path. Decision makers might treat emergency powers as extra-constitutional, an understandable departure from the norms of legality. Justice Robert Jackson's opinion in *Korematsu* suggests how courts could conceptualize emergency powers in this way:

> [I]f we cannot confine military expedients by the Constitution, neither would I distort the Constitution to approve all that the military may deem expedient. . . . [A] judicial construction of the due process clause that will sustain this order is a far more subtle blow to liberty than the promulgation of the order itself. . . . [O]nce a judicial opinion rationalizes such an order to show that it conforms to the Constitution or rather rationalizes the Constitution to show that the Constitution sanctions

such an order, the Court for all time has validated . . . [a] principle [that] lies about like a loaded weapon ready for the hand of any authority that can bring forward a plausible claim of an urgent need. . . . The chief restraint upon those who command the physical forces of the country, in the future as in the past, must be their responsibility to the political judgments of their contemporaries and to the moral judgments of history.[27]

Jackson does not quite make the point I extract from his opinion, which is that it is better to have emergency powers exercised in an extra-constitutional way, so that everyone understands that the actions are extraordinary, than to have the actions rationalized away as consistent with the Constitution and thereby normalized. We might call this a claim that the actions have an extra-constitutional validity, one that the *courts* can neither endorse nor condemn but that is consistent with the persistence of the constitutional regime, which is sustained by the vigilance of the public acting, as it was put in the era of the American Revolution, "out of doors."[28]

Why, then, worry about whether emergency powers are rationalized within the law, or treated as extra-constitutional? If emergency powers are extra-constitutional, decision makers can then understand that they should regret to find themselves compelled to invoke emergency powers.[29] Once the emergency has passed they should not only revert to the norms of legality that were suspended during the emergency, but do what they can to make reparation for the actions they took.[30] Here too Lincoln should be our guide, for among his observations in his Second Inaugural Address, delivered in anticipation of a successful conclusion of the Civil War, was the injunction that we "strive on . . . to bind up the nation's wounds."[31]

Again, it is important to note that according to this analysis, decision makers must be aware that they are acting extra-constitutionally in an emergency. They can be brought to that awareness by, among other things, the repeated assertions of civil liberties alarmists that the officials are acting, not extra-constitutionally, but *illegally*.

Posner and Vermeule treat this problem as a simple variant of the more common problem of finding a conflict between the requirements of law and those of morality. Officials can, they say, always choose to act morally, in disregard of the law, and then hope to persuade others that their actions were justified. The problem of the justified suspension of legality is related to, but not the same as, the one that Posner and Vermeule describe.

The differences are these. First, in the ordinary case, the official says, "My obligations under the law direct me to do X, but my moral duties require that I do Y." In the case of suspension of legality, the official says, "The law gives me the power that I have, but in exercising that power morality requires that I disregard the law — all the law, including the law that enables me to deploy the power at hand." The circularity is apparent. It arises from the use of a position created by law to suspend the law. In the ordinary case, the official has the option of resigning his or her position to avoid acting immorally. In the case of the suspension of legality, that option is unavailable.

Second, and probably more important, the ordinary case involves a discrete, limited-issue departure from legality in the service of morality. The official who acts morally but illegally can take some comfort in knowing that his or her actions do not pose a threat to the ideal of the rule of law. Certainly, there will be occasional conflicts between morality and law in a well-functioning rule-of-law system, but the overlap between law and morality in such a system is likely to be so large that an official who disregards the law to act morally will not cast doubt on the continuing value of the rule-of-law system itself. In contrast, the entire point of suspending legality in emergencies is to displace the rule of law. Perhaps this means only that the stakes are much higher when legality is suspended, but I think the difference in degree justifies distinctive analytic treatment.

The problem of taking action in emergencies raises deep questions of constitutional theory — questions that are not well addressed by treating emergencies as occasions for deploying either ordinary constitutional law or a special kind of constitutional law adapted to emergencies, the course recommended by those who are complacent about the relation between war and constitutionalism. I have argued that we can get a better handle on thinking about constitutional law during emergencies by treating emergencies as occasions for the extra-constitutional suspension of legality. The dangers of such a course are apparent, which gives the constitutional alarmists an important social role. From a more detached position, though, the primary observation must be that neither complacency nor alarmism is an intellectually satisfactory course. The situations in which questions of emergency powers arise are too complex for either. Perhaps the best we can hope for is the development of a more satisfactory structure of analysis to help us think about what policy makers should do.

NOTES

1   I believe this to be the position that Posner and Vermeule describe in their chapter as the *strict* approach to constitutional law during wartime.

2   I believe this to be the position that Posner and Vermeule describe as the *accommodationist* approach.

3   Abraham Lincoln, Annual Message to Congress, 1 December 1862.

4   Home Building & Loan Ass'n v. Blaisdell, 290 U.S. 398, 426 (1934).

5   Schenck v. United States, 249 U.S. 47, 52 (1919).

6   For one thing, Holmes was himself a member of a court that was at the very moment deciding whether the speech in question was constitutionally protected.

7   Woods v. Cloyd W. Miller Co., 333 U.S. 138, 146 (1948) (Jackson, J., concurring).

8   As Lino Graglia puts it, in *Blaisdell* "the Court missed its best, if not its only, chance to hold unconstitutional a law that really was." Lino A. Graglia, "Constitutional Law: A Ruse for Government by an Intellectual Elite," 14 *Georgia State Law Review* 767, 772 (1998).

9   McCulloch v. Maryland, 17 U.S. (4 Wheat.) 316, 407, 415 (1819).

10   Oren Gross distinguishes three types of "separation," of which the temporal one I use here is one. (The others involve separations of space and between the true domestic community and mere temporary residents.) He argues, I believe correctly, that the analytic points are the same for all three types. Oren Gross, "Chaos and Rules: Should Responses to Violent Crises Always Be Constitutional?," 112 *Yale Law Journal* 1011, 1073–96 (2003).

11   Although perhaps fewer judges than executive officials will feel that need, or perhaps judges will feel the need to a lesser extent.

12   David Dyzenhaus, "Humpty Dumpty Rules or the Rule of Law: Legal Theory and the Adjudication of National Security," 28 *Australian Journal of Legal Philosophy* (2003).

13   See David Dyzenhaus, "The Permanence of the Temporary: Can Emergency Powers Be Normalized?," in Ronald J. Daniels, Patrick Macklem, and Kent Roach eds., *The Security of Freedom: Essays on Canada's Anti-Terrorism Bill* (2001), 21. Dyzenhaus notes that the title of his chapter comes from a work written by two South Africans dealing with emergency powers under apartheid. *Id.* at 23.

14   Available at http://www.bartleby.com/124/pres61.html (visited 7 November 2002).

15   In this connection, it is worth noting one possibility: according to the most relevant retrospective evaluation of current policies, those policies might be found to have rested on the proposition that the United States was engaged in a

war on terrorism, whereas in fact the United States will seem in retrospect to have been experiencing a condition of terrorism. Judge Michael Mukasey's discussion of the possibility that indefinite detention of a U.S. citizen as an enemy combatant might become "moot" may perhaps be understood as the judge's recognition that what is today perceived as a war will later become perceived as a condition, although there are other reasons one might have for thinking that a detention justified today might become unjustified in light of later events. (Judge Mukasey's opinion is Padilla v. Bush, 233 F. Supp. 2d 564 (2002).)

16 Gross, "Chaos and Rules," refers to the subject of this section as the Extra-Legal Measures Model.

17 In referring to interest among governing élites in exercising this sort of power, I do not mean to suggest that the élites will be unified either on the appropriateness of exercising emergency powers in any particular situation or on the choice of policies to pursue in that situation. What matters for me is that some significant members of the governing élites will press for the adoption of expansive powers, in the face of a constitution that apparently fails to anticipate the emergency confronting the nation (in the view of these members of the élites) and that also constrains the adoption of policies in response to the perceived emergency.

18 U.S. Constitution, article I, § 9, clause 2.

19 Other constitutions provide a more extensive list of occasions and criteria, and identify substantive constitutional protections that can be suspended during periods of emergency. These provisions are sometimes described as following a "reference model" for emergency powers. See, for example, Joan Fitzpatrick, *Human Rights in Crisis: The International System for Protecting Rights during States of Emergency* (1994), 21 (drawing the term from a report by Nicole Questiaux to the United Nations Sub-Commission on the Prevention of Discrimination and Protection of Minorities). My view is that the Suspension Clause is all that is needed to protect substantive constitutional rights against violation: Guaranteeing the existence of a remedy for claimed constitutional violations is equivalent to guaranteeing substantive rights themselves.

20 Committing the decision to suspend the writ to Congress seems to deal with the problem of aggressive assertions of executive authority in emergencies. But the commitment may be illusory. Perhaps the Constitution can be read, as Lincoln thought it could, to authorize the president to suspend the writ as long as he seeks congressional approval as speedily as possible thereafter. Even more, presidents will almost always be able to identify some statute that authorizes them, they will say, to suspend the writ. A court might eventually find that the president's interpretation of the statutes is erroneous, but in the meantime the writ will have been effectively suspended by action of the president alone.

21 If the threat of another attack similar to the ones of September 11 counts as an invasion, why would not the threat of an attack from Iraq?

22 Gross, "Chaos and Rules," 1023.

23 Louis Michael Seidman, "The Secret Life of the Political Question Doctrine," 37 *John Marshall Law Review* 441 (2004).

24 See, for example, Brian Loveman, *The Constitution of Tyranny: Regimes of Exception in Spanish America* (1993).

25 Carl Schmitt, *Political Theology* (George Schwab trans., 1988), 1.

26 For a discussion, see Gross, "The Normless and Exceptionless Exception: Carl Schmitt's Theory of Emergency Powers and the 'Norm-Exception' Dichotomy," 21 *Cardozo Law Review* 1825–68 (2000).

27 323 U.S. at 245–46 (Jackson, J., dissenting).

28 I am indebted to Wayne Moore for this term. Moore suggests as well that the first two approaches I described could be called *constitutional legality* and *extralegal constitutional validity*.

29 That is why I describe the invocation of emergency powers as an understandable departure from legality rather than a justified one. A justified departure from legality would not be regrettable. Wayne Moore suggests that we might distinguish between the decision makers, who might not be in a position to regret taking the decisions they do, and others, such as Supreme Court justices, who might regret being required to allow others to make extra-constitutional decisions.

30 The Civil Liberties Act of 1988, 50 U.S.C. §§ 1989a et. seq., can then be understood as an expression of the view developed here.

31 Second Inaugural Address, in *Abraham Lincoln: Speeches and Writings, 1859–1865* (D. Fehrenbacher ed. 1989), 697.

Accommodating Emergencies

Eric A. Posner and Adrian Vermeule

Two Views

There are two main views about the proper role of the Constitution during national emergencies. We label them the "accommodation" view and the "strict" view. The accommodation view is that the Constitution should be relaxed or suspended during an emergency. During an emergency, it is important that power be concentrated. Power should move up from the states to the federal government, and within the federal government from the legislature and the judiciary to the executive. Constitutional rights should be relaxed, so that the executive can move forcefully against the threat. If dissent weakens resolve, then dissent should be curtailed. If domestic security is at risk, then intrusive searches should be tolerated. There is no reason to think that the constitutional rights and powers appropriate for an emergency are the same as those that prevail during times of normalcy. The reason for relaxing constitutional norms during emergencies is that the risks inherent in expansive executive power — the misuse of the power for political gain — are justified by the national security benefits.

The second major view about emergencies is that constitutional rules are not, and should not be, relaxed during an emergency. This view starts from the observation that the Constitution already varies the level of protection for civil liberties depending on the interest of the government. Consider, for example, "compelling interest" standards used to evaluate laws that discriminate against protected classes. When an emergency exists, the government has a "compelling interest" in responding to it in a vigorous and effective way. Thus, laws that would not be tolerated during non-emergencies are constitutionally permissible during emergencies. Racial or ethnic profiling, for example, is likely to be seen as less objectionable when used to prevent a terrorist attack than when used to interdict the distribution of illegal drugs. The Constitution should be enforced "strictly" — that is, the rules should be the same during emergencies as during non-emergencies, even if outcomes differ — so that both civil liberties and government interests such as national security can be appropriately balanced, as they always need to be.

As a practical matter, the difference between the two views will be reflected in the aggressiveness of the courts. Under the first view, the courts will defer to emergency policy once they determine that an emergency exists. The courts do not demand that the government justify emergency measures by showing that they serve a compelling interest. Under the second view, courts may permit many emergency measures, but only after subjecting them to review, and courts are likely to strike down many emergency measures as well. The first view has generally been adopted by American courts during emergencies; the second view is the favored position among civil libertarians and law professors.[1]

Defenders of accommodation argue that rules that are appropriate during normal times are not appropriate for emergencies. Judges are not capable of evaluating the actions of the executive and therefore should defer to its judgment rather than subject emergency policies to constitutional review. National security is a preeminent value; when national security is at stake, vigorous action is needed, and the public has no choice other than to put its trust in the executive. The underlying calculus is that the costs of temporary dictatorship (including the risk that it will become permanent) and suppression of civil liberties are less than the cost of national destruction.

Defenders of the strict enforcement view might deny that this calculus is correct. They might argue that national security is not so important, that the loss of civil liberties is more important than the accommodators think, or that the executive invariably discounts civil liberties and exaggerates national security. But this argument is a dead end. There is no reason to think that judges are more likely to make the right tradeoff between security and civil liberties than the executive is; nor is there any reason to think that the constitutional rules evolved during peacetime reflect the appropriate tradeoffs during emergencies. That the executive's hands are on the levers of power is a sufficient reason for vesting him with the authority to make this tradeoff rather than deferring to peacetime constitutional rules developed by the courts.

Defenders of the strict enforcement view have proposed two other rationales for their position. These rationales provide two special reasons for thinking that executives, whether acting on their own or in response to public demand, will typically put too much weight on security, and not enough on civil liberties.

One rationale for strict enforcement during emergencies is institutional. The argument is that emergencies work like a ratchet: with every emergency, constitutional protections are reduced, and after the emergency is over enhancement of constitutional powers is either maintained or not fully eliminated, so that the executive ends up with more power after the emergency than it had before the emergency. With each successive emergency, the executive's power is ratcheted up. Or, to change the figure, the Constitution loses some of its spring every time it is pushed out of shape.

The other rationale is psychological: during an emergency people panic, and when they panic they support policies that are unwise and excessive. Relaxation of constitutional protections would give free rein to the panicked reaction, when what is needed is constraint. Normal constitutional protections hinder the enactment of bad laws during emergencies. To the critic who argues that normal constitutional protections also prevent the needed concentration of power in the executive, the defender of strict enforcement argues that any hindrances on forceful executive action would be justified by the benefits, namely the avoided laws and acts that reflect fear rather than reason.

Both the ratchet theory and the panic theory have conceptual, normative, and empirical difficulties. The ratchet theory lacks a mechanism that permits constitutional powers to rise and prevents them from falling, and makes implausible assumptions about the rationality of individuals who consent to constitutional changes during emergencies. Those who fear the ratchet's power often point to constitutional trends — such as the rise of executive power — that are the result of long-term technological and demographic changes, not of recurrent emergencies; and they ignore the possibility of constitutional trends in the opposite direction, such as the rise of individual rights. (If there is such a trend, it is not a ratchet process either; we include a critique of an optimistic variant of the emergency ratchet, in which a succession of emergencies causes government to display ever-increasing respect for civil liberties.) As for the panic theory, it assumes that people can, while panicked, get outside themselves and constrain their own fear. Although people and officials do panic, we have found little evidence that constitutions or other laws or institutions can control the panic and cause people to lose their fear, or else to choose, while panicked, laws that they would choose if they were not panicked. Finally, defenders of each theory do not examine their normative premises sufficiently: it is not clear that panics and ratchets, if they occur, are bad things. Fear is often the correct response to a threat; panics can shatter constitutional structures, but sometimes constitutional structures should be shattered. Ratchets put the status quo out of reach, but sometimes that is where it should be.

Our argument is negative. We do not defend the current level of accommodation; instead, we criticize two special arguments that the current level of judicial deference is wrong. To show that the current level of deference is correct, one would need to compare the institutional capacities of the judiciary and the executive. Although we will say more about this comparison in our conclusion, the comparison is not the focus of this chapter.

RATCHETS

Ratchets, in General

The "ratchet" (or, redundantly, the "one-way ratchet") is a favored analytic tool of legal theorists. For a genuine ratchet to occur, highly specialized conditions must obtain. The essential features of a ratchet are *unidirectional* and *irreversible* change in some legal variable.[2] First, the policy space in which the ratchet occurs is assumed to be one-dimensional, so that the ratchet produces ever-increasing values of a variable — more and more and more of something. Second, the incremental increases are fixed or costly to undo once they occur. At time 1, some legal rule or practice emerges endogenously from political processes, including the legal system; at time 2, the rule or practice is cemented by some mechanism, and has become an exogenous constraint; at time 3 some dimension of the rule increases endogenously; at time 4 the increase is cemented into place; and the process repeats indefinitely. These conditions are rare, perhaps even nonexistent. The danger here is that the "ratchet" label is being bandied about too freely, and is often confused with a simple trend that happens to extend over time, or with endogenous but easily reversible change in some variable that would quickly revert to its original value if other legal or social conditions changed.

Despite the ubiquity of ratchet accounts, few such accounts are fully specified, and often there is no plausible way to cash them out. Take a popular idea, or intuition, in constitutional theory: if conservative judges respect precedent while liberal judges freely overrule precedents, and conservative courts alternate with liberal ones, then a ratchet effect is created, whereby the existing stock of precedents becomes increasingly liberal over time. But this account is either out of equilibrium, or arbitrarily assumes that the two camps have wildly disparate preferences. If the implicit picture is that both liberal and conservative judges are political, seeking to embody their preferences and attitudes in legal decisions, then conservative judges are myopic in refusing to overrule liberal decisions; they are repeatedly, and inexplicably, duped by the equally unprincipled but more cunning liberals. So the picture must instead be that liberal judges are political while conservative judges have a strong and principled preference for adhering to any past decision, whatever its political valence; but this seems arbitrary.

Perhaps history contains a few genuine ratchet processes. The continual, and doubtless irreversible, expansion of the political franchise in liberal democracies over the course of the nineteenth and twentieth centuries might qualify. But even here there are problems; although it seems intuitive that voting rights, once granted, are difficult to revoke (assuming that the recently enfranchised may themselves vote on any revocation proposal), it is not obvious why enfranchised groups would continually admit politically powerless groups into the political system. In general, ratchet arguments are methodologically suspect, and are invoked with far greater frequency than is warranted by theory or evidence. This pattern holds true for ratchet arguments about emergency powers, to which we now turn.

The Statist Ratchet

The statist ratchet identifies a putative tendency of emergency policies to "become entrenched over time and thus normalized and made routine. . . .

The maintenance of emergency powers may be accompanied by expansion over time of the scope of such powers. At the same time, built-in limitations on the exercise of emergency authority and powers tend to wither away."[3]

As it turns out, however, the statist ratchet account has only a surface sheen of plausibility, and no core. It assumes that emergencies produce unidirectional and irreversible change in the direction of official intrusion on civil liberties. But there is no obvious reason to think that any such process occurs; the statist ratchet fails to supply a mechanism that would explain such a process if it did occur; and if there is such a mechanism, it is not clear that the resulting ratchet process is bad.

Conceptual Problems

The statist ratchet, like all ratchet accounts, assumes a finite, one-dimensional policy space. In this space, government policies vary from minimally to maximally intrusive; the statist ratchet assumes that emergencies produce a continual increase that is unidirectional on this dimension, moving steadily from less official oppression to more.

But this picture is far too crude. The policy space is not one-dimensional but multidimensional: official policies, whether instituted during an emergency or not, can intrude more (or less) on some margins while intruding less (or more) on others. At time T the government policy for airport security is to search passengers who fit a given ethnic and religious profile. At time T + 1 the policy changes to random searches; the new policy, let us say, imposes a cost (at least in an expected sense) on a greater number of people, but reduces the stigma of being searched. Here it is senseless to ask whether liberty has been increased or decreased; instead it has been redistributed, by imposing a smaller deprivation more widely. Second, there is the standard problem of conflicts or tensions between and among libertarian rights, arising from budget constraints on the government that funds the institutions needed to protect those rights. More money for airport searches may reduce the need for ethnic profiling, but it may mean less money for public defenders, or a longer court queue for citizens asserting constitutional liberties against government.

These two problems mean that officials face the difficult problem of aggregating incompatible liberties across different individuals. In rare cases,

Pareto-improving moves will enable greater security at a given level of official intrusion, or less intrusion with a constant level of security; but in most cases more liberty for some means less liberty for others. Because aggregative judgments are inescapable, it is not so much wrong as incoherent to speak generally of "society" having "more" or "less" liberty. The simplistic picture of unidimensional, unidirectional change embodied in the statist ratchet does not begin to engage these problems.

Finally, the boundaries of the policy space themselves change over time. Exogenous shocks arising from technological, economic, and social change can transform the policy arenas in which the balance between security and liberty is played out. Unanticipated change undermines government's ability to control liberties. In place of the menacing picture drawn by the statist ratchet, envisaging a continuous increase of official power over information and personal conduct, we might imagine government as a rat on a treadmill, constantly struggling to keep pace with new forms of technology and new modes of citizen behavior.

Institutional Mechanisms?

Statist ratchet accounts fail to specify any institutional mechanism by which legal and political measures intended to combat emergencies become irreversible. Why, exactly, do temporary measures stick after the emergency has passed? Although statist ratchet accounts usually gloss over this point, we can imagine several related mechanisms. First, judicial precedent developed in times of emergency might distend or spill over into the ordinary legal system, and precedent will be costly to overrule. Second, legal rules developed in times of emergency may be protected by the status quo bias built into the legislative system, or by the formation of bureaucracies and interest groups that coalesce around the new measures and block subsequent efforts to repeal them. We critique these ideas in turn.

PRECEDENT. The locus classicus for the argument from precedent is Justice Jackson's dissent in *Korematsu v. United States*, with its famous claim that "once a judicial opinion rationalizes [an emergency] order to show that it conforms to the Constitution or rather rationalizes the Constitution to show that the Constitution sanctions such an order, the Court for all time has validated . . . [a] principle [that] lies about like a loaded weapon ready for the hand of any authority that can bring forward a plausible claim of an urgent need."[4]

Jackson's idea is obscure. Suppose that judicial precedents explicitly uphold government actions in a time of crisis on the ground that the emergency justifies the order, even if a similar order would be invalid in ordinary times. Why must the precedent both (1) spill over into ordinary law and (2) remain entrenched "for all time," as Jackson puts it? As for the first condition, the precedent will itself have a built-in limitation to emergency circumstances. Presumably the idea is that precedents are extremely malleable, and the category of "emergency" is a fluid and unstable one. But if this is so it is so in both directions; later judges may either distend the precedent to accommodate government power or else contract the precedent to constrain it. Jackson's exegetes need to supply an independent account to explain why the former possibility is more likely, and more harmful, than the latter, and they have not done so.

The best stab at an account of this sort appears in another opinion by Jackson. Institutional incentives will cause the executive to press the boundaries of the "emergency" category to ever-broader extremes, and that will be possible because the category of "emergency" is extraordinarily nebulous and difficult to specify through legal formulations. Cognitive limitations will induce the courts to acquiesce in this expansion. Because the courts will be aware of the limits of their information and the high risks of error if they frustrate executive action in a genuine emergency, they will adopt a deferential stance.[5] This reconstructed argument seems plausible as far as it goes, but rational judges who are aware of their cognitive limitations — and this account assumes self-awareness — can anticipate the slippage and forestall it, by *initially* defining the category of emergency more narrowly than they otherwise would. The eventual expansion of the category will simply reinstate its optimal scope, rather than exceeding it.

At bottom, Jackson's view must rest on a simple empirical conjecture: the expansion of emergency powers, once begun, will inevitably culminate in total executive domination. But this seems hysterical; there is no evidence for it in the study of comparative politics. Many constitutions contain explicit provisions for emergency powers, either in text or in judicial doctrine. Sometimes executive domination has overtaken the relevant polities, sometimes it has not; other variables probably dominate, such as the nation's stage of development, or its susceptibility to economic shocks, or the design of legislative and judicial institutions. Jackson's exegetes bear the burden of showing, systematically, that recognizing a legal category of emergency powers automatically sends the constitution reeling to the bottom of the slippery slope. A casual citation to a few salient examples, typically the emergency provisions of the Weimar constitution, will not carry that burden.

As for the second condition, it is hard to see why precedents granting government emergency powers should be irreversibly entrenched, at least if precedents denying the government emergency powers are not. Stare decisis will be either strong or weak. If it is weak, then past precedents granting emergency powers can be overruled, even if they cannot be cabined to emergency situations. If stare decisis is strong, then courts will be unable to overrule precedents that previously denied government emergency powers in particular settings, or that strongly entrenched liberties, as well as precedents that granted emergency powers. Here too the argument from precedent cuts in both directions. There is no ratchet mechanism that uniquely applies to precedents upholding government claims of emergency power; the general stickiness of precedent is a far broader point.

LEGISLATION (AND CONSTITUTIONAL AMENDMENT). The argument from precedent points to the inertia built into the judicial system; there is a similar argument that points to the inertia of the lawmaking system, embodied in the costly procedures for statutory enactment and constitutional amendment. These design features partially entrench the legal status quo; the statist ratchet account might implicitly suppose that temporary legislation or constitutional provisions, enacted during emergencies, will thus stick after the emergency has passed. But rational and well-motivated legislators can anticipate this possibility by inserting sunset provisions in emergency legislation (as Congress did in the USA PATRIOT Act); rational and well-motivated constitutional drafters can insert sunset provisions in constitutional rules. Gross argues that "[t]ime-bound emergency legislation is often the subject of future extensions and renewals,"[6] and there are current proposals to extend the PATRIOT Act or repeal its sunset clause, but the existence of the sunset clause alters the status quo point: unless proponents of extension can surmount the costly hurdles to legislative action, the statute will lapse automatically. Thus libertarian opponents of renewal still enjoy the advantage of legislative inertia.

The statist ratchet account must suppose that legislators either irrationally fail to anticipate the future termination of the emergency, perhaps because they are gripped by "panic," or else that legislators are motivated to use any and every emergency as a means to expand the permanent powers of government. We address "panic" below. As for motivations, the idea that legislators desire to maximize permanent state power as against the individual is vivid, but it lacks microfoundations in the behavior of the individuals who occupy the legislature. Why, exactly, does it benefit legislators to expand the powers of government? As individuals, they may or may not benefit; even if legislators have an individual stake in the power of Congress as an institution, expanding government power in times of emergency usually benefits the executive most of all, and the executive is Congress's principal institutional rival. The statist ratchet fails to offer a plausible account of legislators' maximands. We might posit that legislators strictly maximize their chances of re-election, but then the question just becomes why constituents demand legislation that (for lack of sunsetting) will outlive the emergency, and the picture must be that during emergencies constituents *irrationally* demand permanent legislation; so we are back to the "panic" idea again.

Even accepting the premise that legislators are frequently irrational or ill motivated, pointing to the status quo bias built into the lawmaking system proves too much. The status quo bias operates neutrally across different types of statutes and constitutional provisions. It not only (1) entrenches liberty-restricting laws (the only case the statist ratchet acknowledges), but equally (2) prevents enactment of liberty-restricting laws, and (3) entrenches liberty-protecting ones. As for case (2), the high costs of statutory enactment can weed out the most draconian proposals for controlling sedition and terrorism; an example is Senator Chamberlin's proposal in 1918 to enact legislation that would allow the government to punish spies by court-martial, which was killed by President Wilson's opposition. As for case (3), the costs of enactment protect from repeal any laws that protect liberties from infringement by later legislatures or the executive. Consider the Posse Comitatus Act, which blocks the executive from using regular armed forces for domestic law enforcement, and thus embodies a traditional libertarian anxiety. The act is just as entrenched by the lawmaking process as the PATRIOT Act would be, had Congress not provided a sunset provision.

BUREAUCRACIES AND INTEREST GROUPS. A related mechanism might posit that emergency policies generate bureaucracies that block repeal of those policies. On this view, creating new agencies to cope with an emergency, perhaps by consolidation of old agencies (as with the Department of Homeland Security), creates a cadre of officials with vested interests in prolonging the new bureaucracy for as long as possible, even after the emergency has passed. Those officials will use their influence, in Congress and with client interest groups, to block repeal of the agency's organic statute or diminution of the agency's power.

It is hardly clear that bureaucratic immortality is a real phenomenon. The same problems we have discussed — the underdeveloped account of officials' maximands, and the mismatch between the scope of the mechanism and the scope of the argument — persist here as well. It is unclear why rational legislators would fail to anticipate and block the future bureaucrats' strategy by inserting a sunset termination provision, a periodic review process, or some other device. And if bureaucratic inertia is a real phenomenon, it operates equally to block moves that would expand government power, restrict liberty, or permanently institutionalize a state of emergency. If an inefficient welter of competing security agencies hampers government's efforts to extend control over unpopular social groups,[7] then those agencies will attempt to block congressional attempts to reorganize them into a more efficient, and more menacing, centralized department. If Congress nonetheless succeeds in doing so, as it recently has, why cannot a future Congress succeed in abolishing or curtailing the agency created to meet the emergency? The dilemma for the statist ratchet account is that either bureaucratic inertia is real, in which case it will block liberty-infringing moves as well as liberty-expanding ones, or it is not real, in which case liberty-infringing moves will not become entrenched.

Generally speaking, there is no reason to suppose that laws, policies, and bureaucratic institutions created during an emergency (1) systematically fail to change, or change back, after a crisis has passed (2) because of institutional inertia and interest-group pressure. The First World War produced a large new cadre of regulatory agencies that persisted into the New Deal and beyond. But a plausible view is that the national economy was previously under-regulated, and that the new institutions satisfied social demand; so this example does not clearly satisfy condition (2). The Second

World War produced espionage and treason laws, and institutions like military tribunals, that were later relaxed and modified, in violation of condition (1); why did the statist ratchet not operate there? These examples are impressionistic, but not more so than the examples adduced by proponents of the statist ratchet. The better working presumption is just that no ratchet effects operate, in any direction; institutional change displays no consistent trend or mechanism, and is determined differently in different contexts by a complex mix of political, economic, and technological forces.

Adaptive Preferences?

We will briefly look at the idea that the statist ratchet operates by virtue of a psychological mechanism. Proponents of the statist ratchet account say, rather vaguely, that government's emergency measures have "a tranquilizing effect . . . on the general public's critical approach toward emergency regimes."[8] The underlying picture here must be some sort of endogenous preference formation, which causes social preferences to conform to government policies, or the related idea of adaptive preferences, in which individuals limit their aspirations, not merely their actions, by reference to the set of feasible policies. Somehow, the intuition runs, society gets used to the post-crisis baseline of expanded governmental power; the ratchet operates not because temporary emergency measures block society's capacity to return to the status quo ante, but because society no longer desires to do so.

The implicit assumption here is that the post-crisis baseline is bad. If it is good — if the pre-crisis baseline represented a society underprepared for emergencies, in which law and institutions were supplying too much liberty and not enough order — then the endogenous formation of preferences for the post-crisis baseline would help to stabilize the new regime, and would thus be good as well. At the very least we would need a very strong account of the value of autonomous preference formation to say that the public's adaptation to new social state is bad; the statist ratchet offers no such account. So the preference-based version of the statist ratchet is, like the institutional version, parasitic on a suppressed and wholly independent judgment that the status quo ante represents the correct balance between liberty and order.

In fact, however, the evidence that endogenous or adaptive preference formation operates in this way is scant indeed. Another view paints just the opposite picture of political and social psychology: in the post-crisis state, a widespread revulsion against the prevailing liberty-infringing policies sets in, and society judges, in hindsight, that the emergency measures were unnecessary. The stock example is the internment of Japanese-American citizens during the Second World War, which is now widely described as an egregious mistake that inflicted unnecessary deprivations of liberty, due in part to racial animus. If this sort of post hoc revulsion operates consistently, then the right account would emphasize contrarian preference formation and hindsight bias, rather than the endogenous preference formation and confirmation bias posited by the statist ratchet. But we will claim that a third account — no ratchets operate systematically, in either a liberty-restricting or a liberty-expanding direction — is the most convincing of all.

Is the Statist Ratchet Bad?

Normatively, the statist ratchet account simply assumes that the status quo ante — the legal baseline before the emergency that produces an irreversible expansion of state control — already embodies the optimal balance between liberty and security. So the statist ratchet in effect makes two normative assertions: (1) the pre-crisis legal rules were optimally balanced for the pre-crisis state; (2) the post-crisis rules are too restrictive for the post-crisis state.

Yet in some settings either or both of these assertions will fail to hold. We might deny (2) while affirming (1), if we think *both* that the pre-crisis rules were optimal for the pre-crisis state *and* that the post-crisis rules are optimal for the post-crisis state. If, for example, the crisis is the product of a permanent change in the polity's political circumstances, such that the value of security is higher after the crisis than before it, then the balance should be recalibrated after the crisis; failing to have that done would constitute social paralysis, rather than a laudable respect for traditional liberties.

More interestingly, we might deny both (1) and (2), if we think that before the emergency society was, in some sense, unprepared for the emergency, under-regulated, or excessively liberty protecting, while after the emergency society has attained the optimal balance. We might believe, for example, that as of September 10, 2001, American governmental institutions were supplying too much liberty and not enough security. Well-documented turf battles between uncoordinated, and arguably inefficient, security and intelligence agencies meant that government failed to anticipate and forestall a major terrorist attack, or even to plan sensibly for its aftermath. On this sort of view, the institutional puzzle would be to explain why government underreacted to the terrorist threat—the opposite of the puzzle for the statist ratchet account, which is to explain why government overreacts to threats. The point here is not to endorse this view of post-9/11 security reorganization on the merits. But the possibility cannot be assumed away a priori.

Proponents of the statist ratchet rarely consider these possibilities. Take Dermot Walsh's argument that the expansion of law enforcement powers in the Republic of Ireland, from about 1970 to the present, has created a legal regime in which the official power to investigate and detain both suspected terrorists and ordinary criminals systematically trumps civil liberties.[9] Walsh's account suggests that legal rules initially formulated to cope with terrorist campaigns and other security emergencies bled over into ordinary policing, resulting in a harsh regime of criminal procedure.

Nothing in Walsh's history suggests any reason to condemn, on substantive civil libertarian grounds, the result of the developments he describes. Walsh notes that the initial impetus for expanded law enforcement authority was "[t]he escalation of subversive activity associated with Northern Ireland," and acknowledges that the existing law was "so heavily biased in favour of the freedom of the individual that the task facing the prosecution could be described fairly as a very tricky obstacle course."[10] So an obvious alternative view is that in Ireland, circa 1970, the law of criminal procedure was too lax for an increasingly complex and heterogeneous society—perhaps because the relevant law was initially impressed with the libertarian mold of nineteenth-century British procedure, and had never been updated. The expansion of police powers after 1970, on this view, would just represent a belated adjustment toward the optimum balance of liberty and security, not a lamentable departure from that balance.

Why, exactly, is it bad if emergency or temporary measures spill over into the ordinary legal system? Spillover of this sort is, in itself, neither good nor bad. The only question is whether the new state of affairs is an improvement on the status quo ante or not; if it is an improvement, then the spillover was a benign event. Perhaps the war or emergency stimulated legal experimentation, the development of new technology, or the creation of ingenious policy mechanisms; in any of these cases it might be wise, not foolish, to incorporate the new information or innovation into the ordinary law after the emergency has passed. The statist ratchet suffers from a virulent strain of the naturalistic fallacy: whatever complex of legal rules happens to exist, at some status quo point, is taken to be good, and any shift in the direction of greater security is taken to be bad. But if the status quo can embody too much liberty, rather than just the right amount, the picture is arbitrary.

The Libertarian Ratchet

If the statist ratchet identifies a sustained and irreversible decline of civil liberties, a mirror-image position — the libertarian ratchet — identifies a progressive and optimistic trend. In this camp are Chief Justice Rehnquist's claim to discern a "generally ameliorative trend" in government's treatment of civil liberties during wartime;[11] an argument by Jack Goldsmith and Cass Sunstein that social evaluation, in hindsight, of government performance during wars and other crises produces a "trend toward greater protection for civil liberties in wartime";[12] and a similar argument by Mark Tushnet.[13] Of these, Rehnquist and Tushnet seem to view the libertarian ratchet as good, while Goldsmith and Sunstein focus on explanation rather than normative assessment. Many of the preceding objections to the statist ratchet apply equally against the libertarian ratchet, mutatis mutandis; we will confine ourselves to a few additional points.

The first is that the libertarian ratchet, like the statist ratchet, extrapolates a trend from an impoverished data set containing too few observations. Proponents of the libertarian ratchet have little to work with: the Civil War, the two World Wars, the armed conflicts in Korea and Vietnam, perhaps the Red Scare of the 1950s if "war" is defined capaciously. Many curves can be drawn through such a small set of points.

Goldsmith and Sunstein claim that "compared to past wars led by Lincoln, Wilson, and Roosevelt, the Bush administration has diminished relatively few civil liberties. Even a conservative Executive branch, it seems, is influenced by the general trend towards civil liberty protections during wartime."[14] Although the first point is indisputable — the Bush administration has not suspended the writ of habeas corpus, punished harmless dissenters, or interned large numbers of American citizens — the second point does not follow from the first, and is methodologically infirm. To know whether the Bush administration would behave with greater respect for civil liberties than the administration of Lincoln, Wilson, or Roosevelt, we would have to observe similar conditions; and we do not. Would the Bush administration show as much restraint if enemy troops were within a short train ride of Washington (Lincoln), if Europe exploded in armed struggle (Wilson), or if an American fleet had been wiped out by the surprise attack of a foreign state (Roosevelt)? It is not hard to imagine, even today, that civil liberties would be extensively abridged in such circumstances. These are counterfactual speculations, but the libertarian ratchet itself rests on a counterfactual speculation—that current administrations would behave with more restraint than past ones, given like conditions.

To establish the libertarian ratchet a large comparative study would be necessary; confining the inquiry to one nation (America) and to a few wars tells us little. This is so even if there has been a constantly increasing respect for civil liberties in America. To construct the general claim solely from the American case is to commit the methodological mistake of selecting cases on the dependent variable. The claim that spring will come early whenever the groundhog sees his shadow cannot be proved by looking solely at years in which, in fact, spring came early.

Perhaps we should understand the libertarian ratchet not as advancing a fully specified hypothesis of this sort, but simply as describing a causal mechanism that operates ceteris paribus: after a series of wars, hindsight tends to produce social judgments that past suspensions of civil liberties were unnecessary. But our second point is that the hindsight-bias mechanism is underspecified; the level of generality at which hindsight operates makes a critical difference. Goldsmith and Sunstein seem to assume that the hindsight judgment operates to bar "unnecessary future invasions of civil liberties," as a general class, but it may equally be true that hindsight condemns only the *specific* policies or programs instituted in past crises. New policies or programs will be categorized differently in the social cognition, and will be assessed strictly ex ante. As Tushnet puts it (in acknowledged tension with his own argument): "Judges and scholars develop doctrines and approaches that preclude the repetition of the last generation's mistakes. Unfortunately, each new threat generates new policy responses, which are — almost by definition — not precluded by the doctrines designed to make it impossible to adopt the policies used last time. And yet, the next generation again concludes that the new policy responses were mistaken. We learn from our mistakes to the extent that we do not repeat precisely the same errors, but it seems that we do not learn enough to keep us from making new and different mistakes."

This is a version of the conceptual point we advanced against the statist ratchet: because the policy space changes over time, it is simplistic to ask whether wars or other emergencies cause an "increase" or "decrease" in governmental respect for civil liberties. As old forms of governmental control become disreputable and disappear (suspension of judicial process, suppression of political speech, and internment), new forms become technologically feasible and normatively freighted (consider sophisticated government monitoring of private communications, including use of the internet, or of lawyers' conversations with clients). Here again, there just is no single dimension of greater or lesser respect for civil liberties — and thus no predicate for the unidirectional trend line that both the libertarian and statist ratchets assume.

Government without Ratchets

The last point emphasizes the common premise of the libertarian and statist ratchets: both accounts assume that the history of civil liberties in America shows a constant trend, or at least that war and other emergencies have a constant, unidirectional ratchet effect on civil liberties. The two accounts simply disagree about whether the direction of the trend is good or bad.

We favor a third view: there are no systematic trends in the history of civil liberties, no important ratchet-like mechanisms that cause repeated wars or emergencies to push civil liberties in one direction or another in any sustained fashion. Wars, crises, and emergencies come in a range of shapes and sizes; the categories themselves are just methodological conveniences, dichotomous cuts in continuous phenomena. It is unclear, given the current state of the empirical work, whether wars and emergencies have any effect on civil liberties at all; if they do, the effects may be complex and multiple, not simple and unidirectional. Especially absent is any convincing reason to think that any political, social, or psychological ratchet operates, under which wars and emergencies have irreversible effects on future policies. The empirical evidence for ratchets in either good or bad directions is absent, and the mechanisms said to create a ratchet are implausible or underspecified.

As a working presumption, then, we should approach each new social state — whether labeled war, emergency, or anything else — without worrying or hoping that our present choices will have systematic and irreversible effects on the choices made by future generations in unforeseeable future emergencies. The better question is just whether, given the circumstances as we know them to be at present, the policies that government pursues are good ones, in light of whatever substantive theory of rights we hold, and in light of the costs and benefits of alternative courses of action. This formulation is deliberately banal. What it rejects is any attempt to structure the inquiry into the merits of particular policies by worrying about the precedential effects of current policies, or in some other way speculating on the irreversible system-level effects of those policies, over time, on future emergencies that future versions of our own society will face. That additional question is a strange attempt, as it were, to get beyond or outside our own historical circumstances; and there is no reason to think that there are any such effects anyway.

Fear

In this part we criticize accounts of emergency that emphasize the Constitution's role in limiting the impact of fear on government policy. The panic thesis argues that because fear causes decision makers to exaggerate threats and neglect civil liberties and similar values, expanding decision makers' constitutional powers will result in bad policy. Any gains to national security would be minimal, and the losses to civil liberties great. Thus, enforcing the Constitution to the same extent as during periods of normalcy would protect civil liberties at little cost.

We argue that the panic thesis is wrong, and does not support the anti-accommodation position. We make three points. First, fear does not play an unambiguously negative role in decision making. Against the standard view that fear interferes with decision making, we argue that fear has both cognitive and motivational benefits. Second, even if fear did play a negative role, it is doubtful that fear, so understood, has much influence on policy during emergencies, or that it has more influence on policy during emergencies than during non-emergencies. Third, even if fear did play a negative role in decision making, and played a greater such role during emergencies than during non-emergencies, it is doubtful that these bad effects could be avoided through the enforcement of the Constitution or other institutional devices, at acceptable cost to national security. All three points suggest that strict enforcement of the Constitution during emergencies will not improve policy choices by restricting the influence of fear.

Preliminaries

Fear can influence government action in two ways. First, government officials themselves might feel fear. Second, even if government officials do not feel fear, the public might feel fear, and government officials might feel compelled to act on the public's fears, lest they be turned out of office for being insufficiently responsive to the public's concerns. In the second case, it is a useful simplification to assume that government officials, by acting as honest agents, act as if they were themselves afraid; thus, the two cases can be treated as though they were the same.

To understand how fearful government officials might make decisions, one can profitably begin by considering the rational actor model as a baseline. The rational actor model assumes that people implicitly use accurate probability distributions to estimate the likelihood of uncertain outcomes. The methodological assumption is obviously strong; the justification is that errors are symmetrical and wash out, so that aggregate behavior obeys accurate probability distributions at a statistically significant level even if individual behavior deviates in both directions. If this assumption is true, then governments act as rationally during emergencies as during normal times. The decision to infringe civil liberties for security purposes may be right or wrong, but it is no more likely right or wrong than the quotidian decision to construct a new highway or reduce funding for education. There is no reason to think that the government will systematically undervalue civil liberties or overvalue security during emergencies, or that it will systematically overestimate the magnitude of a threat, compared to its behavior during non-emergencies. Instead, the government will attach the same weights to these goods as it does during non-emergencies; it will also on average accurately estimate the magnitude of the threat, sometimes underestimating it and at other times overestimating it.

The rational actor model does not clearly support either the accommodation position or the strict enforcement position. The critic of accommodation can argue that a rational executive will disregard civil liberties to the same extent during emergencies as during non-emergencies; therefore, constitutional enforcement should be the same as well. Courts can protect civil liberties while permitting emergency measures by requiring the government to show that infringements on civil liberties serve the compelling interest in national security. The defense of accommodation rests not on the rational actor model, but on an empirical assumption about relative institutional competence: courts are in a bad position to evaluate the executive's emergency measures. Secrecy is more important than during non-emergencies; so are speed, vigor, and enthusiasm. The standard characteristics of judicial review — deliberation, openness, independence, distance, slowness — may be minor costs, and sometimes virtues, during peacetime; but during emergencies they are intolerable.

According to the panic thesis, the problem with emergency measures is not that they may be rational yet objectionable infringements on civil liberties but that they are frequently irrational, and thus infringe civil liberties without also creating sufficient national security benefits. During emergencies, panic interferes with rational assessment of risks. The distortion can take a number of forms: exaggeration of the probability or magnitude of the threatened harm; or, what amounts to nearly the same thing, neglect of competing values such as privacy and equality. As a result, government interests will not usually be as compelling as everyone thinks they are, and government policy, if not constrained, will unnecessarily interfere with civil liberties. Although this argument is conventionally advanced by civil libertarians concerned by wartime restrictions, it also underlies a popular view about the effectiveness of terrorism: that it "trap[s] the authorities into brutal repression and overreaction which then alienates the public and drives them into tacit or active collaboration with the terrorists."[15] The claim is not that the government rationally curtails civil liberties to combat the terrorist threat, but that the government overreacts, and that the public tolerates a rational response but not an overreaction. The source of overreaction could only be fear or some other emotion such as anger or outrage. On this view, strict enforcement of the Constitution has two virtues: preservation of civil liberties, a good in itself, and preservation of the government against its own bad judgment.

This argument, at base, holds that the government's policy will not reflect accurate probability distributions, or else that a rational government will take advantage of the public's inaccurate probability distributions so that it can accomplish ends denied to it during non-emergencies. Fear displaces rational assessment of the risks at one level or the other. Is this view accurate?

Two Views of Fear

The anti-accommodation view depends heavily on a particular theory of fear, a theory implying that fear interferes with cognition and judgment. However, fear is a complex emotion, and generalizing about its relationship to cognition is hazardous.

The simple view of fear underlying the strict enforcement theory springs from one aspect of this emotion, its core noncognitive basis. Fear is in part a purely physiological response to a threat, a response that is outside of conscious control. When a person comes upon a tiger in a jungle, he undergoes certain physiological changes — the chemistry of his blood changes, his heartbeat increases, certain areas of his brain are stimulated — resulting in an urge to flee that can be overcome only with difficulty. One interesting aspect of this phenomenon is that panic responses appear to be asymmetrically distributed: false positives are more likely than false negatives. A person is more likely to flee from a shadow that looks like a tiger than to fail to run from a tiger that looks like a shadow. Evolutionary psychologists argue that the asymmetry of responses is the result of an asymmetry in the payoffs. A person who is eaten by a tiger is worse off than a person who unnecessarily runs away from a shadow. Thus, the noncognitive aspect of fear has two immediate implications: people do not think about threats and react to them "rationally"; and the automatic reaction to threats reflects long-gone evolutionary pressures rather than the needs of an agent in modern society.

This story yields two opposing approaches to the role of fear in decision making. The first view is that fear interferes with cognition: the person who feels fear reacts to the threat instinctively rather than deliberatively, and in a way that is biased rather than neutral. Fear of air travel causes people to drive, which is riskier than flying; fear of pesticides, toxic waste, and genetic engineering causes people to endorse expensive and ineffective policies that cause more harm than good. This fear-interferes-with-cognition view has deep roots in the western philosophical tradition, one piece of which rests on the opposition of reason and passion. Passions interfere with reason, and the rational person attempts to suppress them. When a person is motivated by a passion, it means that his choices are unlikely to be good ones.

The second view is that fear does not interfere with cognition, or if it does, the interference contributes to good action. There are two related points here. First, fear enhances the senses: the person who feels fear is attuned to the threat, and alert to every nuance of the environment. Fear powers a searchlight that illuminates some features of the landscape even as it obscures others. Second, fear provides motivation. Where a fully rational person spends time deliberating, the fearful person acts quickly. Both observations suggest that fear can play a constructive role during national emergencies.

How does fear enhance the senses? Although the fearful person may make the characteristic mistake of seeing a tiger in a shadow, the other side of this error is the sensory arousal allowing the person to pick out in the environment threats that would otherwise be invisible. It has been said that after 9/11, airplane passengers and security officials paid much more attention to other passengers, and were more ready to alert authorities or intervene personally if they saw something suspicious. This alertness resulted in many false positives: conversations were misinterpreted, false conclusions were drawn from swarthy complexions, harmless objects were confiscated as weapons. But in a few cases, hijackings or bombings were, or may have been, prevented. Do the lives saved justify the inconvenience to all passengers and Arabs and Muslims in particular? Civil libertarians might say yes or no, but one's position on this question is not the issue. What recent experience has shown is that fear has generated cognitive gains as well as losses, and part of the reason is that the asymmetry between gains and losses that underlies the evolutionary story may apply to a world threatened by terrorism as well, however imperfectly. The simple story — that fear means error — is too simple.

The motivational benefit of fear for individuals is that it enables a rapid response to a possible threat that would not, if real, give individuals time to deliberate about available options. To the drafter of a rule that constrains the curtailment of civil liberties, or to the judge who seeks to enforce that rule or the general strict enforcement position, the decision maker always has a powerful argument: "your rational assessments — even if they are not clouded by your remoteness from the current emergency — may have resulted from a kind of clear thinking but are fatally undermined by your *motivational* remoteness. If you did not feel fear, then you cannot have put in the necessary effort to make the right decision." Fear compels people to devote resources to solving a problem that for a dispassionate and uninvolved person may be interesting but is not compelling. In this way, fear motivates not only action, but deliberation. Having perceived a threat, and felt fear, people will work hard to think of ways to address it. They are more likely to discard old assumptions and complacent ways of thinking, and to address problems with new vigor.

The second, complex view of fear does not deny the insights of the first view; it incorporates them into a more nuanced account. Fear will produce choices different from those that will be made by a person who does not feel fear, but these choices may be better or worse, depending on context. The argument here mirrors an increasingly influential psychological and philosophical literature on the passions, a literature that stresses the constructive role of the passions in judgment. "Emotions provide the animal [including the human] with a sense of how the world relates to its own set of goals and projects. Without that sense, decision making and action are derailed."[16] Anger can magnify slights and provoke unreasoned violence; but it is also a response to an offense against one's dignity and can motivate legitimate protest.[17] The passions do not always inhibit reason; they also inform reason and provide the motivation for necessary action.

Against the view that panicked government officials overreact to an emergency, and unnecessarily curtail civil liberties, we suggest a more constructive theory of the role of fear. Before the emergency, government officials are complacent. They do not think clearly or vigorously about the potential threats faced by the nation. After the terrorist attack or military intervention, their complacency is replaced by fear. Fear stimulates them to action. Action may be based on good decisions or bad: fear might cause officials to exaggerate future threats, but it also might arouse them to threats that they would otherwise not perceive. It is impossible to say in the abstract whether decisions and actions provoked by fear are likely to be better than decisions and actions made in a state of calm. But our limited point is that there is no reason to think that the fear-inspired decisions are likely to be worse. For that reason, the existence of fear during emergencies does not support the strict enforcement theory that the Constitution should be enforced as strictly during emergencies as during non-emergencies.

The Influence of Fear during Emergencies

Suppose now that the simple view of fear is correct, and that it is an unambiguously negative influence on government decision making. Critics of accommodation argue that this negative influence of fear justifies skepticism about emergency policies and strict enforcement of the Constitution. However, this argument is implausible. It is doubtful that fear, so understood, has more influence on decision making during emergencies than during non-emergencies.

The panic thesis holds that citizens and officials respond to terrorism and war in the same way that an individual in the jungle responds to a tiger or snake. The national response to emergency, because it is a standard fear response, is characterized by the same circumvention of ordinary deliberative processes: thus, (1) the response is instinctive rather than reasoned, and therefore subject to error; and (2) the error will be biased in the direction of overreaction. While the flight reaction was a good evolutionary strategy on the savannah, in a complex modern society the flight response is not suitable and can only interfere with judgment. Its advantage — speed — has minimal value for social decision making. No national emergency requires an *immediate* reaction — except by trained professionals who execute policies established earlier — but instead people make complex judgments over days, months, or years about the appropriate institutional response. And the asymmetrical nature of fear guarantees that people will, during a national emergency, overweight the threat and underweight other things that people value, such as civil liberties.

But if decision makers rarely act immediately, then the tiger story cannot bear the metaphoric weight that is placed on it. Indeed, the urge to flee has nothing to do with the political response to the bombing of Pearl Harbor or the attack on September 11. The people who were there — the citizens and soldiers beneath the bombs, the office workers in the World Trade Center — no doubt felt fear, and most of them probably responded in the classic way. They experienced the standard physiological effects, and (with the exception of trained soldiers and security officials) fled without stopping to think. It is also true that in the days and weeks after the attacks, many people felt fear, although not the sort that produces an irresistible urge to flee. But this kind of fear is not the kind in which cognition shuts down. (Some people did have more severe mental reactions and, for example, shut themselves in their houses, but these reactions were rare.) The fear is probably better described as a general anxiety or jumpiness, an anxiety that was probably shared by government officials as well as ordinary citizens.

While there is psychological research suggesting that normal cognition partly shuts down in response to an immediate threat, we are aware of no research suggesting that people who feel anxious about a non-immediate threat are incapable of thinking, or thinking properly, or systematically overweight the threat relative to other values. Indeed, it would be surprising to find research that clearly distinguished "anxious thinking" and "calm thinking," given that anxiety is a pervasive aspect of life. No one argues that people's anxiety about their health causes them to take too many precautions — to get too much exercise, to diet too aggressively, to go to the doctor too frequently — and to undervalue other things like leisure. So it is hard to see why anxiety about more remote threats, from terrorists or unfriendly countries with nuclear weapons, should cause the public, or elected officials, to place more emphasis on security than is justified, and to sacrifice civil liberties.[18]

Fear generated by immediate threats, then, causes instinctive responses that are not rational in the cognitive sense, not always desirable, and not a good basis for public policy, but it is not this kind of fear that leads to restrictions of civil liberties during wartime. The internment of Japanese Americans during the Second World War may have been due to racial animus, or to a mistaken assessment of the risks, but it was not the direct result of panic; indeed there was a delay of weeks before the policy was seriously considered. Curtailments of civil liberties after 9/11, aside from immediate detentions, followed a significant delay and much deliberation. The civil libertarians' argument — that fear produces bad policy — trades on the ambiguity of the word "panic," which refers both to real fear that undermines rationality and to collectively harmful outcomes driven by rational decisions (such as bank runs, in which it is rational for all depositors to withdraw funds if they believe that enough other depositors are withdrawing funds). Once we eliminate the false concern about fear, the panic thesis becomes indistinguishable from the argument that during an emergency people are likely to make mistakes. But if the only concern is that during emergencies people make mistakes, there would be no reason for demanding that the Constitution be enforced normally during emergencies. Political errors occur during emergencies and non-emergencies, but the stakes are higher during emergencies, and that is the conventional reason why constitutional constraints should be relaxed.

In sum, the panic thesis envisions decision makers acting immediately when in fact government policymaking moves slowly even during emergencies. Government is organized so that general policy decisions about responses to emergencies are made in advance, and the implementation of policy during an emergency is trusted to security officials who have been trained to resist the impulse to panic. The notion of fear causing an irresistible urge to flee is a bad metaphor for an undeniable truth: that during an emergency the government does not have as much time as it usually does, and as a result will make more errors than it usually does. But these errors will be driven by normal cognitive limitations, and not the pressure of fear: thus, the errors will be normally distributed. It is as likely that the government will curtail civil liberties too little as too much.

Institutional Problems

Having registered our skepticism that citizens and officials are less capable of judgment during emergencies than during normal times, we now consider the panic thesis on its own terms, and assume for the sake of argument that people predictably panic during national emergencies while remaining calm at other times, and that the panic has unambiguously negative consequences for decision making. Recall the panic thesis — that because of the danger of panic, constitutional constraints should not be relaxed during emergencies. Higher stakes do not justify relaxation of constitutional constraints because with the higher stakes comes the danger of panic, and constitutional constraints are needed to prevent fear from generating bad political outcomes such as the unnecessary restriction of civil liberties.

We now examine how those constitutional constraints could be enforced. The anti-accommodation view — that the Constitution should be enforced as strictly during an emergency as during a non-emergency — depends on giving citizens, executive officials, or judges the ability to enforce the Constitution strictly despite their own fear-addled judgment that a policy is justified by a threat to security. Is this assumption realistic? How can a person bind himself against his own bad judgment? We examine three mechanisms: (1) intrapersonal self-restraint; (2) reliance on rules; and

(3) insulation of decision makers. Each mechanism specifies a different trade-off between discretion, which results in cognitive errors, and constraint, which prevents needed action. None provides reason for endorsing the panic thesis.

Intrapersonal Self-Restraint

The panic theory, which assumes that fearful officials make worse judgments than calm officials, is not the same as the anti-accommodation view. The panic theory is just one rationale; the ratchet theory, as we saw, is another. Indeed, the panic theory is broader than the anti-accommodation view: it holds that officials in a state of fear should always discount their own risk assessments, whereas the anti-accommodation view refers to one particular circumstance, that of emergency. We might therefore ask: If the panic justification for the anti-accommodation view is correct, why not constrain policy choices whenever officials are panicked, not just when there is an emergency, and give calm officials free rein, even if there is an emergency? Officials could be made to understand that whenever they feel fear, they are likely to discount civil liberties and exaggerate the threat.[19] When they know themselves to be afraid, they should engage in a kind of intrapersonal overcompensation, and assume that their own estimate of the threat is too high. Having pushed down a risk assessment that they know to be high, they can make a rational decision even when afraid.

This "panic rule," as we will call it—discount your own estimate of a threat if you feel fear—captures the panic theory more precisely than the anti-accommodation view does. The panic rule is, in legal parlance, a standard: its contours are those of the underlying normative goal, that of preventing fear from interfering with decision making. Thus, the panic rule tells officials to discount their risk assessments if and only if they feel fear. The accommodation position is a rule: it tells officials to discount their risk assessments if and only if there is an emergency. The fact of emergency serves as a proxy for the normative concern, that of fear.

The benefit of the panic rule is that it allows the Constitution to accommodate calm officials, and requires strict enforcement only against those who panic. The problem is its psychological unrealism. To see this problem, suppose that third-party enforcement of the Constitution is not feasible: the officials who determine policy or law in a state of fear are the same as the officials charged with enforcing or respecting the Constitution. Executives who know that judges will defer to their foreign policy are nonetheless expected to obey the Constitution. And judges themselves may feel fear to the same degree as the decision makers whose laws are being reviewed in court. The panic rule asks these officials to discount their own threat assessments whenever they feel fear.

The problem with this rule is that it assumes that decision makers can accurately determine the conditions under which they should not trust their own judgment. Suppose that some event such as a terrorist attack occurs, and then the question facing decision makers is whether to use ethnic profiling to prevent further attacks. If, as we must assume, the decision makers are afraid, then they will overestimate the probability of another terrorist attack, and thus be more likely to infringe civil liberties than they would be if they were calm. Self-restraint could occur only if decision makers could also realize that they overestimate the risk because they afraid. But this is psychologically unrealistic: either decision makers are afraid and exaggerate the risk, or are not afraid and assess the risk accurately or with normal, unbiased error.

The contrary view would have one think that officials could both believe that a threat exists and, knowing that they are afraid, doubt their own belief. But if officials take the existence of fear as an indication that they should discount their own beliefs, then why should they credit the belief that there is a threat in the first place? People feel fear because they perceive a threat; they cannot step outside themselves and doubt their own beliefs just because they know that fear can interfere with cognition.

Rules

The psychological unrealism of the panic rule might be avoided through the use of a more rule-like rule, one that does not require a decision maker to hold incompatible beliefs. People have foresight and can design rules and institutions that will dampen the influence of panic on political outcomes. People might be able to design a rule that provides that when some event associated with a panic occurs, people should be cautious about passing laws or endorsing other political actions. The mechanism involves a distinction between the identification of conditions that can be accurately perceived and acted upon even when the subject is emotionally aroused, and the exercise of judgment that the emotional state precludes. People would, even in their fear-clouded minds, realize that they are afraid because a significant event has occurred, and thus that they should discount their own judgments or at least delay acting on them.

The condition or proxy could be an emergency described in relatively clear terms: an invasion or attack by foreign soldiers, a natural disaster, a spike in the death rate, a decline in the GDP. When these events occur, people could — in a Pavlovian fashion? — feel themselves committed to discounting their own assessments of risk. The rule might say that after a terrorist attack, one should divide one's updated probability assessments by two. If people think that a subsequent attack is certain, they should discount the perceived probability to 50 percent; if they think the second attack will kill millions, they should cut the estimate in half. As a result, people will be less willing to permit police to single out Arabs or Muslims for suspicion, shut down the airports, and eavesdrop on the mails.

The argument depends on several assumptions, all of them troublesome. First, it must be the case that people can, while panicking, accurately identify the conditions under which they panic: that is, they must be able to determine that their current probability estimates are made under the relevant conditions, and not independently of these conditions. People must think, "Because there was a terrorist attack six months ago, my current predictions are inaccurate"; and not, "The terrorist attack occurred long enough ago for me to recover my cognitive abilities." Second, the conditions must actually be correlated with panic. If the rule is "discount one's assessment of the risks if a terrorist attack occurred within two (four?, ten?) years," then it must be the case that people's assessments are exaggerated within that time frame, and to a sufficient extent, and not reasonably accurate in a substantial portion of the cases. Third, the conditions must be capable of being specified in advance with reasonable accuracy, and must in fact generate more benefits than costs. People must be able to know what kind of events are likely to generate fear and thus interfere with probability estimates, as well as the time frame during which the effect lasts: airplane crashes, terrorist attacks, military interventions, and the like, all with their own associated time frames. If the conditions are misspecified, then the rule will cause people to discount their own beliefs when they are accurate, and thus fail to deliver an adequate response to an authentic emergency. But because we have so little information about how people exaggerate risks when afraid, and how much of a discount is appropriate, it is hard to believe that any rule would improve behavior.

Critics of accommodation do not typically argue that detailed rules such as these should be institutionalized. Instead, they attempt to evade the difficult calculus illustrated by the discussion so far by flatly asserting that whatever the optimal rule, emergency policies will be better if they comply with normal constitutional restrictions than if they do not.

There are two problems with this argument. The first is that it does not fully escape the psychological unrealism of intrapersonal self-restraint. People in the grip of fear will rationalize their decisions on the basis of their exaggerated assessment of the threat. Because the threat is significant, they will think, a compelling government interest justifies intrusions on civil liberties. Although it is possible that they will choose less restrictive laws than they would under the accommodation view, we doubt that officials in the grip of fear are capable of making such fine distinctions. Fear, according to the simple view endorsed by the panic thesis, focuses attention on the threat and away from civil liberties. Officials will reach for any policy that addresses the threat, and are likely to find a compelling government interest in the fact of the emergency. This is the lesson of history. One can say in favor of the anti-accommodation rule that it is, with respect to psychological realism, superior to intrapersonal self-restraint. Intrapersonal self-restraint requires people to discount their own judgments, whereas the anti-accommodation rule appears to tell them to act the same during emergencies as otherwise. But it is not much of an improvement.

The second objection is even more important. Like all rules, the anti-accommodation view reduces decision costs through overinclusion. The anti-accommodation rule applies to officials who remain calm despite the emergency, and prevents them from implementing rational policies. It also applies to fearful officials whose policies might be based on exaggerated notions of risk but are still better policies than those available under the Constitution strictly construed. A policy of detaining immigrants, for example, may be based on an exaggerated notion of the threat but still be preferable to no policy at all. If unconstrained officials choose policies that are biased against civil liberties, it remains unlikely that enforcing the Constitution rather than making accommodations will ensure that policies reflecting the optimal balancing of liberty and security will be chosen.

The panic rule and the anti-accommodation rule reflect different trade-offs between discretion and overinclusion, but neither is satisfactory. Both rules require people to act as if they did not believe their own judgments—under the first rule, by recognizing that fear may hamper their judgments; under the second, by recognizing relatively objective conditions associated with fear that may hamper their judgments. The first vests too much discretion in the person who, by hypothesis, cannot trust his own judgment. The second reduces discretion but then relies on the wholly unsupported claim that the objective conditions can be identified and specified in advance, and are sufficiently correlated with periods of public and official fear.

Insulation of Decision Makers

The third mechanism is to vest emotionally disciplined people with political authority and insulate them from popular opinion. Emotionally disciplined people are less likely to panic than normal people are, and thus more likely to choose good policies if unconstrained by popular opinion; but they might rationally implement policies demanded by a panicking citizenry if the alternative is ejection from office. There are two versions of this argument. One possibility is to reduce popular accountability at all times, so that political leaders will be insulated when an emergency occurs. The other possibility is to vest authority in particular individuals when an emergency is identified or declared; for example, the president could declare an emergency and the military would then have temporary police powers. Both versions assume that the people with leadership positions will actually be calmer than the public during an emergency: ordinary politicians in the first case, and the president (at the point of declaring the emergency) and military officials (after the emergency is declared) in the second case. Both versions also assume that the insulation materials cannot be pierced by public sentiment.

These assumptions are all questionable. The U.S. Constitution already insulates political officials from popular pressures to some extent—more so than in a direct democracy, for example—and it is probable that executive officials, who are constantly exposed to crises large and small, do not panic as frequently as ordinary people do. But the usual fears about relaxing constitutional protections during emergencies are based on the assumption that elected officials do panic sometimes; so their being insulated already is no comfort. Insulating them further would be perverse: it would make officials less accountable during non-emergencies so that they would be less likely to be influenced by panicking citizens during emergencies. But this would just mean that civil liberties will be violated more often during times of calm. Civil libertarians don't want to reduce civil liberties during times of calm; they want government officials to respect normal constitutional barriers during emergencies. If government officials are not willing to do that — either because they are panicking or because they need to respond rationally to a threat — then giving them greater insulation against popular fears will not improve their decisions.

It also is questionable whether elected officials can resist political pressures when citizens panic. During the Second World War, the internment of Japanese-Americans was not motivated by the threat that they posed to security; it was motivated, to a great degree, by concerns about the morale of the majority of citizens in key states like California, who falsely believed that Japanese-Americans posed a threat to security or else associated them with the enemy and therefore did not trust them. A large part of dealing with a national emergency is to calm the fears of citizens. Government's usual response is to channel and dam up these fears rather than dismiss them as irrational. If the public believes that a threat exists, official assurances to the contrary do no good — instead, they are evidence to the public that the government is unprepared and insufficiently vigorous — and waving the Constitution at the public will not help when the public believes that the Constitution itself is being threatened.

Finally, people do not usually choose officials on the basis of their ability to stay calm during emergencies. There are too many other relevant considerations. Most politicians are elected on the basis of their ability to deliver the goods during ordinary times. Although sometimes a politician's background contains indications of emotional discipline, the latter is not a salient issue in political contests.

What can be said for the insulation method is that it is psychologically realistic. If emotionally disciplined people can be identified in advance and given positions of authority, then it is not psychologically unrealistic to assume that they will make rational decisions. Strict enforcement of the Constitution will ensure that they do not violate civil liberties for rational but impermissible reasons, such as political advantage; but the compelling interest standard will give them the freedom to make proper responses to the emergency. Along the dimension of psychological realism, then, the insulation method dominates the other two rules. But the insulation method does much worse on the cost-benefit dimension. Insulated officials are not democratically responsive. This means that they are not likely to make good policy choices and that the public will not trust them with significant power.

Federal judges are highly insulated officials in the American constitutional system. For this reason, civil libertarians argue that judges are well positioned to guard civil liberties against the excesses of panic during wartime and other emergency periods. Yet judges themselves do not appear to share this view. American judges have almost always deferred to the executive during emergencies.[20] The reason is apparently that the judges have done the cost-benefit balancing that the civil libertarians have neglected, and found themselves wanting.[21] If insulation gives them the advantage of calm, the price is lack of information and lack of power. Judges do not have the information that executives have, and are reluctant to second-guess them. They also do not have access to the levers of power, so they can delay a response to an emergency only by entertaining legal objections to it. They do not have such access because such power cannot be given to people who are not politically accountable. All of this explains why during emergencies judges rarely feel that they have their ordinary peacetime authority to interfere with executive decision making.

Indeed, the champions of civil liberties during emergencies in American history have usually been officials in the executive or legislative branches, not the justices of the Supreme Court. During the Palmer raids, the attorney general's attempt to exploit public fears for political gain was resisted by the acting secretary of labor, whose approval was needed for deportations. The labor department, unlike the Supreme Court, had the political power to block or delay deportations because it had the legitimacy conferred by its expertise concerning immigration, and authority over it. During the Second World War, many members of the Roosevelt administration opposed the internment of Japanese-Americans, and though they could not prevent the military's decision, they ensured that the interment would be carried out in as humane a fashion as possible; it was also the Justice Department that opposed Roosevelt's schemes to squelch dissent. During the cold war, although neither Truman nor Eisenhower took brave public stands against McCarthy, they criticized his methods and tried to undermine his influence, and he was eventually defeated by opposition from high-level appointees in the executive branch and elected officials in the legislative branch. The Supreme Court was, throughout these events, largely passive. It did not have the political authority to oppose the executive (or legislative) branch during emergencies, and so it did not act. The justices could not have made the case that they understood the nature of the emergency better than executive officials did. Only officials within the political branches, who could make a credible case that they had better information and motives than the opponents of civil liberties, and had the proper institutional responsibility for handling the emergency, had the necessary public legitimacy.

Anti-Accommodation as a Precommitment Device

The anti-accommodation view relies on a simple and much-criticized theory that constitutional or other rules can be properly thought of as rational (good) precommitments against emotional (bad) decisions. But fear plays a valuable role as well as a negative role, and no commitment device can be designed in advance that can prevent fear from influencing behavior; nor is there reason to think that such a device would produce good outcomes. It is simply perverse for a state to commit itself not to respond vigorously to emergencies, and we have argued that fear may be an angel rather than a demon. A purely rational response to a crisis sounds good in the abstract, but some motivational oomph is necessary as well, and when fear is needed to supply that motivation, constitutional restrictions on its influence can do much harm.

Legal scholars dwell on the many historical events in which fear appeared to produce bad policy choices. These are the Red Scares, the banking panics, and so forth. Fears about Hitler may have resulted in appeasement rather than resistance. But there are as many cases where the absence of fear may have resulted in policies that were weak when they should have been vigorous. Here we count the failed Weimar government before Hitler and the Kerensky government before Lenin. Conventional wisdom attributes unpreparedness for the 9/11 attacks not to lack of information but to bureaucratic inertia. Leading officials assessed the risks correctly but could not summon the necessary political will. Fear changed this instantly. In the United States before the Second World War, public complacency about

American security behind two oceans hamstrung public officials who were better informed. Roosevelt sought to stir up fear so as to motivate the war effort, by contrast to his effort to suppress fear during the early years of the Great Depression. His contrary actions just show how fear has both good and bad effects, and fear that can be disabling in one context may provide needed motivation in another.

We have criticized two common arguments against the long-standing judicial practice of deferring to the political branches, and especially to the executive branch, during wartime and other emergencies. Our point is that if one wants to criticize the current level of deference, one ought to depend on arguments different from the ratchet and panic arguments.

What would these arguments be? Courts have long recognized that they face a tradeoff when they evaluate the actions of the executive branch. On the one hand, the executive branch has advantages that courts lack: information about current threats to national security, and control over the military, police, and other institutions that can meet a threat. To counter threats to national security, the executive must be able to act on its information quickly, without having to defend its sources (and thereby risk compromising them); rely on its own accumulated experience; and issue orders that will be obeyed without delay. Judicial scrutiny can only interfere with forceful executive action. On the other hand, the officials who hold executive power for the time being may attempt to extend their power or to squash political opponents. Judicial deference would permit these abuses to occur. So a potential cost of deference is the risk of executive (or congressional-executive, as the case may be) abuse, and the benefit of deference is the reduction, as a result of noninterference by judges, of risks to national security and to other goods protected by the executive.

Constitutional practice during normal times reflects one possible tradeoff between these considerations. Police must obtain warrants but not if they are in hot pursuit; the press can be made to pay damages for disclosing government secrets but not usually enjoined; and so forth. Strict enforcement of constitutional rights is justified in normal times as long as the cost of deference exceeds the benefit; and in normal times the benefit of deference is probably low. In the case of emergency, however, the relevant benefit from deference is forceful executive action against a threat to national security; this benefit is higher than the benefit of reducing crime. By contrast, the cost of deference — the risk of abuse of executive power — remains constant during emergencies and non-emergencies. Because the cost of deference remains constant, while the benefit of deference rises during an emergency, judges should be more deferential during emergencies than during non-emergencies. This view is not unique to the American system; it can be found in many liberal democracies, and has long antecedents: republics and democracies have often put their security in the hands of even (temporary) dictators during emergencies. However, there is a difference between saying that deference should be higher during emergencies and saying that the current level of judicial deference — what we have called "accommodation" — is correct. To show that the latter proposition is true, one would have to describe in more detail the relative institutional capacities of the executive and the judiciary. If, for example, courts can process national security information securely, quickly, and accurately, then judicial deference need not be as high as otherwise. All we have before us is evidence about what judges think, and judges appear to have doubts about whether they can do this. Those who criticize this position need to show in what respects the courts are wrong.

NOTES

1 For completeness, we should mention a variant of the second view, which holds that not only rules but outcomes should remain the same during emergencies and non-emergencies. On this view, emergency measures are permissible only if they would be permissible if taken during non-emergencies. Racial profiling, for example, if not permitted for drug interdiction, is also not permissible for deterring terrorism. Although we do not know of anyone who clearly endorses this view, it approximates the position of those who are most hostile to the Bush administration's anti-terrorism policies after 9/11. See, for example, David Cole, "The New McCarthyism: Repeating History in the War on Terrorism," 38 *Harvard Civil Rights–Civil Liberties Law Review* 1 (2003).

2 Of course, the change need not be literally irreversible; it may be merely sticky, because more or less costly to undo. Weak ratchet accounts are more plausible than strong ones, but they also pack less punch. In what follows we will take these qualifiers to be understood whenever we speak of "irreversibility."

3 Oren Gross, "Chaos and Rules: Should Responses to Violent Crises Always Be Constitutional?," 112 *Yale Law Journal* 1011, 1090 (2003). See also Terry M. Moe

and William G. Howell, "The Presidential Power of Unilateral Action," 15 *Journal of Law, Economics & Organization* 132, 157 (1999).

4 Korematsu v. United States, 323 U.S. 214, 246 (1944) (Jackson, J., dissenting).

5 See Woods v. Cloyd W. Miller Co., 333 U.S. 138, 146 (1948) (Jackson, J., concurring) (describing the federal government's war power as "dangerous" because "[i]t is usually invoked in haste and excitement [and] . . . is interpreted by judges under the influence of the same passions and pressures. Always, [the] Government urges hasty decision to forestall some emergency or serve some purpose and pleads that paralysis will result if its claims to power are denied or their confirmation delayed").

6 Gross, "Chaos and Rules," 1090.

7 For an example, see Tushnet, "Defending Korematsu?," this collection.

8 Gross, "Chaos and Rules," 1093–94.

9 Dermot P. J. Walsh, "The Impact of the Antisubversive Laws on Police Powers and Practices in Ireland: The Silent Erosion of Individual Freedom," 62 *Temple Law Review* 1099, 1102 (1989).

10 *Id.* at 1128–29.

11 William Rehnquist, *All the Laws but One* (1997), 221.

12 Jack Goldsmith and Cass R. Sunstein, "Military Tribunals and Legal Culture: What a Difference Sixty Years Makes," 19 *Constitutional Commentary* 261, 262 (2002).

13 Tushnet, "Defending Korematsu?"

14 Goldsmith and Sunstein, "Military Tribunals and Legal Culture," 28.

15 Paul Wilkinson, *Terrorism and the Liberal State* (2d ed. 1986), 81 (discussing the ideas of Carlos Marighela).

16 Martha C. Nussbaum, *Upheavals of Thought* (2001), 117.

17 *Id.* at 394.

18 Kuran and Sunstein argue that during emergencies the availability heuristic comes into play, and that it may be magnified by social influences. People observe a dramatic event, overestimate the likelihood of its recurrence, and then support bad policies based on this error. See Timur Kuran and Cass Sunstein, "Availability Cascades and Risk Regulation," 51 *Stanford Law Review* 683 (1999). This argument is about cognition, not emotion, and so not strictly relevant to our claims about fear. However, we note that for this view to favor the strict enforcement policy, it must be the case that threats to security (like terrorist attacks) are more salient, and thus more susceptible to the availability heuristic, than examples of official oppression (like detentions and torture). There is no evidence for such an asymmetry.

19 An intrapersonal analogy can be found in a favored technique of anger management: when one feels angry, one should take a deep breath and count to ten

before acting. If one trains oneself to respond in a Pavlovian fashion to an event or condition, and the response is likely to restore or improve judgment, then irrational actions can be avoided. Note, however, that this technique works by invoking a device by which one's judgment can return to normal; no one thinks that fear can go away after a deep breath.

20 Issacharoff and Pildes argue that judges are less deferential during emergencies than is commonly thought; but their examination of the cases shows that judges *are* deferential during emergencies; it is just that they are more deferential when the executive and legislature speak with one voice than when the executive acts alone. See the chapter by Samuel Issacharoff and Richard H. Pildes, "Between Civil Libertarianism and Executive Unilateralism."

21 For explicit discussions, by judges, of their own lack of information in wartime cases, see, for example, Hamdi v. Rumsfeld, 337 F. 3d 335, 343 (4th Cir. 2003) (Wilkinson, J., concurring in the denial of rehearing en banc); Hamdi v. Rumsfeld, 316 F.3d 450, 471, 473–74 (4th Cir. 2003); Korematsu, 323 U.S. at 245 (Jackson, J., dissenting).

Part II

Counter-stories: Maintaining and Expanding Civil Liberties in Wartime

Mark A. Graber

Constitutional lawyers and historians frequently tell stories about how civil liberties and civil rights in the United States are restricted during wartime. The first major federal restrictions on civil liberties, the Alien and Sedition Acts of 1798, were enacted while the federal government was dealing with its first major military conflict, the undeclared naval war with France.[1] President Abraham Lincoln during the Civil War unilaterally imposed martial law in the North and censored the Copperhead press.[2] Left-wing dissidents and aliens who opposed military intervention were persecuted during the First World War.[3] During the Second World War, martial law was imposed in Hawaii and Japanese-Americans were forcibly removed to internment camps.[4] The cold war inspired McCarthyism.[5] Massive detentions without trial or aid of counsel are taking place during the present war against terrorism.[6]

These common accounts of restrictive policies during wartime do not tell the complete tale of how military conflicts and tensions influence civil rights and liberties in the United States. Some civil rights and liberties have historically been unaffected by war. Military action in American history is not associated with any substantial rise in the annual rate of executions or new restrictions on reproductive rights. Many restrictions on civil liberties are selectively applied. Right-wing critics of American policymaking during the First World War were not persecuted. German-Americans during the Second World War were not sent to internment camps. Restrictive policies adopted during one war are not adopted in subsequent wars.[7] Contempo-

rary left-wing opponents of the war against terror are far freer to criticize government policy than were left-wing opponents of the First World
War. American Muslims have no curfew and are not being rounded up en
masse. Some military conflicts are never mentioned when the canonical
stories about civil rights in wartime are told. The War of 1812, the Mexican-
American War, and the Spanish-American War were fought without any
substantial federal restrictions on civil rights and civil liberties.[8]

The canonical narratives also omit numerous instances in which military conflict inspired some government officials to increase protections for
civil rights and liberties. The national commitment to racial equality increased substantially during the Civil War, the Second World War, and the
cold war.[9] The Supreme Court in *West Virginia State Board of Education v.
Barnette* (1943)[10] held that the government could not compel students to
salute the flag, overruling its pre-war decision in *Minersville School Dist. v.
Gobitis* (1940).[11] Government repression aimed at socialists and communists eased substantially during the Second World War. Persons who criticize the Bush administration for violating the constitutional rights of aliens
do not praise that administration's unyielding commitment during the war
against terrorism to the rights of gun owners. Some of these stories are told,
but as part of other narratives such as the history of racial equality or free
speech in the United States. Some are hardly ever recounted. None is pres-
ently part of a grand narrative about civil liberties and rights policy in the
United States during wartime.

This chapter is a preliminary attempt to integrate these counter-stories
of when rights were protected and expanded during wartime into the general narrative of civil liberties policy during war and periods of military tension.[12] The first part recounts numerous instances when civil rights and civil
liberties were either protected or expanded during hot or cold wars. These
accounts, while not intended to be comprehensive, provide evidence that
policies protective of rights in the United States during wartime have been
approximately as frequent, have affected approximately as many people, and
have been as concerned with fundamental liberties as restrictive policies. The
second part of the chapter sketches some counter-stories of civil rights protected or expanded during the present war against terrorism. The same
factors that have historically explained why some rights are restricted, others
protected, and still others expanded during particular wars, the analysis
suggests, continue to structure contemporary responses to military conflict.

The chapter concludes by noting how incorporating the counter-stories into grand narratives about civil rights and liberties in wartime provides a better perspective on the policies of the Bush administration.

Protection and expansion of civil rights and civil liberties during hot and cold wars do not occur at random, but take place regularly whenever some combination of the following four conditions is present:[13]

1. "[A] large-scale war requir[es] extensive economic [or] military mobilization of [the beneficiaries of a rights protective policy] for success."[14]

2. "[T]he nature of America's enemies . . . prompt[s] American leaders to justify such wars and their attendant sacrifices by emphasizing the nation's inclusive, egalitarian, democratic traditions"[15] or, at least, the national commitment to particular civil rights and liberties.

3. The beneficiaries of the civil right or liberty are, for reasons of race, ethnicity, or ideology, identified as loyal Americans, as aligned with American allies or countries whose support the United States is seeking, or at least as enemies of America's enemies.

4. Powerful political actors inside and outside government see the military conflict as an additional reason for advancing existing commitments to particular civil liberties and rights. Other crucial government actors can be persuaded or pressured to support those rights or liberties.[16]

Civil rights and liberties are likely to be restricted, by comparison, whenever the beneficiaries of protective policies are ideologically or ethnically identified with America's enemies or when government officials see the military conflict as an additional reason for advancing existing commitments to further limit the right or liberty in question.

This fuller but by no means complete story of civil liberties policy during wartime supports two additional conclusions.[17] First, civil liberties policy has historically varied by war and issue. Rights policies vary within wars and between wars. The Civil War witnessed substantial restrictions on free speech rights and substantial increases in the rights enjoyed by persons of color. The Second World War was easy on political dissidents and hard on Japanese-Americans. Speech rights were substantially restricted during the American Revolution, the undeclared war with France, the Civil War, the First World War, and the cold war, but not during the War of 1812, the Mexican War, the Spanish-American War, the Second World War, or during the present war against terrorism. Second, decisions to restrict civil rights and liberties during a war result from subjective choices rather than from objective necessities. Political dissent has been as widespread and as intense during wars in which speech was not restricted as during wars in which speech was restricted. Japanese-Americans during the 1940s were no more disloyal or loyal than German-Americans (and they were probably far more loyal than German-Americans during the First World War). Whether government officials restrict liberty, history suggests, depends more on ethnic stereotypes and contestable beliefs about the value of civil liberties than on clear threats presented by the exercise of a particular right during a particular war.

SOME COUNTER-STORIES

Four kinds of stories can be told about civil liberties and civil rights in wartime. The conventional stories are about restrictive policies adopted in the name of national security. Non-stories are about the absence of any or particular civil liberties issues during war or particular wars. These narratives, analogous to the tale of the dog that did not bark in the night, counter careless claims that military conflicts or tensions consistently produce generalized pressures to limit all existing individual rights. Some counter-stories are about how wartime proposals for new restrictive policies were defeated. These narratives demonstrate that Americans, at least under certain conditions, are capable of resisting efforts to limit civil liberties and rights during wartime. Other counter-stories are about how particular civil rights and civil liberties were expanded during wartime. These narratives demonstrate that Americans, in almost every major instance of military conflict or tension, have thought that mobilization needs, rewards for loyalty, or concerns not to emulate policies identified with national enemies have justified providing more protection for *some* individual rights.

The stories told below are about political actors making explicit connections between domestic civil liberties and an existing military situation. The canonical stories about occasions when civil liberties were restricted in wartime tell of policymakers claiming that the exercise of a particular right threatens national security. The counter-stories about occasions when civil liberties were expanded in wartime tell of policymakers claiming that protective policies promote national security or are intertwined with the justification for military force. Other stories about the relationship between war and civil liberties can be told, focusing on the unintended consequences of war.

Abortion policies after the Second World War are a good example of the difference between conscious and unintended consequences of war on civil rights policy. European policymakers frequently justified cold war abortion policies by pointing to the consequences of past military conflicts on future military needs. "[T]he devastating effects of World War II on the population," Berta Hernandez-Truyol notes, "prompted many Eastern European states to outlaw abortion in the hopes of increasing population to re-establish the labor force and rebuild armies."[18] The leading postwar opponents and proponents of abortion rights in the United States, by comparison, did not point to the cold war when justifying their preferred policy. National security concerns played, at most, a very minor role in arguments about family policy. Proponents of abortion rights rarely emphasized the need to distinguish American abortion policies from those implemented by national enemies. The Second World War significantly influenced family policy in the United States, primarily through the further loosening of sexual mores and the resulting postwar demands for a return to normalcy.[19] The terrain in which arguments about abortion were made was altered by war, but war did not directly affect those arguments.

The remainder of this chapter focuses on the connections that political actors self-consciously drew between civil rights policy and the military conflicts in which they were engaged.

Non-stories

War throughout American history has not exerted any general, across-the-board pressure to restrict all civil rights and civil liberties. Government officials during particular wars at most propose to limit particular civil rights and liberties. They do not propose to restrict civil rights and liberties whenever the United States is faced with a military threat, and they have never responded to a military threat by proposing to restrict all civil rights and liberties. No major rights controversies are associated with the War of 1812 or the Mexican War. No significant changes in the rate of executions or in birth control policies are directly associated with any military conflict. Some civil liberties controversies have erupted only during certain wars. The Second World War is the only military conflict associated with significant increases or decreases in religious freedom. More than two hundred years passed before even a minor Second Amendment controversy flared during a war. The Third Amendment has never been tested while the United States is at war.

Racial (and Gender) Equality

The struggle for racial equality provides numerous counter-stories of how civil rights were expanded during wartime and periods of military tension. During the cold war, support for desegregation was partly rooted in perceived needs to increase American popularity abroad. *Brown v. Board of Education*, Derrick Bell declares, "helped to provide immediate credibility to America's struggle with Communist countries to win the hearts and minds of emerging third world peoples."[20] Mary Dudziak elaborates Bell's insight at great length and with much sophistication when detailing the ways in which the cold war inspired, structured, and limited racial liberalism during the mid-twentieth century. Her study emphasizes that government officials regarded measures aimed at expanding African American freedom as crucial to American struggles against the Soviet Union. "[E]fforts to promote civil rights within the United States," Dudziak details, "were consistent with and important to the more central U.S. mission of fighting world communism."[21] Legal briefs frequently reminded courts that decisions furthering civil rights would have favorable national security consequences. The Justice Department in *Brown* informed the justices that "racial discrimination in the United States remains a source of constant embarrassment to this Government in the day-to-day conduct of its foreign relations." Jim Crow, the brief for the federal government continued, "jeopardizes the effective maintenance of [American] moral leadership of the free and democratic nations of the world."[22]

Philip Klinkner and Rogers Smith extend the connection between military threats and the civil rights of African Americans far beyond the cold war. Military conflict, they observe, has historically been the primary vehicle for securing greater racial equality in the United States. Every major improvement in the condition of African Americans, Klinkner and Smith point out, has been closely associated with a war. The rhetoric of liberty that inspired the colonists to declare independence and take up arms against Great Britain was simultaneously employed to justify emancipation in the North, bans on the importation of slaves, and laws easing manumission in the slave states.[23] The Civil War destroyed slavery and, as the heroism of black troops became known, inspired many northern states to repeal racist policies. Racial barriers began falling in northern states as the wartime service of African Americans fostered more egalitarian attitudes. One Union officer wrote, "You have no idea how my prejudices with regard to the negro troops have been dispelled by the battle the other day."[24] The first federal decrees desegregating the workplace were issued during the Second World War, when the United States had substantial need of African American troops and laborers. Military service again proved a vehicle for dispelling racial prejudice, clearing a path for the civil rights movement of the next decade.[25] Americans dissatisfied with the present racial status quo, this analysis might suggest, should consider imitating the fictional duchy of Grand Fenwick and find a powerful opponent to declare war against.[26]

Klinkner and Smith highlight two direct connections between *certain* wars and increased racial equality. Policymakers promote racial equality, they claim, when the war effort requires African Americans to fight for victory, and when egalitarian commitments are intertwined with the justification for the war.[27] African American troops played significant roles in the Civil War, the Second World War, and to a lesser extent the American Revolution. The Confederacy, Nazi Germany, and the Soviet Union inspired renewed commitment to the principles of human liberty and equality that inspired the American Revolution. Just as significantly, African Americans had no ethnic, racial, or ideological ties to the American South or Nazi Germany that might have created the suspicions of a "fifth column" that haunted Japanese-Americans during the Second World War. Some black communists did have ideological ties to the Soviet Union, but most policymakers during the 1950s and 1960s placed greater emphasis on the racial ties between African Americans and those third world countries deemed crucial supporters of American efforts during the cold war.

Proponents of racial equality were well positioned to take advantage of their windows of opportunity during the Civil War, the Second World War, and the cold war. Klinkner and Smith emphasize that strong protest movements were already in place that could pressure government officials to improve the status of African Americans.[28] Of equal importance, government officials during the Civil War, the Second World War, and the cold war were either sympathetic to racial liberalism or not implacably wedded to the racial status quo. President Andrew Johnson's actions during Reconstruction suggest that the favorable conditions for improving the status of African Americans during the Civil War would have had a much lesser impact on public policy had a northern Democrat been president during the conflict. The different civil rights policies adopted in the First and Second World Wars reflect the differences between a nascent and a full-blown civil rights movement, between President Wilson's commitment to segregation and President Roosevelt's aristocratic indifference to most racial issues, and between a Justice Department indifferent to civil liberties and a Justice Department staffed by committed racial liberals.

War often promotes gender equality as well as racial equality. The same mobilization concerns that provide increased opportunities for persons of color typically increase opportunities for women. The domestic needs for labor generated by a large-scale war offer new opportunities for women to gain positions from which they were previously excluded by law or by practice. When "men [are] away at war," Sara Evans notes, "women of all classes and races ha[ve] to assume a range of tasks traditionally allocated to men."[29] Women are particularly likely to be beneficiaries of wartime labor shortages because they are perceived as Americans, at least as loyal as their fathers, husbands, and sons on the battlefield. When the absence of men creates labor shortages, women can be trusted to take their place. Legal and nonlegal barriers to their participation fall by the wayside. During the Second World War, for example, women were given opportunities to volunteer for military service, businesses dropped formal and informal bans on women in certain jobs, and the War Labor Board fought to ensure that women who went to work were paid the same as men performing the same tasks.[30]

The ebb and flow of women's rights in the United States runs opposite to what the conventional story predicts. The traditional narrative highlights restrictive policies adopted during wartime, then regretted and abandoned when peace is restored. Lincoln's imposition of martial law was declared unconstitutional after Appomattox.[31] The Japanese internment became a national embarrassment after the Second World War.[32] The story of women's rights, however, is the opposite: liberties gained during wartime are abandoned when peace is restored. Women are encouraged to join the work force during wars when they are replacing absent men. They face renewed assertions of male supremacy after the troops come home and are accused of replacing present men.

Jehovah's Witnesses (and Other Religious Minorities)

The experience of Jehovah's Witnesses during the Second World War demonstrates that civil liberties as well as civil rights have been expanded during wartime. The Supreme Court of the United States in *Minersville School Dist. v. Gobitis* (1940) by an 8–1 vote ruled that a mandatory flag salute in public schools violated neither the free exercise nor free speech provisions of the First Amendment.[33] That decision provoked two intense reactions. The first was a mass assault on Jehovah's Witnesses. Members of the sect who refused to salute the flag found their children expelled from schools, their property vandalized, and themselves victims of mob violence.[34] The second was an élite assault on the Supreme Court. Prominent jurists and journalists excoriated the justices for failing to declare a constitutional right to refrain from saluting the flag.[35] A judicial change of course soon ensued. Two years after *Gobitis* was decided, Justices Hugo Black, William O. Douglas, and Frank Murphy in an unprecedented opinion publicly confessed error.[36] The next year, the Supreme Court by a 6–3 vote overruled *Gobitis*.[37] Justice Robert Jackson's majority opinion in *West Virginia State Board of Education v. Barnette* famously asserted, "[i]f there is any fixed star in our constitutional constellation, it is that no official, high or petty, can prescribe what shall be orthodox in politics, nationalism, religion, or other matters of opinion or force citizens to confess by word or act their faith therein."[38]

Gobitis may have been abandoned legislatively or by executive degree before being overruled judicially. Disturbed that the existing pledge of allegiance ceremony bore too close a resemblance to the Nazi salute, Congress in 1942 with the support of the American Legion passed a new law regulating public displays of loyalty. One provision in the bill stated that "citizens will always show full respect to the flag when the pledge is given merely by standing at attention."[39] In an interpretation that was probably not intended by Congress, the executive branch immediately determined that the national legislature had preempted all state and local laws requiring students to salute the flag and recite the pledge of allegiance. "State and local regulations demanding a different standard of performance," Justice Department lawyers declared, "must give way entirely, or at least be made to conform." After 1942 officials in the Roosevelt administration specially decreed that "a school board order respecting flag salute exercises should not now be permitted to exact more of the pupil with religious scruples against the flag salute than that he should stand at attention while the exercise is being conducted."[40]

Roosevelt's Justice Department more directly contributed to the overthrow of *Gobitis* by securing the appointments of two additional justices on record as thinking the case wrongly decided. Robert Jackson had expressed reservations about *Gobitis* before his nomination.[41] Wiley Rutledge, when a federal circuit court judge, condemned laws that required "Jehovah's Witnesses . . . to choose between their consciences and public education for their children."[42] These executive actions meant that in 1943 the Supreme Court did not stand alone against a national majority committed to restricting religious freedom. *Barnette* was the consequence of a wartime effort sponsored by the executive branch of the national government to promote civil liberties.

Barnette belies two conventional claims about civil liberties during periods of military tension. First, constitutional decision makers during times of military tension are said to balance individual rights against national security. One value must, at least in part, be sacrificed to better secure the other value. Second, the balancing scale is thought to be biased toward national security. Military tensions, constitutional commentators generally agree, typically provide occasions for new, drastic limits on civil liberties and rights. Justice Oliver Wendell Holmes summed up accepted knowledge when in a unanimous opinion upholding a wartime restriction on political dissent, he declared, "When a nation is at war many things that might be said in time of peace are such a hindrance to its effort that their utterance will not be endured so long as men fight and that no Court could regard them as protected by any constitutional right."[43] When deciding the second flag salute case, however, Justice Jackson neither balanced free speech against national security nor ruled that national security justified new limits on political dissent. The judicial majority that struck down mandatory flag salutes insisted that protecting individual rights during a war promoted national security. Justice Jackson's opinion in *Barnette* referred specifically to "the fast failing efforts of our present totalitarian enemies" when commenting that "[c]ompulsory unification of opinion achieves only the unanimity of the graveyard." Contrary to Justice Holmes, Americans were freer to refrain from saluting the flag during the Second World War than they were before Pearl Harbor.

Barnette was a wartime civil liberties decision, not merely a civil liberties case that happened to be handed down when the United States was at war. The flag salute ceremony became a national controversy only after Hitler took power in Germany and embroiled the world in total war. Disputes over whether persons in the United States had a right to refrain from saluting the flag arose as early as 1918, but garnered little public attention.[44] During the 1920s and early 1930s, only members of tiny religious sects refrained from saluting the flag, few communities passed laws requiring children to salute the flag in school, and those communities that did pass such laws often did not strictly enforce them. Members of the Jehovah's Witnesses in the United States began refusing to salute the flag en masse only after being inspired by the example of Jehovah's Witnesses in the Third Reich who were persecuted for refusing to give the Nazi salute.[45] American communities began rigidly enforcing laws mandating flag salutes only during the late 1930s, when the prospect of war in Europe heightened concerns with patriotism and inspired fears that members of Jehovah's Witnesses were fifth columnists.[46] Justice Felix Frankfurter's opinion in *Gobitis* was clearly influenced by the fall of France only a few months earlier.[47]

The Second World War played a prominent role in the arguments for and against the constitutionality of the mandatory flag salute. Proponents regarded the Jehovah's Witnesses as "professed Nazi agents"[48] and insisted that loyalty ceremonies were particularly vital during wartime. "[T]his is not the time for Jehovah's Witnesses . . . to be engaged in a nationwide program teaching disloyalty to our flag," the national commander of the American Legion declared, "when our supreme effort is needed for the unification of all elements toward our national safety."[49] Prominent citizens, who during the 1940s defended the right to refrain from saluting the flag, consistently analogized mob violence against Jehovah's Witnesses to "nazi methods"[50] and compulsory flag salutes in the United States to compulsory saluting in Germany. The *New Republic* in an editorial condemning *Gobitis* asserted that the United States was "in great danger of adopting Hitler's philosophy in the effort to oppose Hitler's legions."[51] "Such procedure . . . would be understandable in Germany," the *Christian Century* complained when welfare was denied to Jehovah's Witnesses who refused to take part in flag ceremonies. "There a man either gives the nazi salute and votes *Ja* when ordered or else he starves."[52]

The Second World War did much to promote religious freedom in general by linking religious bigotry with the Nazi state. Fighting an enemy identified with religious persecution, American leaders highlighted the more religiously inclusive elements of the country's political and constitutional heritage. "The gruesome persecution of religious minorities in Germany," Shawn Francis Peters asserts, "horrified many Americans and prompted them to tout the religious liberties enjoyed by members of all faiths in this country."[53] Many cases that served as vital precedents for expanding religious and other liberties during the Warren Court era were decided during the Second World War, partly as a judicial response to Nazism.[54] Jews, in particular, were *domestic* beneficiaries of increased calls for religious tolerance.[55] "With the Japanese attack on Pearl Harbor" and America's entry into the Second World War, Benjamin Ginsburg declares, "anti-Semitic activity was temporarily discredited through its association with the national enemy."[56] Immigration curbs remained, but greater governmental efforts were made to prevent assaults on Jews by various hate groups. Businesses and universities began abandoning religious discrimination during the waning years of the Second World War.[57]

The Eight-Hour Day during the First World War

The First World War was a boon to workers who supported the war effort. Mobilization needs, combined with an executive predisposed to support moderate labor demands, led to increased federal power to mandate the conditions of labor and new statutory rights for workers. Pre-war constitutional doctrine had cast doubt on whether government could give statutory rights to workers that they could not gain at the bargaining table.[58] Congress was disinclined to pass such measures. The threat of war changed the direction of public policy. When railway workers in 1916 threatened a strike to achieve an eight-hour day, the Wilson administration proposed and Congress passed the Adamson Act, mandating the eight-hour day.[59] The Supreme Court sustained that law in *Wilson v. New*.[60]

The impending war in Europe played a crucial role in these decisions to expand the rights of workers. President Wilson's address to Congress in

1916 demanded passage of the Adamson Act because "we cannot in any circumstances suffer the nation to be hampered in the essential matter of national defense."[61] When management in the winter of 1917 refused to adhere to the law, seeking a test case in the Supreme Court, Wilson placed great pressure on industrial leaders to grant the eight-hour day for reasons of national security. Shortly after the Germans torpedoed three American ships, he informed the National Conference Committee of the Railroads that "in this time of national peril . . . , a general interruption of the railway traffic of the country . . . would entail a danger to this nation."[62] Presidential threats to do whatever was necessary to avoid a strike succeeded. Management agreed not only to accept the eight-hour day, but to maintain the eight-hour day even if the Supreme Court ruled the Adamson Act unconstitutional.[63]

The Supreme Court's decision the next day to uphold the constitutionality of the Adamson Act was similarly influenced by a war which would be declared a mere three weeks after the ruling was handed down.[64] Chief Justice Edward White's opinion spoke of emergencies in general as providing justification for powers.[65] All recognized that the threatened emergency was not simply the train strike, but a train strike when the United States was about to engage in military action.[66] Attorney General Thomas Gregory observed that the Chief Justice "knew, as we all knew, that we were on the very verge of War; for the moment he forgot the facts of the case that was before him and his prophetic eye was resting on the immediate future when every proper energy of our country would be called upon to sustain it in its hour of greatest need."[67] Justice Pierce Butler was more explicit when in *Highland v. Russell Car & Snow Plow Co., No. 8* he declared that "the war power of the nation" was an instance where "Congress may regulate the making and performance of . . . contracts whenever reasonably necessary to effect any of the great purposes for which the national government was created."[68]

Labor issues complicate assertions that war provides occasions for restricting civil rights and liberties. Conflicts between union and management are often over whose rights are to be protected and to what degree. Workers during the progressive era declared they had a right to limits on the workday. That right, while not recognized in American constitutional practice, is enshrined, along with the right to join a union, in the Universal Declaration of Human Rights.[69] Employers during the Progressive era asserted that they had the right to determine the conditions under which they would contract for labor. This right was recognized in previous Supreme Court decisions protecting the freedom of contract.[70] Thus, government labor policy during the First World War (and other wars) could not simply balance individual rights against national security. Contested notions of national security inevitably determined whose individual rights the government protected.

Procedural Rights during the Cold War

Many procedural reforms that took place during the due process revolution were self-consciously associated with the Second World War and the cold war. One consequence of military conflicts and struggles with totalitarian nations was that policymakers and justices increasingly regarded constitutional protections for criminal suspects as central to the democratic values that the United States was championing throughout the globe. Scholars note the influence of "aversive constitutionalism"[71] on American constitutional practice during the 1940s and 1950s. "Precisely because they provide a sharp idea of what the U.S. does *not* stand for," Kim Lane Scheppele documents, "Nazi Germany and the Soviet Union became irresistible points of reference . . . on numerous occasions and in many doctrinal conceptions."[72] "[T]he desire to articulate principles that distinguished America from the Soviet Union and Nazi Germany," Richard Primus writes, "contributed to a long line of liberal Supreme Court decisions from the Second World War through the Warren Era."[73] Margaret Raymond agrees that "American constitutional criminal procedure and norms during the postwar period were defined in part in reaction to those negative totalitarian models."[74]

Numerous majority, concurring, and dissenting opinions defending and extending the constitutional rights of persons accused of crimes pointed to the practices of nations with which the United States was engaged in hot and cold wars as models that Americans could not emulate.[75] Justice Hugo Black's majority opinion in *Ashcraft v. Tennessee*, when declaring unconstitutional a coerced confession, favorably compared the United States to "certain foreign nations . . . which convict individuals with testimony obtained by police organizations possessed of an unrestrained power to seize persons suspected of crimes against the state, hold them in secret custody, and wring from them confessions by physical or mental torture."[76] The majority opinion in *Escobedo v. Illinois* contrasted the right to counsel guaranteed by the Sixth Amendment to practices in the Soviet Union forbidding the presence of counsel when criminal suspects were interrogated.[77] Permitting certain listening devices without adequate safeguards, Justice Douglas declared in *Berger v. New York*, "would take us closer to the ideological group we profess to despise."[78] Liberal commentators agreed with the Court. Erwin Griswold's lectures on the Fifth Amendment observed that the privilege against self-incrimination "would never be allowed by communists, and thus it may well be regarded as one of the signs which sets us off from communism."[79]

Aversive constitutionalism was primarily a wartime phenomenon. American élites promoted civil liberties by distinguishing the United States from totalitarian countries only when the United States was involved in a hot or cold war with those countries. Law reviews and judicial opinions during the 1930s did not treat the gross violations of human rights in Stalinist Russia or Nazi Germany as reasons for Americans to provide greater protection for civil liberties at home. Germany became the model not to emulate only with the onset of the Second World War.[80] The Soviet Union became the basis of comparison only with the onset of the cold war.[81] When the cold war thawed, so did aversive constitutionalism.[82] South Africa was rarely held up as a model to be avoided, even though that country's inhumane practices were well known.[83]

Anti-imperialist Dissent during the Spanish-American War

The McKinley administration's decision to declare war against Spain and send troops to quell rebellion in the Philippines brought forth the most vigorous dissent to the use of military force in American history. Professor Charles Eliot Norton of Harvard University "urged Harvard students not to enlist in a war in which 'we jettison all that was most precious of our national cargo.'"[84] American military intervention in the Philippines inspired even greater criticism of government policy. Such prominent politicians as William Jennings Bryan and Benjamin Harrison joined the Anti-Imperialist League, which issued frequent condemnations of administration policy.[85]

Charles Francis Adams Jr. praised the "very gallant resistance the unfortunate Filipinos are making against our wholly unprovoked assault upon them."[86]

These caustic attacks on military policy, which included explicit calls not to volunteer for military service, were not subject to any domestic censorship. The McKinley administration did make an abortive attempt to prevent Edward Atkinson from mailing anti-imperialist pamphlets to prominent figures in the Philippines, but Atkinson was allowed to mail more than 100,000 copies domestically. Encouraged by the sharp attacks on the administration's refusal to mail antiwar literature abroad, Atkinson issued another pamphlet intended as his "strongest bid yet for a limited residence in Fort Warren."[87] Chastened by the failure of its previous efforts, the McKinley administration did nothing. Attacks on military imperialism at the dawn of the twentieth century were allowed to be "uninhibited, robust, and wide-open," even though they "include[d] vehement, caustic, and sometimes unpleasantly sharp attacks on government and public officials."[88]

Two factors explain why during the eighteenth and nineteenth centuries political dissent was suppressed during some military conflicts but not others. Persons not identified ideologically, ethnically, or racially with American enemies were free to protest against military involvements. Norton, Adams, and Atkinson were white conservatives protesting a war against an Asian opponent. White Whigs similarly protested against the Mexican War without having their loyalty challenged. When white critics of military policy had ethnic or ideological ties to national enemies, however, as during the American Revolution, the undeclared war with France, and the Civil War, dissent was suppressed. Until the Second World War, the War of 1812 was the only instance of military combat in American history when white critics without official interference condemned a war against another nation identified as white. Existing attitudes about national power may have had an even greater influence on speech policies during wartime, correctly predicting national policy in every military engagement fought before the Second World War. For the first 150 years of national existence, free speech was restricted only during wars in which the political party with the broader conception of national power controlled the presidency. Federalists (undeclared war with France) and Whig-Republicans (Civil War) limited political dissent when wars occurred on their watch. Jeffersonians (War of 1812) and Jacksonians (Mexican War) did not. The stand-pat Republicans of the McKinley administration who did not repress speech during the Spanish-American War had a narrower conception of national power than the progressives in the Wilson administration who restricted speech during the First World War.

Communists during the Second World War

The good war was good for American communists. In the political environment of the early 1940s, they were increasingly perceived as loyal Americans or identified with the main ally of the United States in the Second World War. The alliance between the United States and the Soviet Union inspired increased toleration for socialists, Marxists, and other members of the radical left. Americans, "appreciat[ing] the tremendous sacrifices in blood the Soviet Union was making to defeat Nazi Germany," developed a more "benign view" of the country.[89] American liberals, appreciating the support that domestic communists gave to the New Deal, frequently supported communists seeking leadership positions in labor unions and running for local, state, and federal offices.[90]

Communist support for the domestic and foreign policy of the Roosevelt administration, combined with concomitant perceptions of communists' loyalty, helped reduce significantly the number of Americans who favored legislation curtailing subversive activities. Opinion polls by 1945 found that popular majorities no longer supported new bans on radical left-wing speech.[91] Government officials, responding to both communist support and shifts in public attitudes, sharply reduced the repression of radical activists. William Wiecek declares, "the wartime Grand Alliance temporarily abated antisubversive activity aimed at leftists." The Second World War, he continues, "marked the nadir of anticommunism" in the United States.[92] Federal prosecutors remained on the sidelines as communist influence in American life increased substantially. Mobilization as well as loyalty concerns fostered a more tolerant public policy. The Roosevelt administration did not aggressively pursue efforts to deport radical labor leaders for fear of inducing strikes and work stoppages.[93] This reduced government surveillance hardly made the early 1940s halcyon days for the radical left. Still, Americans during the Second World War were far freer to join groups associated with the Communist Party and express support for communist goals than either before or after.

The Supreme Court during and immediately after the Second World War upheld the civil liberties claim in all three cases brought by communists or persons affiliated with communists. Justice Black in *Lovett v. United States* ruled that legislation cutting off the salaries of named federal employees declared by Congress to be subversives was an unconstitutional bill of attainder. His opinion noted administration opposition to the bill and quoted representatives who declared the law a "legislative lynching."[94] The justices in *Bridges v. Wixon* ruled that labor leaders who cooperated extensively with communists were not affiliated with communists for purposes of federal deportation law. Justice Douglas highlighted the Grand Alliance as establishing that good Americans could legitimately cooperate with organizations associated with the Soviet Union. "Certainly those who joined forces with Russia to defeat the Nazis," he wrote, "may not be said to have made an alliance to spread the cause of Communism."[95] Most significantly, the judicial majority in *Schneiderman v. United States* made clear that long-standing members of the Communist Party could be "attached to the principles of the constitution of the United States" as that phrase was used in citizenship law. Justice Murphy declared, "we certainly will not presume in construing the naturalization and denaturalization acts that Congress meant to circumscribe liberty of political thought by general phrases." The procedures for amending the Constitution set forth in Article V "and the many important and far-reaching changes made in the Constitution since 1787," he continued, "refute the idea . . . that one who advocates radical changes is necessarily not attached to the Constitution."[96]

The Supreme Court proved just as receptive during the Second World War to the civil liberties of persons who sympathized with the Nazi cause, at least those who did so in word but not in deed.[97] The federal government moved far more aggressively against domestic Nazis than domestic communists during the first half of the 1940s, but six of the seven convictions that reached the Supreme Court were reversed.[98] Each reversal was on statutory grounds. Nevertheless, the justices made clear that they would be far less willing to find Nazi activities illegal under federal law than courts had been in analogous cases during and immediately after the First World War. "[M]en are not subject to criminal punishment because their conduct offends our patriotic emotions or thwarts a general purpose sought to be effected by specific commands which they have not disobeyed," the majority opinion in *Viereck v. United States* declared.[99] The justices in *Keegan v. United States* ruled that persons could not be convicted of obstructing the draft for counseling others that the draft was unconstitutional, a claim nearly identical to assertions that had sent Charles Schenck to jail in 1918.[100] Justice Murphy in *Hartzel v. United States*, while not questioning whether the Espionage Act of 1917 was constitutional, cited Justice Holmes's dissent in *Abrams v. United States*[101] as authority for interpreting the statute as requiring proof of a specific intent to interfere with military recruitment. Pamphlets that "depict[ed] the war as a gross betrayal of America, denounce[d] our English Allies and the Jews and assail[ed] in reckless terms the integrity and patriotism of the President of the United States," under this standard, were "not enough by [themselves] to warrant a finding of criminal intent."[102] Justice Jackson, after ruling in *Cramer v. United States* that the government had failed to produce two witnesses to an overt act of treason, concluded with Thomas Paine's admonition: "[h]e that would make his own liberty secure must guard even his enemy from oppression."[103]

Existing attitudes toward free speech and civil liberties explain why persons identified ideologically and ethnically with Germans were less likely to be prosecuted and convicted, and to have their convictions sustained on review, during the Second World War than during the First. Paul Murphy points out that progressives during the first fifteen years of the twentieth century were not sympathetic to civil liberties claims of any sort, whether claims of property rights or of free speech rights. Most progressives were committed utilitarians who believed that individual rights were subordinated to the public good. When war broke out, progressives in all branches of the national government were predisposed to restrict both rights to free speech and rights to public property in the name of national security.[104]

Civil liberties enjoyed far more support in the Roosevelt administration. Franklin Roosevelt may not have belonged to the American Civil Liberties Union, but many of his trusted advisors did. Attorney General Francis Biddle was a particularly strong supporter of civil liberties. He entered office believing that "[t]he extravagant abuse of prosecutions for sedition had been the most serious example of hysteria in the First World War." When local federal attorneys arrested opponents of the war for utterances that Biddle thought "palpably innocuous," he "ordered that the men be released and the prosecutions dropped."[105] Federal justices were similarly far more predisposed to protect civil liberties during the Second World War than during the First World War. The Supreme Court during the first two decades of the twentieth century rejected every free speech claim presented to the justices.[106] The justices during the 1930s provided increased support for civil liberties[107] and, in an important footnote, indicated that protecting free speech was a central judicial function.[108]

Overall

These counter-stories, while not presenting a comprehensive account of freedom when the United States is at war, seem at least as representative of individual rights policies during wartime as the well-known instances when the government restricted rights. For every instance in which government restricted civil liberties during wartime, another instance exists when government policy remained the same, and still another when an individual right was expanded. For every Japanese-American sent to an internment camp, there is an African American freed from Jim Crow. For every A. Mitchell Palmer, there is a Francis Biddle. Developing more precise measures of civil rights and liberties during wartime may be impossible. Any effort to determine statistically whether the restrictions on Japanese-Americans during the Second World War were greater than the improvements in the status of African Americans will depend too heavily on the researcher's values implicit in the measurements. Like the proverbial apples and oranges, some policies are simply not capable of precise comparison.

The best that scholars are likely to do is identify certain patterns in wartime behavior. If the analysis above is correct, these patterns have less to do with war per se than with the presence of specific conditions during a war. Both the conventional stories and counter-stories suggest that civil rights policies when the United States is at war are determined by mobilization needs, the ideological justification for the war, the identity of potential rights holders, and the predispositions of crucial political actors. These conditions help explain policy in previous wars and in the contemporary war against terrorism, which has created opportunities for expanding rights unrecognized by too many commentators.

WAR AND POLITICS

Many stories are already being told about civil rights and civil liberties during the present war against terrorism. As always, the narratives tend to be of civil rights and civil liberties restricted in wartime. Critics complain about decisions by the Bush administration to engage in ethnic profiling, hold numerous persons in detention without trial, deprive detainees of the assistance of counsel, use military courts, and remove previous restrictions on the means that law enforcement officials may use when investigating both terrorists and ordinary criminals. As has historically been the case, the victims of these policies are typically identified ideologically or, more important, ethnically with the enemy. Liberal white critics speak freely against the war, while many ethnic Arabs previously uninterested in politics have been detained and humiliated by government officials.[109]

Important counter-stories can also be told about civil liberties and civil rights protected and expanded during the war against terrorism. Military experts long indifferent to privacy rights are now insisting that bans on gays in the military be abandoned during the present crisis. The Bush administration is steadfastly refusing to adopt anti-terrorist policies that might infringe the claimed Second Amendment rights of gun owners. (The administration's successful defense of gun rights during the war against terrorism is a counter-story, no matter what the proper interpretation of the Second Amendment. Gun control at present is a counter-story because the Bush administration believes that citizens have a constitutional right to bear arms and is successfully preserving this claimed liberty during a time of military conflict.) The Supreme Court's decision in *Grutter v. Michigan*, sustaining an affirmative action program, was heavily influenced by a brief submitted by retired military officers which asserted that race-conscious measures were necessary for national security.[110] These counter-stories highlight ongoing themes about civil liberties during wartime and raise questions about the extent to which contemporary policy is driven by objective national security needs or the low value that the Bush administration places on particular civil rights and liberties.

Several contemporary policies illustrate how previous commitments shape official responses to a military conflict. When governing officials had previously championed a particular civil liberty (as members of the Bush administration did with gun rights), they are likely to regard the military conflict as either supporting their position or having no bearing on it. Thus, in addition to defending the rights of gun owners during the war against terrorism, President Bush has maintained that the military situation makes imperative the enactment of tax cuts that his administration was touting before the attack on the World Trade Center. Liberals exhibit a similarly steadfast commitment to pre-war policies. Senator Edward Kennedy and others seek to restrict only those rights that they sought to restrict before terrorist concerns occupied policymakers. The major critics of Bush administration gun and tax policies after September 11 were also the major critics of administration gun and tax policies before September 11.

These recent counter-stories indicate the ways in which war may exercise a powerful indirect effect on civil rights and civil liberties by changing the power relationships between political actors. Military tensions affect institutional support in fairly predictable ways. Presidents experience strong short-term surges in popularity.[111] Power flows to the national government at the expense of the states.[112] Trust in the military increases substantially.[113] These shifts in public opinion privilege policies favored by the president as opposed to Congress, by national officials as opposed to state officials, and by the military as opposed to civilians. The fate of particular civil liberties and rights in wartime thus may depend on whether the military crisis effectively transfers power to political actors inclined to support that liberty or right. Affirmative action was a beneficiary of the war against terrorism because that war increased the power of a military previously committed to obtaining a racially diverse armed forces.

Civil liberties and civil rights policies during previous wars are also at least partly explained as indirect consequences of changes in public support for various political institutions and actors. The First World War was good for labor because a president favoring an eight-hour day had strong public support in 1917. The Second World War facilitated racial liberalism by transferring power from conservative states and a Congress dominated by a conservative bloc to presidents that had fairly liberal Justice Departments. The war against terrorism has served as a vehicle for restricting civil liberties largely because the events of September 11 increased public support for an administration predisposed to regard foreign nationals as having few rights and more than willing to find any excuse to abandon existing legal limits on criminal investigations.

The counter-stories about civil rights and civil liberties that can be told about past and present wars require a reworking of the conventional case against the Bush administration's policies. Most civil libertarians contend that while civil rights and liberties are always restricted in war, the Bush administration is going too far. War, in their view, inevitably requires citizens to sacrifice some liberties, just not as many as John Ashcroft and his political associates demand. Alan Brinkley's sharp attack on contemporary policy nevertheless acknowledges that "in times of national emergency, . . . the relative claims of order and security naturally become stronger."[114] Critics are right that civil rights and civil liberties have often been limited during war in the name of national security. Restrictive policies, however, are hardly inevitable when war breaks out. No particular civil right or liberty has been restricted whenever the United States has been involved in a hot or cold war. War has often generated arguments for protecting and increasing civil rights and liberties. History makes clear that when faced with similar circumstances in past wars, other administrations have made policy choices different from those of the Bush administration. Every contemporary policy to restrict some rights while protecting others is a subjective choice, not mandated by historically recognized national security needs.

A different administration would have made a different, more civil libertarian response to the events of September 11. Concerned with American reputation abroad, a Justice Department staffed by civil libertarians would have emphasized the need to treat foreign nationals with increased respect during the war against terrorism. As during the Second World War and the cold war, American élites during a war that has been advertised as necessary to protect American freedoms would have highlighted such paladins of liberty as the right to counsel and trial by jury. Gun ownership would have been the paradigmatic liberty that had to be restricted in time of war. Increased taxes would be defended as simply a pale imitation of the sacrifices that American soldiers are making abroad.

Americans need to be more fully aware of the counter-stories about civil rights and liberties. War, history demonstrates, simultaneously creates opportunities to increase and restrict the freedom in the United States. Which opportunities are taken advantage of depends largely on who has the power to tell the official stories. One moral of the above story is that the major threat to civil rights and liberties at present is less what happens to civil liberties in wartime than what happens to civil liberties when George Bush is presiding during wartime. Another moral is that if the war against terrorism involves a struggle for the hearts and minds of persons in the third world, crucial battles are more likely to be won by a renewed emphasis on American commitments to diversity and respect for the strangers among us than by championing conceptions of individual rights largely limited to gun ownership and low tax rates.

NOTES

1 John C. Miller, *Crisis in Freedom: The Alien and Sedition Acts* (1951).
2 Mark E. Neely Jr., *The Fate of Liberty: Abraham Lincoln and Civil Liberties* (1991).
3 William Preston, *Aliens and Dissenters* (1963); Paul L. Murphy, *World War I and the Origin of Civil Liberties in the United States* (1979); Schenck v. United States, 249 U.S. 47 (1919).
4 Jacobus tenBroek, Edward N. Barnhart, and Floyd W. Matson, *Prejudice, War and the Constitution* (1968); Duncan v. Kahanamoku, 327 U.S. 304 (1946); Korematsu v. United States, 323 U.S. 214 (1944); Hirabayashi v. United States, 320 U.S. 81 (1943).
5 Stanley I. Kutler, *The American Inquisition: Justice and Injustice in the Cold War* (1984); Dennis v. United States, 341 U.S. 494 (1951).
6 Richard C. Leone and Greg Anrig Jr., eds., *The War on Our Freedoms: Civil Liberties in an Age of Terrorism* (2003).
7 See Mark Tushnet's chapter "Defending *Korematsu?*"
8 Samuel Eliot Morison, Frederick Merk, and Frank Freidel, eds., *Dissent in Three American Wars* (1970).
9 See Mary L. Dudziak, *Cold War Civil Rights: Race and the Image of American Democracy* (2000); Philip A. Klinkner and Rogers M. Smith, *The Unsteady March: The Rise and Decline of Racial Equality in the United States* (1999).
10 319 U.S. 624.
11 310 U.S. 586.
12 In keeping with the story-telling nature of the analysis, I offer no rigid definition of war or a period of military tension. The exclusion or inclusion of a few borderline cases would not change the analysis.
13 The conditions below are largely derived from the pioneering work of Philip Klinkner and Rogers Smith on war and racial equality. Klinkner and Smith, *The Unsteady March*. Their study suggested that three conditions were necessary for Americans to make substantial progress toward racial equality. My more general analysis of civil rights and civil liberties adopts their first condition in toto,

slightly modifies their second condition, significantly expands their third condition, and adds a new condition.

14 Klinkner and Smith, *The Unsteady March*, 3.

15 *Id.* at 3.

16 Klinkner and Smith emphasize "domestic political protest movements willing and able to bring pressure upon national leaders." *Id.* For reasons discussed below, the predispositions of national leaders have historically had as great an influence on civil rights and civil liberties policy in wartime.

17 Neither the conventional stories nor the counter-stories tell of the Vietnam War. That conflict generated significant efforts to limit, maintain, and expand civil liberties. The reason for the intense conflict, which I hope to explore in a later essay, is that conditions were present for both increasing civil liberties (Congress predisposed to protect rights, white Americans protesting a war against a nation of color) and restricting civil liberties (executive branch predisposed to limit rights, protestors identified with communist enemies).

18 Berta Esperanza Hernandez-Truyol, "Women's Rights as Human Rights: Rules, Realities and the Role of Culture: A Formula for Reform," 21 *Brooklyn Journal of International Law* 605, 652 (1996).

19 Sara M. Evans, *Born for Liberty: A History of Women in America* (1989), 227–29, 244–50.

20 Derrick A. Bell Jr., "*Brown v. Board of Education* and the Interest-Convergence Dilemma," 93 *Harvard Law Review* 518, 524 (1980).

21 Dudziak, *Cold War Civil Rights* (2000), 12.

22 *Id.* at 100–101.

23 Klinkner and Smith, *The Unsteady March*, 12–23.

24 *Id.* at 63, see also 52–71.

25 *Id.* at 161–287.

26 See Leonard Wibberley, *The Mouse That Roared* (1985).

27 Klinkner and Smith, *The Unsteady March*, 3.

28 *Id.* at 4.

29 Evans, *Born for Liberty*, 53.

30 *Id.* at 222.

31 See Ex parte Milligan, 71 U.S. 2 (1866).

32 Tushnet, "Defending *Korematsu*?," this collection.

33 310 U.S. 586 (1940).

34 Shawn Francis Peters, *Judging Jehovah's Witnesses: Religious Persecution and the Dawn of the Rights Revolution* (2000), 1–11, 72–95, 110–13, 124–27, 134–78, 211–16, 267–73, 281–84; Victor W. Rotnem and F. G. Folsom Jr., "Recent Restrictions upon Religious Liberty," 36 *American Political Science Review* 1053, 1061–63 (1942).

35 Peters, *Judging Jehovah's Witnesses*, 67–69.

36 Jones v. Opelika, 316 U.S. 584, 623–24 (1942) (Black, Douglas, and Murphy, JJ., dissenting).

37 West Virginia State Board of Education v. Barnette, 319 U.S. 624, 642–43 (1943).

38 *Barnette*, 319 U.S. at 642. One month before handing down *Barnette*, the Supreme Court in *Murdock v. Pennsylvania*, 319 U.S. 105 (1943), held that Jehovah's Witnesses selling religious books could not constitutionally be required to pay a generally applicable licensing fee on peddlers. This decision overruled *Jones v. Opelika*.

39 Peters, *Judging Jehovah's Witnesses*, 246.

40 Rotnem and Folsom, "Recent Restrictions upon Religious Liberty," 1064. See Peters, *Judging Jehovah's Witnesses*, 245–46, 252; *Barnette*, 319 U.S. at 638.

41 Peters, *Judging Jehovah's Witnesses*, 238–39.

42 Busey v. District of Columbia, 129 F.2d 24, 38 (D.C. Cir. 1942) (Rutledge, J., dissenting). See Francis Biddle, *In Brief Authority* (1962), 193.

43 Schenck v. United States, 249 U.S. 47, 52 (1919).

44 David R. Mainwaring, *Render unto Caesar: The Flag-Salute Controversy* (1962), 11.

45 Peters, *Judging Jehovah's Witnesses*, 24–25.

46 *Id.* at 9, 12–13, 16, 73–76, 80, 84, 92, 100, 106–8, 112.

47 *Id.* at 52–60, 65.

48 Peters, *Judging Jehovah's Witnesses*, 73.

49 *Id.* at 110, see also 156–57, 161, 194–95.

50 *Id.* at 97 (quoting Francis Biddle), see also 75, 86, 96–98.

51 *Id.* at 69. See Rotnem and Folsom, "Recent Restrictions upon Religious Liberty," 1063 ("How much more effective an instrument of patriotic education it would be if the flag salute itself were made a practical daily exercise of a fundamental liberty, a liberty which is one of the four great freedoms for which this nation is now fighting!").

52 Peters, *Judging Jehovah's Witnesses*, 163.

53 *Id.* at 16.

54 *Id.* at 14–16, 290–94.

55 Increased tolerance at home did not, however, translate into any greater willingness to prevent horrible Jewish suffering abroad. See David S. Wyman, *The Abandonment of the Jews: America and the Holocaust, 1941–1945* (1984).

56 Benjamin Ginsburg, *The Fatal Embrace: Jews and the State* (1993), 119.

57 *Id.* at 99.

58 See, for example, Lochner v. New York, 198 U.S. 45 (1905).

59 See Arthur S. Link, *Woodrow Wilson and the Progressive Era, 1910–1917* (1954), 235–37.

60 243 U.S. 332 (1917).

61 38 *The Public Papers of Woodrow Wilson* (Arthur Link ed. 1982) 101.

62 41 *The Public Papers of Woodrow Wilson* (Arthur Link ed. 1982) 414.

63 *Id.* at 431 n. 2; see Link, *Woodrow Wilson and the Progressive Era*, 237 n. 34.

64 See Michal R. Belknap, "The New Deal and the Emergency Powers Doctrine,"
    62 *University of Texas Law Review* 67, 79 (1983).

65 Link, *Woodrow Wilson and the Progressive Era*, 347–52.

66 See also Oren Gross, "Chaos and Rules: Should Responses to Violent Crises
    Always Be Constitutional?" 112 *Yale Law Journal* 1011, 1063–64 (2003).

67 Belknap, "The New Deal and the Emergency Powers Doctrine," 80 n. 93.

68 279 U.S. 253, 261–62 (1929). See Belknap, "The New Deal and the Emergency
    Powers Doctrine," 82–84.

69 Article 24 declares, "Everyone has the right to rest and leisure, including reason-
    able limitation of working hours and periodic holidays with pay." Article 23,
    Section 4, declares, "Everyone has the right to form and to join trade unions
    for the protection of his interests." Universal Declaration of Human Rights,
    www.un.org/rights/50/decla.htm.

70 See note 58, above.

71 Kim Lane Scheppele, "Aspirational and Aversive Constitutionalism: The Case for
    Studying Cross-constitutional Influence through Negative Models," 1 *ICON* 296,
    312 (2003). This paragraph is heavily indebted to Scheppele's important article.

72 *Id.* at 313.

73 Richard Primus, "A Brooding Omnipresence: Totalitarianism in Postwar Con-
    stitutional Thought," 106 *Yale Law Journal* 423, 423 (1996).

74 Margaret Raymond, "Rejecting Totalitarianism: Translating the Guarantees of
    Constitutional Criminal Procedure," 76 *North Carolina Law Review* 1193, 1197
    (1998).

75 For the examples discussed below and others, see Raymond, "Rejecting Totali-
    tarianism," 1203–20.

76 Ashcraft v. Tennessee, 322 U.S. 143, 153 (1944).

77 378 U.S. 478, 488 n. 9 (1964) ("[t]he Soviet criminal code does not permit a
    lawyer to be present during the investigation").

78 388 U.S. 41, 67–68 (Douglas, J., concurring).

79 Erwin N. Griswold, *The Fifth Amendment Today* (Cambridge: Harvard Univer-
    sity Press, 1955), 81.

80 Primus, "A Brooding Omnipresence," 429, 437.

81 Raymond, "Rejecting Totalitarianism," 1210.

82 See Raymond, "Rejecting Totalitarianism," 1220.

83 For the rare exception, see Florida v. Bostick, 501 U.S. 429, 443 (1991) (Mar-
    shall, J., dissenting).

84 Frank Freidel, "Dissent in the Spanish-American War and the Philippine Insurrection," Morison, Merk, and Freidel, eds., *Dissent in Three American Wars*, 74.

85 See Robert L. Beisner, *Twelve against Empire: The Anti-Imperialists, 1898–1900* (1985).

86 Freidel, "Dissent in the Spanish-American War," 83.

87 *Id.* at 85.

88 New York Times Co. v. Sullivan, 376 U.S. 254, 270 (1964).

89 Harvey Klehr and John Earl Haynes, *The American Communist Movement: Storming Heaven Itself* (1992), 102.

90 *Id.* at 100–101.

91 *Id.* at 101.

92 William M. Wiecek, "The Legal Foundations of Domestic Anti-Communism: The Background of *Dennis v. United States*," 2001 *Supreme Court Review* 375, 403.

93 Biddle, *In Brief Authority*, 300–302.

94 Lovett v. United States, 328 U.S. 303, 309 (1946).

95 Bridges v. Wixon, 326 U.S. 135, 143 (1945).

96 320 U.S. 118, 132, 137 (1943).

97 The justices had no difficulty permitting Nazi saboteurs to be tried by a military court, even though civilian courts were open in the jurisdictions where their offenses were alleged to have taken place. Ex parte Quirin, 317 U.S. 1 (1942).

98 In addition to the cases discussed below, see Fiswick v. United States, 329 U.S. 211 (1946) (claim that petition in 1940 concealed membership in the Nazi party cannot be proved by evidence that petitioner supported the Nazis after 1940); Baumgartner v. United States, 322 U.S. 665 (1944) (evidence that a naturalized citizen supported the Nazis during the late 1930s cannot be used to prove that he falsely declared loyalty to the United States when becoming a citizen in 1932). The one case in which the Court ruled against a Nazi sympathizer was Knauer v. United States, 328 U.S. 654 (1946) (evidence at the time of naturalization supported finding that petitioner falsely swore allegiance to the United States).

99 318 U.S. 236, 245 (1943).

100 Keegan v. United States, 325 U.S. 478 (1945). See Schenck v. United States, 249 U.S. 47 (1919).

101 250 U.S. 616, 627 (1919).

102 322 U.S. 680, 683, 689 (1944).

103 Cramer v. United States, 325 U.S. 1, 48 (1945).

104 Paul L. Murphy, *World War I and the Origin of Civil Liberties in the United States* (1979). See Mark A. Graber, *Transforming Free Speech: The Ambiguous Legacy of Civil Libertarianism* (1991), 78–86.

105 Biddle, *In Brief Authority*, 233–34. Significantly, perhaps, the decision to intern Japanese-Americans was made by War Department officials not noted for their

previous commitment to racial and ethnic equality. The Justice Department under Biddle privately opposed the policy. See *id.* at 219, 226.

106 See Fox v. Washington, 236 U.S. 273 (1915); Patterson v. Colorado, 205 U.S. 454 (1907).

107 See Herndon v. Lowry, 301 U.S. 242 (1937); Near v. Minnesota, 283 U.S. 687 (1931); Stromberg v. California, 283 U.S. 359 (1931).

108 United States v. Carolene Products Co., 301 U.S. 144, 152–53 n. 4 (1938).

109 See Alan Brinkley, "A Familiar Story: Lessons from Past Assaults on Freedoms," Leone and Anrig, eds., *The War on Our Freedoms*, 46; Lelyveld, "The Least Worst Place," Leone and Anrig, eds., *The War on Our Freedoms*, 124.

110 539 U.S. 306 (2003).

111 See John E. Mueller, "Presidential Popularity from Truman to Johnson," 64 *American Political Science Review* 18, 20–22 (1970).

112 Richard C. Leone, "The Quiet Republic," Leone and Anrig, eds., *The War on Our Freedoms*, 16.

113 See David C. King and Zachary Karabell, *The Generation of Trust: Public Confidence in the U.S. Military since Vietnam* (Washington: AEI Press, 2003).

114 Brinkley, "A Familiar Story," 23. See Stephen J. Schulhofer, "No Checks, No Balances: Discarding Bedrock Constitutional Principles," Leone and Anrig, *The War on Our Freedoms*, 74; Leone, "The Quiet Republic," 12.

Defending *Korematsu*?
Reflections on Civil Liberties in Wartime

Mark Tushnet

Introduction

Writing in 1945 shortly after the end of the Second World War, Professor Eugene Rostow of Yale Law School described recently decided cases upholding the detention of Japanese-American citizens as a "disaster." They deserved that description, Rostow believed, because "[t]he course of action which we undertook was in no way required or justified by the circumstances of the war." For Rostow, "[t]he internment of the West Coast Japanese is the worst blow our liberties have sustained in many years."[1]

Rostow's criticism of *Korematsu v. United States* has become the common wisdom.[2] Indeed, it has been generalized into an observation about the typical response of the U.S. government to perceived national security needs in wartime. The Latin phrase *inter arma leges silent*, which literally means that in times of war law is silent, has been translated to mean that in wartime the U.S. government frequently adopts policies that are simultaneously exaggerated responses to real security threats and substantial restrictions on civil liberties.[3] As David Cole has put it, "there is reason to think that as a general matter in times of crisis, we will overestimate our security needs and discount the value of liberty."[4] And according to Justice William J. Brennan, "After each perceived security crisis ended, the United States has remorsefully realized that the abrogation of civil liberties was unnecessary. But it has proven unable to prevent itself from repeating the error when the next crisis comes along."[5] This chapter examines that observation, using *Korematsu* as a vehicle for refining the claim and, I think, reducing it to a more defensible one.

KOREMATSU AND THE EX ANTE PERSPECTIVE

There *is* a pattern in our responses to government actions taken in wartime, but it is not the pattern of systematic overreaction that has become the conventional wisdom. And there seems to have been a process of social learning, which reduces the significance that policies adopted in the past have as a basis for evaluating current policies.

The pattern is this: The government takes some action that its officials — and frequently the courts — justify by invoking national security. In retrospect, once the wartime emergency has passed, the actions, and their endorsement by the courts, come to be seen as unjustified in fact (that is, by the facts as they existed when the actions were taken). The explanation is this: The actions are taken under conditions of uncertainty, when the officials do not know how the war is going to turn out, but they are evaluated retrospectively in, as Holmes put it, calmer times, and often when the war has been won. The glow of success reflects backward and affects our evaluations.[6] The social learning is this: Knowing that government officials in the past have exaggerated threats to national security or have taken actions that were ineffective with respect to the threats that there actually were, we have become increasingly skeptical about contemporary claims regarding those threats, with the effect that the scope of proposed government responses to threats has decreased.

The Pattern and Explanation: Ex Ante Decision, Ex Post Evaluation, and Ex Ante Knowledge

As I have said, it is commonly asserted that wartime emergencies elicit policy responses that in retrospect are seen as unjustified. I will sketch the history that supports this assertion, making no claims that I can provide a comprehensive view of either the episodes I discuss or the entire sweep of history.[7]

The first period is the 1860s.[8] President Abraham Lincoln suspended the writ of habeas corpus, obtaining congressional approval only after the event.

He directed that military courts operate in areas threatened by Southern forces even though the civilian courts remained open.[9] Sitting as a circuit judge, Chief Justice Roger Taney condemned the suspension of the writ,[10] but the Supreme Court never ruled on the constitutionality of Lincoln's action. In February 1864, while the Civil War was still in progress, the Supreme Court disclaimed jurisdiction to review the constitutionality of military trials by the statutory route the defendant chose,[11] and then in 1866, after the war had ended, held that the military trials were unconstitutional.[12] During Reconstruction the Supreme Court evaded challenges to the constitutionality of military reconstruction,[13] although its decision in *Texas v. White* (1869) adopted a theory that simultaneously endorsed the Republican Party position that secession was illegal and cast some doubt on the legality of the Republican position on military reconstruction.[14]

The historical judgment on these events is divided. Critics of Lincoln's actions make a strong case that Congress must authorize the suspension of the writ of habeas corpus *before* the president acts. And continued military occupation of a pacified domestic territory seems inconsistent not only with federalism but with core constitutional concerns about civilian self-government. Yet in both instances the practical imperatives of the circumstances, and the evident justness of the Northern cause, seem to support the legality of the government's actions.

The second period typically referred to in discussions of civil liberties during wartime is the period near the end of the First World War and extending into the early 1920s, when — for a time — the United States provided support for anti-Soviet forces in the Russian Civil War. The attorney general of the United States and state prosecutors brought charges against a large number of domestic radicals for seditious speech, essentially speech critical of the nation's wartime positions,[15] and the attorney general directed a roundup of radical aliens, seeking their deportation.[16] The Supreme Court upheld the use of laws making unlawful the criticism of government policy. The Court adopted the famous "clear and present danger" test in *Schenck v. United States*,[17] but applied it relatively loosely, allowing juries to find a defendant guilty if the defendant's speech had a natural tendency to induce listeners to violate the laws being criticized.[18] The Court continued to apply loose First Amendment standards through the 1920s,[19] but as we will see, later courts repudiated the Court's application of its First Amendment standards.

The Japanese internment cases are the central examples of civil liberties violations during the Second World War, and for the moment I will simply note the immediate adverse response to the Supreme Court's decision in *Korematsu*, a response that has not changed since 1945.

During the hottest periods of the cold war, prosecutions were brought against members of the Communist Party. Government officials took various other adverse actions against members of the party, people associated with the party, and people of a general left-wing cast who were thought to be associated with the party. In 1951 the Supreme Court upheld the convictions of the party's main leaders.[20] It endorsed the "clear and present danger" test, restating it in a way seemingly more protective of expression. Chief Justice Vinson's plurality opinion expressly asserted that the *dissenting* views expressed by Justices Holmes and Brandeis in the cases of the 1920s were the ones later cases "inclined" toward.[21] Still, the Court did uphold the convictions. Later in the 1950s the Court invoked the heightened standard to reverse convictions of the party's second-line leaders,[22] and developed related constitutional rules that made it harder for the government to impose sanctions on mere "fellow travelers." Its most important decision, for present purposes, allowed the government to convict a person for associating with a group that had both legal and illegal goals only if the government showed that the person was an "active" member who specifically intended to carry out the group's *illegal* goals.[23] Again, this restatement occurred in an opinion *upholding* a conviction. Still later, in 1968, in the midst of protests against the Vietnam War that made the Court well aware of the significance of its decision for potential prosecutions of antiwar protestors, the Court further tightened the standard in *Brandenburg v. Ohio*,[24] now allowing convictions only where advocacy of illegal action "is directed to inciting or producing imminent lawless action and is likely to incite or produce such action."[25]

This quick survey indicates the pattern commonly attributed to the civil liberties implications of government policies in wartime: The government acts, the courts endorse or acquiesce, and — sooner or later — society reaches a judgment that the action was unjustified and the courts mistaken. The retrospective critical view is a compound of two other judgments: that the threat to which the actions were responses was exaggerated, and that the responses were excessive in relation to the real threats (obviously) and even to the exaggerated threats. So, for example, critics say that the Japanese internments were supposed to limit the possibility that Japanese-Americans would engage in sabotage and espionage on the West Coast, but that there was a much smaller risk of sabotage and espionage from that community than policymakers thought. Or, critics might acknowledge that the threats to the United States from Soviet espionage were substantial, but assert that prosecuting members of the U.S. Communist Party was a badly designed policy response to the threat of espionage, which would have been countered better by devoting investigative and prosecutorial resources to intensified scrutiny of people associated with embassies and consulates.

The critical reactions to policies made in wartime circumstances may be mistaken. The reason is that the reactions occur after the event, but policymakers must act before the event. Even more, the reactions have all occurred after the United States succeeded in combating the wartime enemy, and usually under circumstances where there is no plausible case to be made that the actions in question—the Japanese internment, for example—actually played a significant role in its success. The policymakers were acting in real time, when they did not know that the United States would win the war, when they could not be sure of the size of the threats they were dealing with or of the effectiveness of various strategies to respond to these threats of uncertain size. From the ex ante perspective of the policymakers, the actions they were taking might be entirely rational and ought not be criticized in retrospect. And to the extent that we are concerned with developing a law that will guide policymakers, we should be careful not to constrain them because of our hindsight wisdom—unless we are pretty confident that the constraints we put in place really do respond only to tendencies to *exaggerate* uncertain threats or to develop *ineffective* policy responses to real threats.

Developing appropriate responses to decision making under uncertainty may be less difficult than it might seem, though. The reason is that there is another feature of the pattern that I have not yet discussed. The ex ante defense of policymakers assumes that they are doing the best they can to respond in conditions of uncertainty. The historical record rather strongly suggests that this assumption is often incorrect. Examination of the decision-making process in detail reveals that quite often—perhaps almost always—at the time the policies were chosen at least some of the relevant decision makers knew, and more should have known, that the policies they were adopting either were responses to exaggerated threats or were likely to be ineffective in countering the real threats.

The evidence is clearest in connection with the Japanese internment.[26] General John L. DeWitt, the West Coast military commander, was a racist who simply assumed without evidence that Japanese-Americans posed a threat of sabotage and espionage. General DeWitt made his final recommendation in favor of internment on 14 February 1942, more than two months after the attack on Pearl Harbor. In support of his recommendation, General DeWitt wrote, "The very fact that no sabotage has taken place to date is a disturbing and confirming indication that such action will be taken."[27] DeWitt's inference of a threat from the absence of sabotage rested on his racist assumption that "[t]he Japanese race is an enemy race," and that it was wrong to assume "that any Japanese, barred from assimilation by convention as he is, . . . will not turn against this nation when the final test of loyalty comes."[28] Rostow points to another indication of General DeWitt's cast of mind: General DeWitt's final report, prepared in 1943 and published in the following year, mentioned three episodes when the western coast was shelled by Japanese submarines. Two of the three episodes, though, occurred after the removal of Japanese-Americans from the region and, as Rostow pointed out, "These were the only such items in the Final Report which were not identified by date."[29]

The story of the first Red Scare is a bit more complicated. The problem was that the policy response should have been known to be ineffective. The reason is bureaucratic. The Department of Justice conducted the raids that rounded up aliens to be processed for deportation. The immigration statutes in place at the time did authorize the deportation of aliens who believed in or advocated the violent overthrow of the government, or who were members of organizations that did so. But the Department of Justice did not control the deportation process. Rather, that was in the hands of the Department of Labor. Justice Department agents prepared affidavits supporting the arrest, detention, and deportation of aliens, but the secretary of labor had to decide whether the affidavits and other evidence were sufficient to justify deportation. And the acting secretary of labor, Louis Post, was much more skeptical about the radical threat than officials in the Department of Justice were.[30] Post believed that a person could be deported as a member of an organization only if the person knew he was a member of the organization. Further, he believed that many aliens were "members" of Communist parties with unlawful aims only because leaders of the Socialist party assigned their names to the new Communist parties when radicals split off from the Socialist party. Post also insisted that a person must know of the organization's illegal aims, and he enforced rules against relying on uncounseled confessions and illegally seized evidence such as membership lists. Post's recalcitrance provoked efforts to remove him from office, but in the end nothing happened, precisely because Post was able to show how little evidence the Department of Justice had to support its claims that the aliens it sought to deport were dangerous radicals. I emphasize that this is not entirely a story of a heroic decision maker resisting wartime hysteria, although the story does contain that element. It is also a story about the inevitable incompatibility between one bureaucracy and another—a predictable failure of coordination.

A stronger case can be made for the effectiveness of the actions taken during the second Red Scare. The legal attacks on the Communist party undoubtedly reduced its organizational effectiveness, and—at least during the Second World War—U.S. citizens affiliated with the Communist party did engage in espionage on behalf of the Soviet Union. Disrupting the party might have impeded the Soviet Union's espionage efforts somewhat. A complete analysis, though, would require examining what might have been done with the resources devoted to undermining the Communist Party had those resources been devoted directly to investigating espionage. One would have to know, as well, how easy it would have been for the Soviets to develop spies *not* affiliated with the Communist Party. I do not know of relevant studies of these questions, although I should note my sense that the investigations of the Communist Party were probably too extensive—consumed too many resources—relative to the role that the party played in espionage, the availability of other channels of espionage, and the possibility that the resources might have been deployed more effectively in investigating espionage directly.

Some General Observations: The Relevance of Bureaucracy and Limits on Social Learning

The story of the first Red Scare suggests a complication with some bearing on defending *Korematsu*. The decisions we are examining all are taken by government *bureaucracies*, and an analysis of their effectiveness must take that fact into account. Assume for the moment that General DeWitt really did see in the presence of Japanese-Americans a threat of sabotage and espionage (concededly, a belief predicated on racism). He did not act on his own. Rather, he presented to bureaucratic superiors his assessment of the threat, and of the possible responses. Although General DeWitt's reasons for action may have rested on racist assumptions, the decisions of the higher-ups, relying on DeWitt, did not. Now, consider the situation from General DeWitt's perspective. He is the front-line decision maker, whose actions must receive the endorsement of bureaucratic superiors. Being on the front lines, he may believe that he knows better than his superiors what the true risks are. But, he might fear, were he to present *accurate* information about those threats, his superiors would mistakenly think that they were small, or that his proposed policy response was inappropriate. So, he presents to his superiors distorted information—knowingly distorted information—to ensure that they will make accurate decisions.

One aspect of the preceding account of decision making in uncertain conditions deserves particular note, as a prelude to the discussion of social learning below. At the time decisions are made, decision makers say to the public that the decisions are responses to threats of uncertain size and scope. The decision makers, or at least some of them, may have information available suggesting rather strongly that the policies being adopted either are ineffective or are exaggerated responses to the threats as the decision makers themselves understand them. But that information is, understandably, available only to the decision makers (or, worse, only to some of them). That policies are developed in uncertain times on the basis of information not fully available outside the decision-making bureaucracy may account for the courts' initial acquiescence in the policies, and for the subsequent critical reactions when the previously unavailable information becomes available.

Another consequence of bureaucracy is perhaps so obvious that it might be overlooked. Decision makers rarely like to admit that they made a mistake, particularly recently. In the present context the background of *Ex parte Quirin* is the most relevant example.[31] In brief: Several Nazi saboteurs landed on Long Island in 1942. One of them immediately went to federal authorities, informing them of the Germans' mission of sabotage. The officials did nothing for a few days. Then they rounded up the saboteurs, heralding the arrests with press releases touting the effectiveness of the Federal Bureau of Investigation in finding and capturing the saboteurs.

Fearing that a public trial would expose the FBI's claims for the nonsense they were, the Departments of the Army and of Justice agreed to prosecute the saboteurs in military tribunals convened for that purpose. The Supreme Court upheld the constitutionality of tribunals in an action that Justice Frankfurter, one of the leaders inside the Court for validating the government's action, later called "not a happy precedent."[32] The bureaucratic interest in avoiding disclosure of mistakes suggests that the public should be particularly skeptical about claims that government officials know their actions to be justified but unfortunately, for good policy reasons, are unable to disclose the foundation for their claims.

A final general observation should also occasion skepticism, this time about the limits of social learning. The pattern I have described is one that might be called fighting the last war.[33] That is, the legal world's retrospective evaluation of actions taken the last time around is that those actions were unjustified. Judges and scholars develop doctrines and approaches that preclude the repetition of the last generation's mistakes. Unfortunately, each new threat generates *new* policy responses, which are — almost by definition — not precluded by the doctrines designed to make it impossible to adopt the policies used last time. And yet, the next generation again concludes that the new policy responses were mistaken. We learn from our mistakes to the extent that we do not repeat precisely the same errors, but it seems that we do not learn enough to keep us from making new and different errors.[34]

Some Contemporary Examples

We can now consider some contemporary examples in light of the patterns I have identified. The first involves the general pattern of retrospective adjustment of our understanding of civil liberties; the second involves the bureaucratic interest in keeping mistakes from the public eye.

We know from the Communist Party cases that a person cannot be convicted of an offense defined as membership in a proscribed organization, unless the prosecution establishes that the person knew of and agreed with the proscribable goals of that organization. The reason is that people sometimes become members of organizations with mixed goals, legal and illegal, because they agree with and hope to advance the legal goals, and do not know of the illegal ones (or know of the illegal goals but seek to change them), and that making mere membership an offense would unduly limit the exercise of those members' freedom of speech and association. But, knowing that we cannot make mere membership a crime, can we nonetheless make paying dues a crime? Recent statutes suggest that we can, when they make it an offense to give material support to an organization with both legal and illegal (terrorist) goals.[35] In ordinary language, paying dues to an organization with terrorist and non-terrorist goals does give the organization material support. The statute on its face does not require the government to show that the defendant paid the dues knowing that some of the funds would be used to support the illegal goals, perhaps on the theory that because money is fungible, even money paid with the strictest of intentions that it be used for benign activities frees up money to be used for malign ones. If the patterns I have described persist, we can expect courts to uphold convictions in the face of claims that the government failed to show the defendant's having shared the illegal goals. And we can expect that several years later courts will begin to require such a demonstration from the government.

Notably, and in a way relevant to much of what follows, one reason for the pattern is that prosecutors are likely to single out the easiest cases for prosecution first, those in which the claim of lack of knowledge of malign goals is quite implausible. But sometimes — perhaps because of litigation strategy, or because of slip-ups in the prosecution — the trial records will not show the defendant's state of mind or knowledge even though it is clear enough what that state of mind was. From a court's point of view, the easiest way to rectify the problem is to say that no evidence of state of mind was really necessary: the government was really trying only to catch true terrorists and those who did support them, and really did bring such people before the court; the only problem is a small litigation error that the courts will feel inclined to overlook. Then, as weaker cases come along, courts will begin to realize that prosecutors have taken the statute too far, sweeping up defendants who really were not terrorist supporters in any commonsense way. They then will impose a state-of-mind requirement on the prosecution.

My second example is the government's imposition of secrecy in deportation hearings involving "sensitive" detainees. Defending the closure of the hearings, the government has argued that even the disclosure of the names and addresses of the people whose cases were being heard might provide information useful to terrorists. The argument is that terrorists could use the names of the people, along with other information they could gather about them, to infer the behavior that brought the people to the government's attention and then adjust their own behavior accordingly. It is important to acknowledge that this argument is *not* senseless and may even have substantial merit. But two points about the argument must also be noted. First, the government's position has the advantage, from a bureaucrat's point of view, of making it difficult for the public to determine whether the government's policy was a sensible response to a realistically evaluated threat. Second, the argument rests on premises the evidence for which cannot be made public by the terms of the argument itself.[36] In short, just as judges and ordinary citizens must — and probably do — trust executive officials to make appropriate decisions about whom to prosecute under laws that *could* be construed broadly to threaten free expression, so here citizens and judges must trust executive officials to have made realistic evaluations of threats and to have developed sensible policy responses to those threats.

The general point I wish to make is that the process I have sketched is one in which courts implicitly rely on the good faith of executive officials — here, the officials' good faith effort to prosecute only true terrorists and their supporters — as the unstated basis for overlooking civil liberties problems with the legal positions that the executive officials have staked out. These two examples demonstrate the role that deference to executive judgment plays in developing the pattern I have described.

SOCIAL LEARNING: THE WHIG VERSION

The optimistic view of the pattern I have described is that it demonstrates a valuable form of social learning.[37] The threat to civil liberties posed by government actions has diminished in successive wartime emergencies.[38] We ratchet down our reaction to what we perceive to be a threat each time we observe what we think in retrospect were exaggerated reactions to threats.[39] To take the obvious example, nothing on the scale of the Japanese internment has yet been proposed during the current situation. And no substantial policy of racial profiling has been openly adopted, though there has been an increase in expressed support for certain forms of racial profiling at airports (or, more properly, nationality-based profiling).

Other essays in this collection explain one source of the social learning: politics. Those most enthusiastic about expansive presidential power — the shills — have come to acknowledge the practical political reality that they must scale back their actions, if not their claims. Social learning elsewhere in society appears to have produced a political dynamic that restrains the administration.

Another dimension of the question of social learning is revealed by examining other actions that have been described as threats to civil liberties. These include the detention of resident aliens for suspected visa violations, nondisclosure of the names of those detained, deportations when violations were found, and seemingly intrusive invitations by federal agents to Arab-Americans to discuss what they knew about potential terrorist activities in their communities.[40] Putting aside the question of whether any of these actions should be treated as threats to civil liberties, I would emphasize that the threats have affected almost exclusively non-citizens resident in the United States. Some, it turns out, were law violators: that is, they had violated immigration law. These law violators were subjected to deportation even though their violations, before September 11, would not have led to such action, at least not immediately. The government simply changed its previous policy of respectful consideration of a law violator's personal circumstances. The new policy, while perhaps not the policy best suited to a humane government, does not seem to me a violation of civil liberties.

In some instances, the actions taken might be true violations of civil liberties. But again, they are violations of the rights of residents who are not U.S. citizens. David Cole argues that such violations might have spillover effects on the rights of citizens.[41] That is, once we get accustomed to these actions when taken against non-citizens, we will be more comfortable about extending them to citizens. That may be true, but the threat to citizens has not yet materialized, except, as I have suggested, in connection with the detentions of citizens as members of an enemy army. In Cole's words, "Measures initially targeted at noncitizens *may well* come back to haunt us all."[42] My claim about social learning is that while the possibility identified by Cole is a real one, its magnitude is smaller than he suggests.

Cole uses the example of the Red Scare of the 1920s and its extension in the McCarthy era to illustrate his claim.[43] We learned during McCarthyism, in his view, that rules applied at first against non-citizens could then be applied to citizens. Similarly, the rules applied today against non-citizens might be applied in the future to citizens. But one might describe the process of social learning differently.[44] After all, the McCarthy era involved not just the application of rules proscribing various forms of expression, but the development of constitutional doctrine constraining the application of those rules. So it might be that what we learned is this: actions that seem constitutionally permissible when taken against non-citizens will be treated as constitutionally problematic when they are taken against citizens.

The social learning process, that is, couples learning about exaggerated reactions to perceived threats with a persistent creation of an Other — today, the non-citizen — who is outside the scope of our concern. Perhaps, indeed, we are able to discern exaggerated reactions, and learn to reduce their reach, only because we are able to displace our concerns on to that Other. The Whig version of social learning does identify a real process in which government policy in response to emergencies has a decreasingly small range, but a more pessimistic view would direct our attention to continued focus of the policy on the Other.

Have I truly "defended" *Korematsu*? In one sense, yes. I have tried to explain how decision makers faced with what they understood to be a threat to the nation might have engaged in actions that in retrospect seem quite unjustified. I have suggested that those actions should look different not only to those who evaluate them in the future, but to ordinary citizens and judges at the time the actions are taken. Judges should refrain from giving in to an understandable urge to make exercises of emergency powers compatible with constitutional norms as the judge articulate them, to avoid normalizing the exception. And ordinary citizens should take a stance of watchful skepticism about claims from executive officials that the actions of the officials are in fact justified by, and are sensible policy responses to, threats to national security.[45] This is particularly true when the officials assert that the nature of the threat makes it impossible for them to disclose fully the reasons for the actions they take. The officials may be right, which is why ordinary citizens should not be flatly outraged by the actions,[46] but there is a good chance that they are wrong, which is why we should be skeptical about their assertions.

NOTES

1 Eugene Rostow, "The Japanese-American Cases: A Disaster," 54 *Yale Law Journal* 489 (1945).

2 323 U.S. 214 (1944).

3 See, for example, William H. Rehnquist, *All the Laws but One: Civil Liberties in Wartime* (1998), 224.

4 David Cole, "Enemy Aliens," 54 *Stanford Law Review* 953, 955 (2002).

5 William J. Brennan Jr., "The Quest to Develop a Jurisprudence of Civil Liberties in Times of Security Crises," 18 *Israel Yearbook on Human Rights* 11, 11 (1998), quoted in Oren Gross, "Cutting Down Trees: Law-Making under the Shadow of Great Calamities," in *The Security of Freedom: Essays on Canada's Anti-Terrorism Bill*, ed. Ronald J. Daniels, Patrick Macklem, and Kent Roach (2001), 39, 54.

6 The fancy description of this is hindsight bias. For an accessible discussion, see Jeffrey J. Rachlinski, "A Positive Political Theory of Judging in Hindsight," 65 *University of Chicago Law Review* 571 (1998).

7 I am especially concerned that the common use of a few episodes might be misleading, and that examination of every period in which the United States (whether the government or the people) believed itself to be under significant external threat might disclose a far more random set of responses than the common story identifies.

8 Sometimes the story is told about the Civil War only, omitting Reconstruction. I think that doing so may lead one to give a bit too much credit to the Supreme Court, which was somewhat more receptive to challenges to executive actions taken during the Civil War than it was to challenges to Reconstruction, even though civil liberties concerns could arise in connection with both periods.

9 The classic overview of Lincoln's actions from a constitutional perspective is James G. Randall, *Constitutional Problems under Lincoln* (rev. ed. 1964).

10 Ex parte Merryman, 17 Fed. Cas. 144 (1861).

11 Ex parte Vallandigham, 68 U.S. (1 Wall.) 243 (1864).

12 Ex parte Milligan, 71 U.S. 2 (1866).

13 See Mississippi v. Johnson, 71 U.S. 475 (1867); Georgia v. Stanton, 73 U.S. 50 (1868); Ex parte McCardle, 74 U.S. 506 (1869).

14 74 U.S. 700, 725 (1869) (describing the nation as "an indestructible Union, composed of indestructible States").

15 For a study of the sedition prosecutions, see Richard Polenberg, *Fighting Faiths: The Abrams Case, the Supreme Court, and Free Speech* (1987).

16 On the Palmer Raids and the Red Scare of the 1920s, see Robert K. Murray, *Red Scare: A Study of National Hysteria, 1919–1920* (1964); Regin Schmidt, *Red Scare: The FBI and the Origins of Anticommunism in the United States* (2000).

17 249 U.S. 47 (1919).

18 See also Abrams v. United States, 250 U.S. 616 (1919).

19 Gitlow v. New York, 268 U.S. 652 (1925); Whitney v. California, 274 U.S. 357 (1927).

20 Dennis v. United States, 341 U.S. 494 (1951).

21 *Id.* at 507.

22 Yates v. United States, 354 U.S. 298 (1957).

23 Scales v. United States, 367 U.S. 203 (1961).

24 395 U.S. 444 (1969).

25 *Id.* at 447.

26 The standard account is Peter Irons, *Justice at War* (1983).

27 Quoted in Rostow, "The Japanese-American Cases," 521. (Here and elsewhere I rely on Rostow's article in the service of the rhetorical goal of showing that information about the decision makers' state of mind was available roughly contemporaneously with the decisions themselves.)

28 Quoted in *id.* at 520, 521.

29 *Id.* at 523. Rostow also noted that "[t]hose subsequently arrested as Japanese agents were all white men." *Id.*

30 Post's memoir is Louis F. Post, *The Deportations Delirium of Nineteen-Twenty: A Personal Narrative of an Historical Official Experience* (1923).

31 317 U.S. 1 (1942). The best source on the Quirin case is David Danelski, "The Saboteurs' Case," 1 *Journal of the Supreme Court Historical Society* 61 (1996).

32 Quoted in Danelski, "The Saboteurs' Case," 80.

33 As Geoffrey Stone puts it, "[O]ne might say that the Court learns just enough to correct the mistakes of the past, but never quite enough to avoid the mistakes of the present." *Eternally Vigilant: Free Speech in the Modern Era*, ed. Lee C. Bollinger and Geoffrey R. Stone (2002), 8 (comment of Geoffrey Stone).

34 For a similar observation, see David Cole, "The New McCarthyism: Repeating History in the War on Terrorism," 38 *Harvard Civil Rights–Civil Liberties Law Review* 1, 3–4 (2003) ("While it has adapted slightly the tactics of prevention to avoid literally repeating history, in its basic approach the government today indeed is replaying the mistakes of the past. All we have learned from history is how to mask the repetition, not how to avoid the mistakes.").

35 See AEDPA, Pub. L. § 303(a), codified at 18 U.S.C. § 2339B and 8 U.S.C. § 1189.

36 Richard Pildes has pointed out an important distinction. The government's argument rests on two premises: (1) Terrorists have proven adept at using public information as a basis for adapting their behavior to avoid detection. (2) The aggregate information provided by public disclosure of the names and addresses of subjects of deportation hearings is an example of the type of infor-

mation terrorists have used. I suppose the government could be required to present evidence supporting the first premise, and that doing so would not give the terrorists more information than they already have — although the premise seems to me so obviously true that perhaps it need not be supported in any particular case. The problem lies in demonstrating the validity of the second premise without giving the terrorists information they do not already have about how the government responds to terrorist threats.

37 Jack Goldsmith and Cass R. Sunstein, "Military Tribunals and Legal Culture: What a Difference Sixty Years Makes," 19 *Constitutional Commentary* 261 (2002), offer a different version of the Whig account, attributing the different reactions to *Ex parte Quirin* and the Bush administration's proposal for military tribunals to broad changes in the legal and popular culture, including greater skepticism about government and greater concern for the rights of the accused. This account is not inconsistent with the Whig story I offer, but it is more limited along one dimension, focusing only on one policy rather than on all policy responses to wartime emergencies, and more expansive along another, given its attention to broad cultural changes rather than to the specifics of wartime emergencies.

38 Other things might be learned from the pattern as well. For example, *Korematsu* and similar cases might teach us that courts should treat military decisions just as they treat decisions by other bureaucracies, giving no *special* deference to military judgments. Or, we might learn that our retrospective attention to overestimated threats of danger has obscured our attention to questions about whether policy responses are appropriate even if the threat is *properly* evaluated.

39 I think it worth noting that one part of the process of social learning might be an exaggerated contemporaneous response to present-day policies: overstated claims that present policies threaten deep incursions on civil liberties might help us learn, over time, that the present policies were unsound, even if not quite as unsound as their present-day critics contend.

40 For an overview of these actions, see Cole, "Enemy Aliens," 959–77.

41 See, for example, *id.* at 959 ("what we are willing to allow our government to do to immigrants creates precedents for how it treats citizens.")

42 *Id.* (emphasis added).

43 Cole's other example is the extension of the Enemy Alien Act, adopted in 1798 (and still in effect), to the Japanese internment, and the extension of red-baiting from an action directed against immigrants in the 1920s to one directed against citizens in the McCarthy period. As I have suggested, if the Japanese internment cases are a precedent for anything today, it is as a precedent cautioning against imprudent actions.

44 In addition, the length of time between the episodes described by Cole brings

into question the claim that the earlier one caused the later one, or even was a precedent for it.

45 I am aware of the significance of my using the term "citizens" here.

46 Except insofar as the process of social learning I described requires that *some* citizens publicly characterize the actions as outrageous.

Part III

The War Powers outside the Courts

William Michael Treanor

The Problems

Few areas of constitutional law have produced as much heated debate as that of war powers, heat produced in no small part by the passionate belief that this is a subject of incalculable consequence. But stunningly and ironically, there is little connection between the issues that scholars debate and the constitutional issues involving war that government officials and political leaders confront.

War powers scholarship continues to be haunted by the war in Vietnam, and the dominant question continues to be whether Congress must approve large-scale, sustained military action. But this is not the central issue now (if ever it truly was, since President Johnson could always point to the Gulf of Tonkin Resolution).[1] Concededly, there are political actors who still articulate the view that the executive can unilaterally initiate major conflict and sustain the conflict in the absence of congressional authorization of some form. The first President Bush, for example, made claims to that effect before and after the Gulf War.[2] But he ultimately went to Congress for authorization.[3] The debate about whether Congress must authorize large-scale military conflict in the absence of some emergency is one in which champions of Congress have prevailed as a practical matter. As defenders of the executive branch justify military action already taken or prepare justification for actions being considered, they either rely on congressional authorization of some type or argue that there is some exception warranting departure from the general principle that Congress must authorize conflict. Thus, to the extent that I can deduce internal deliberations from reading newspapers, as the current administration prepared for war against Iraq, it was not ready to do so simply on the grounds that there is a general executive power to start and wage war without congressional authorization. But administration lawyers did conclude that war against Saddam Hussein could be started in 2002 in light of the president's constitutional powers and congressional authorization of the Gulf War in 1991.[4] Although the administration eventually decided to seek express congressional authorization, its apparent consideration of a statute enacted eleven years earlier as justification highlights an issue that *does* have enormous bite: How focused must congressional consideration be for it to constitute authorization? Is it necessary that Congress explicitly authorize a particular conflict for it to be constitutional?

I don't mean: Must Congress authorize major conflict by formally declaring war? The issue of whether Congress must formally declare war for large-scale conflict to be constitutional—like the broader issue of whether Congress must authorize sustained conflict—appears to be of great significance for many scholars. I should add that it is hard for me to see that this is actually a difficult issue. Formal declarations of war were increasingly rare at the time of the founding, as Hamilton observed in the Federalist 25,[5] and after 1798 Congress clearly approved the quasi-war against France without a formal declaration of war.[6] Background understanding and early practice thus make clear that the framers—in granting Congress the power to "declare war"—were using the term in a nontechnical way and did not intend that formal declarations of war should be the only mechanism by which Congress could initiate major conflict. Of greater relevance for my point here, the argument that Congress must formally declare war to initiate major conflict is not one that engages with a current controversy. The United States has repeatedly engaged in military conflict since the Second World War without once formally declaring war, and there is no political constituency clamoring for a different practice under which a declaration of war would be necessary. In contrast, the issue that is of great moment is whether congressional authorization must be explicit and addressed to a particular controversy. As I noted above, my sense is that the current administration considered going to war against Iraq in 2002 on the basis of the congressional authorization of the Gulf War in 1991. During the Clinton administration, the Office of Legal Counsel (OLC) justified the planned invasion of Haiti in 1994 on the basis of implied authorization found in an appropriations bill,[7] and in 2000 it provided a similar justification for the intervention in Kosovo.[8] So the executive has controversially taken the position that Congress's authorization need not be explicit.

Leading scholars have recognized that there can be disagreement about *when* Congress has authorized military action in a way that is constitutionally sufficient. There is, for example, an ongoing debate about whether the Tonkin Gulf Resolution was sufficient justification for the war in Vietnam or whether the War Powers Resolution should be understood to authorize sixty days of military action before the executive needs further approval from Congress. But there has been little thinking about the broader question of how one determines as a matter of law when Congress has signed off on military action and, as the Kosovo and Haiti opinions indicate, this is a question of great moment.

A connected issue of similar import is: In what situations is congressional approval unnecessary? Even champions of a pro-Congress understanding of the Constitution, such as Ely, recognize that there are *some* situations in which the president can move in advance of congressional authorization — such as when the nation is under attack or to rescue U.S. citizens abroad.[9] The critical question, and one that has received little attention, is: What are the contours of this category? How do we determine when the executive can proceed unilaterally? This is, again, a fundamental issue. In the Clinton and first Bush administrations, military actions such as those in Somalia, Haiti, and Bosnia were justified by the Department of Justice on the grounds that the deployment of troops did not amount to "war" in the constitutional sense.[10] Under the test employed by Walter Dellinger, then an assistant attorney general, the nature, scope, and duration of the conflict must be assessed. If they do not rise to a certain level, the conflict is not "war" and thus Congress need not approve it.[11] In Somalia, Dellinger's predecessor, Timothy Flanigan, took the position that the president did not need congressional approval when he deployed troops to protect both U.S. citizens and non–U.S. citizens.[12] In contrast, the War Powers Resolution suggests that the president can act unilaterally only when the United States or its territories, possessions, or troops are under attack.[13] The gap between the Department of Justice position and the War Powers Resolution is vast. The president's ability to act alone is, under one approach, great; under the other, it is reserved for particular types of emergencies.

Beyond its failure to focus on the issues of primary practical consequence today, a basic failing of most current scholarship on the war powers is that it has not adequately addressed either the question of constitutional role or how political actors should engage in constitutional discourse. Classically, legal scholars have focused either on how courts should interpret the Constitution or on how scholars should interpret it. In recent years, scholars such as Mark Tushnet have pushed to "tak[e] the Constitution away from the courts." I think the case that Tushnet has made is compelling, but we need now to focus more on *how political actors should engage in constitutional interpretation.* The war powers question is an extraordinarily rich area for consideration of this question, both because the courts have historically retreated from the area and because there is a significant body of OLC opinions that provide evidence of how one set of political actors has interpreted the Constitution. At the same time, there is a difficult area to think through. How does the presence of a body of executive branch precedent (the opinions of the Office of Legal Counsel) affect the constitutional interpretations of executive branch actors? Should they interpret the Constitution differently from members of Congress? More broadly, are members of the three branches of government entitled to interpret the Constitution differently precisely because the Constitution in the war powers area contemplates, to use Corwin's phrase, an "invitation to struggle" in which the different branches of government promote different institutional interests?[14]

It is also a challenge to work through political actors' constitutional obligations precisely because the area is so difficult. As the next section will suggest, there is a range of legitimate interpretations to constitutional questions in the war powers area, such as the two I am focusing on here (What constitutes congressional authorization? When is congressional authorization unnecessary?). What should a political actor do when there is a range of appropriate interpretations? Should she try to be principled? What does it mean to be principled, and what would a principled approach be? Should the political actor instead be opportunistic, because the constitutional system—like the adversary system—works best when players pursue self-interest, rather than try to take an Olympian view? These are hard issues that have received relatively little exploration.

Finally, I have found much of the scholarship in this area wanting because it typically treats the question of the proper role of executive and

Congress in the war powers area as an easy one. Scholars disagree about what the proper role is, but even as they disagree, they treat the position they hold as clearly correct. But for reasons that will be outlined below, this is not an area that admits of easy answers.

The rest of this chapter represents an attempt to start exploring these issues. In the next section, I sketch out why normal methodologies of constitutional interpretation fail to give us concrete answers to the questions of what constitutes congressional authorization and when authorization is unnecessary. In the final section, I offer a foray into why principled decision making is important here and how a political actor might engage in it.

LIMITS OF TRADITIONAL METHODOLOGIES

When I write a law review article, I typically get a certain number of letters from people who disagree with me. But the only time I have ever gotten truly angry letters was when I wrote about the original understanding of the war powers clause.[15] What upset people was not my thesis about why the framers gave the power to declare war to Congress, but rather the simple fact that in my view, one could legitimately disagree about what the war clause of the Constitution means. There is a substantial body of scholarly opinion insisting that the constitutional framework is perfectly straightforward, that Congress has to authorize conflicts, and that there is no ground for dispute. As John Hart Ely writes on the first page of his war powers book: "The power to declare war was constitutionally vested in Congress. The debates, and early practice, establish that this meant all wars, big or small, 'declared' in so many words or not — most weren't, even then — had to be legislatively authorized."[16] The record is much more ambiguous, and the ambiguity bears on my questions of what constitutes congressional authorization and when it is not necessary.

Start with text. The Constitution vests in Congress the power "To declare War, grant letters of Marque and Reprisal, and make Rules concerning Captures on Land and War." The president is "Commander in Chief of the Army and Navy of the United States," and he possesses as well whatever power can be derived from the vesting clause of Article II, section 1. There are a number of legitimate ways to read these texts, and they have different implications for the way my two questions are resolved.

Article I's grant of power to Congress can, as a textual matter, plausibly be read as mandating that Congress must authorize *any* conflict for it to be constitutional. Under this approach, while Congress is specifically given only the power to start the biggest conflicts (formally declared wars) and the smallest (the limited operations conducted by those operating with letters of marque and reprisal), these grants should be read almost poetically to stand for the proposition that Congress has to approve the biggest conflicts, the smallest conflicts, and everything in between. Article I, section 8, clause 11, is thus best understood as constitutional synecdoche. (For those with vague memories of the term from long-past high school English classes: the part stands for the whole.) "To declare War [and] grant letters of Marque and Reprisals" is the lawyer's equivalent of "Lend me your ears" and "All hands on deck." Although the synecdoche analogy is original with this essay, the basic point is Ely's.[17]

While Ely's approach to the text would mandate that only congressionally approved conflicts are constitutional, precisely because the text does not speak to the full range of military operation, it does not provide clear guidance as to what form approval must take. In other words, under Ely's reading Congress can sanction conflict by declaring war, by issuing letters of marque and reprisal, and in other ways that are not spelled out. Thus, this textual approach does not resolve one of my two questions — how one can tell when Congress has authorized conflict. In addition, it does not actually resolve my other question. While according to this textual approach the only way the nation can go to war is with congressional authorization, advocates of this view countenance departures from their own textual reading (typically without acknowledging that this is a problem). Thus, as noted, Ely recognizes that there are some emergency situations in which the president can act unilaterally.

Or Article I can be read more literally, for example in the way that then-Assistant Attorney General Dellinger read it in his OLC opinions. Congress has the power to start war — this is how "declare War" is read, under this approach — and it has the power to issue letters of marque and reprisal. But there are conflicts that fall in between — conflicts that are not "war" in the constitutional sense because of their limited "nature, scope, and duration."[18] Congress does not have to authorize these conflicts for them to be constitutional. This reading of the text does not resolve how Congress authorizes the conflicts that it constitutionally must authorize for them to be legitimate. Under Dellinger's approach, while a formal declaration of war is not the only way for Congress to initiate conflict, the textual reading does not answer the question how, other than through declarations of war and grants of the letter of marque and reprisal, Congress starts war. In practice, Dellinger's approach — with its pro-executive tilt — led to finding authorization where congressional authorization was not explicit (as in Haiti).

Alternatively, Article I can be read very literally, in the way that Eugene Rostow, for example, read it.[19] Congress has the power to declare war. It has the power to issue letters of marque and reprisal. And that's it. This approach offers a precise answer to my questions. Congress can authorize conflict in precisely two ways — formally declaring war; issuing letters of marque and reprisal. The president cannot do either of these things. Otherwise, he has a free hand.

With respect to the resolution of my two questions, the issue of which of these readings one embraces is critical. But it is far from obvious which of these readings one *should* embrace. None is baseless, and none is so strong as to command consent.

For a committed textualist, Rostow's reading has a certain power: "to declare war" was a term with significance at international law at the time of the framing, and the founders, Rostow contends, should be understood as intending to incorporate that meaning. Unless one is committed to an acontextual textualism, however, one would find this approach wanting, because it is at odds with the originalist evidence. The founders intended, according to this evidence, that the president not be able to lead the nation into war unilaterally. As James Wilson observed, "This system will not hurry us into war; it is calculated to guard against it. It will not be in the power of a single man, or a single body of men, to involve us in such distress; for the important power of declaring war is vested in the legislature at large."[20] Although they are legitimately subject to competing interpretations, the records of the Philadelphia convention also support the conclusion that the founders did not want wars to start without congressional approval.[21] While the pure textualist might embrace Rostow's reading, then, the reading opens up a door that would allow the executive to subvert the original understanding almost completely.[22]

Ely's reading — like Rostow's — has a plausible textual basis: for Ely, the constitutional text means that wars could only be started with congressional authorization. "Declare" means "start." But like Rostow's reading, Ely's also bumps up against originalist evidence. The debates in Philadelphia indicate that the framers understood the "declare war" clause to leave to the executive the power to meet emergencies. When Madison and Gerry proposed that the phrase "make war," which originated with the Committee on Detail, be changed to "declare," they observed that they would "leav[e] to the Executive the power to repel sudden attacks."[23] Ely's reading of the text does not leave room for military action not authorized by Congress in advance, yet it was clear that the founders intended that—at least "to repel sudden attacks"—unilateral presidential action was permissible. Ely realizes that there were some situations in which the founders countenanced unilateral action, but he does not explain how this can be reconciled with his approach to the text. I should add that Ely's reading is much more satisfactory than Rostow's. Rostow offers a reading at odds with the fundamental purpose of the founders, their belief that the president should not have the general power to take the nation into war unilaterally. Ely's reading is much closer to the founders' vision, but its weakness is that he does not offer a reading of the text consistent with his understanding of the Constitution. Moreover, he does not have a compelling explanation of why his vision of the category in which unilateral presidential action is permissible—response to emergencies—is the correct one.

Which leaves us with Dellinger's reading.[24] Again, it has attractions. Implicitly Dellinger, like Ely, equates "declare" with "start," and that is a textualist reading that squares with originalist evidence. At the same time, by stressing the word "war"—and by interpreting "war" to cover a limited category of conflicts—he avoids the problem that confronts Ely, because Dellinger's textualist reading recognizes, as Ely's does not, that there were some conflicts that did not have to be authorized by Congress in advance. But the problem is that the emphasis on the word "war" does not capture the types of conflicts that did not have to be authorized. Madison and Gerry were concerned about the need for immediate action, not about exempting limited conflicts. While it may be that the framers would not have understood the word "war" to extend to certain very small-scale military conflicts, it is hard to argue that a military action of the scale contemplated in Haiti was not "war," as they understood the term. The strengths and weaknesses of Dellinger's approach mirror the strengths and weaknesses of Ely's: Dellinger offers a more capacious view than Ely of the category of situations in which unilateral presidential action is appropriate, but his justification for the contours of that category, like Ely's, is not wholly convincing.

Now, aficionados of the textualist turn in modern constitutional jurisprudence may expect me to offer at this point a tour de force textualist reading that is absolutely novel and that also squares perfectly with the originalist understanding. There is, however, no such reading. This is an admission that highlights the gap between lawyerly practice and historical reality. The lawyer reads constitutional text (or statutory text) in a way that makes sense of it. She does not say that there is a gap between the original understanding and the words the framers chose. Champions of constitutional textualism, such as Akhil Amar, have come to push the approach further and to ascribe to the founders a sensitivity to words that any poet would envy and an anticipation of future possibility that no seer could even dream of possessing. The framers were not always that careful about what they wrote, however. Sometimes, of course, they were quite careful. They worried, for example, about representation and spent a great deal of time crafting the result. But other times they weren't so careful. We may, for example, try to reconstruct the original meaning of the contract clause (there is a substantial scholarly literature on the topic), but it is hard to figure out what the framers actually intended since the one time they discussed it at the convention they voted it down. Nonetheless, the clause somehow was included in the draft of the Committee of Style, and nobody seems to have noticed its presence in the hurry to approve the document and adjourn.

If one were to do a chart tracking how closely the framers focused on the various clauses of the Constitution, the "declare war" clause would appear near the contract clause toward the bottom. As I was drafting this essay, I read aloud Madison's report of the principal debate on the war powers clause. It took me one minute and thirty-five seconds. Moreover, the people recorded as speaking were by and large not in favor of the clause as adopted — either because they preferred the committee's proposal of "make" war, or because they thought that the power to declare war should be vested in the president. "Declare" war hardly represents the product of close deliberation that reflects deeply held beliefs. It seems as if the formulation was adopted more because Madison and Gerry were dissatisfied with "make" than because they were positively attracted to "declare" and had a clear understanding of what they meant by the term. In any event, this was not a first-order issue for them. As a result, they fashioned a text that neither fully captured their intentions nor resolved the issues that have become pressing to us. Thus, none of the textual readings is fully satisfactory.

Similarly, the originalist evidence is not dispositive of the two issues that I am highlighting here: when congressional authorization is necessary and what constitutes such authorization. As I have noted, with respect to the first issue, Madison and Gerry thought the executive should have the power to repel sudden attacks, and there is no other discussion on point. How do we interpret this brief comment? If Gerry's and Madison's comment reflects the view that the executive has some power to deal with emergencies while Congress convenes and determines how to act, what are the contours of that power? Is it limited to the specific case mentioned in the debates, of "repel[ling] sudden attacks?" Would it also extend to the protection of U.S. citizens abroad, as in Somalia? Non–U.S. citizens, also as in Somalia? How about a preemptive strike responding to what the president believes (but Congress does not) is a threat of sudden attack? Does the executive have other powers beyond the power to address emergencies that allow him to put troops in harm's way? Was it, for example, permissible for President Clinton to deploy troops in Bosnia for peacekeeping purposes, even though there was a risk that they would have to engage in combat?[25] Was it permissible for him to send troops into Haiti at the request of the legitimate national government at a time when the risk to troops seemed minimal?[26] The historical record is far too thin to permit us to answer these questions. While the originalist evidence does not support Rostow's view that there was a general executive power to initiate conflict without congressional approval, the contours of the exception suggested by Madison and Gerry are highly debatable, and both Ely's and Dellinger's views have a plausible originalist basis.

A similar point can be made about the originalist view on what the appropriate forms for Congress to authorize conflict were. If one rejects Rostow's reading of the text because it is at odds with the generally expressed view that wars should not start without congressional sanction, then, one can conclude, the founders anticipated that there were mechanisms other than declarations of war and grants of letters of marque and reprisal for commencing hostilities. But there is no clear understanding of what those alternative mechanisms would be. Again, this open issue is critical in terms of current practice. For example, in 2000 Congress both rejected a concurrent resolution authorizing military operations in Kosovo and, at a time when the War Powers Resolution provided that an appropriations statute did not constitute authorization for military action, nonetheless enacted a statute specifically funding military operations in Kosovo. Did the executive, operating against this backdrop, have congressional authorization for its operations in Kosovo, as it concluded it did because of the appropriations statute?[27] Given the founders' limited focus on the question of congressional authorization, these are not the types of issues on which the original understanding is clear.

Other interpretive guides are similarly unsatisfactory. English precedent is unhelpful. The founders were rejecting the English model, under which the executive was charged with deciding when to start conflict (although one can debate how completely they were rejecting that model). One therefore cannot map previous practice onto the original understanding. Separation-of-powers principles are also unhelpful in working out the issues that are the subject of current controversy. The founders vested different powers in the different branches, as noted above, but it is precisely the contours of these powers and the order of precedence of those powers when they conflict that are unclear. Judicial precedent is also particularly unhelpful because the courts have largely avoided the area.

Nor does evolving tradition yield answers. While one can trace a general expansion of executive power in the war powers area — and this is certainly the case in the years since the Second World War — that expansion has been highly (if episodically) contested by Congress. Thus, we the people cannot be said to have evolved to a new consensus that alters the constitutional framework.

In sum, the methodologies which one normally relies on do not yield clear answers to the questions of what constitutes congressional authorization and when it is not necessary. In the next section, I discuss how political actors should respond to this uncertainty.

PRINCIPLED DECISION MAKING

Evaluation of the constitutional jurisprudence of a judge properly proceeds along two tracks. First, we should look at what her fundamental constitutional commitments are and how they are linked to her constitutional jurisprudence. For example, she may be committed to majoritarian rule and embrace originalism (or a textualism that tracks original usage) as a result. Or she may be fundamentally committed to liberty or equality, and she may construe the Constitution as embodying that commitment. Analyzing a judge's work in this way, we can assess whether her commitments are normatively appealing to us, whether they are our commitments. Second, we should look at whether stances that she takes in specific cases and on particular constitutional questions are consistent with her overall constitutional jurisprudence. Here we are assessing whether her decisions reflect adherence to the rule of law or whether they are driven, instead, by a desire for a particular outcome. When we find that a judge resolves a particular controversy in a way that is inconsistent with her overall jurisprudence, that is a telling criticism. And so, for example, when scholars contend that Justice Scalia's decisions in *Printz* and *Lucas* fail to accord with his textualist methodology, that contention is offered as a sharp critique.

We do not apply the same standards when we review the constitutional jurisprudence of political actors. We don't expect the same consistency. Scholars will still occasionally point out divergences—I recently read a work, for example, that criticized Senator Joseph Biden for having made inconsistent statements about evolving constitutional meaning during the confirmation hearings of Robert Bork and Clarence Thomas—but we rarely try to make sense of political actors' views in the same way that we try to make sense of judges' views, and when inconsistencies are found, the point is generally made is that the politician is a politician and that changing positions is what politicians do.

If we are to take the Constitution outside the courts seriously, however, this dual standard is inappropriate. If political actors are also, as they should be, constitutional actors whose interpretive role is as significant as the interpretive role of courts, their constitutional acts should be measured against precisely the same standards that we use when assessing judicial acts. We should ask: What normative vision does the constitutional actor adopt? Is a particular action consistent with that vision or is she disregarding her overall vision to achieve a particular outcome? If political actors cannot satisfy the same standards of consistency that we apply to judges, then their constitutional commitments are not truly their constitutional commitments. They are policy views dressed as constitutional commitments.

What does this mean to the political actor confronting a war powers question, such as the question of when congressional authorization is not necessary or the question of what constitutes congressional authorization? As I have previously suggested, there is a range of principled stances that one could take in resolving these problems. In deciding which to follow, the political actor should seek to adopt one of these stances on the basis of principle, rather than out of a desire to further a particular policy outcome in a particular case.

Principle in part means that the individual should take a consistent approach to constitutional interpretation. The war powers area is one in which, famously, right and left are attacked for abandoning their normal methodologies. People on the left, like Ely, are criticized for embracing originalism; people on the right, such as Meese, are criticized for rejecting it. This criticism is significantly overstated. I believe that Ely's writings on war powers can be squared with his writings in other contexts. Similarly, as I suggested in the preceding section, the questions of what the original understanding was and how the text should be read are more complicated than generally thought, particularly as they apply to the questions of congressional authorization on which I am focusing here. Nonetheless, principled decision making means that one should not embrace an approach in the war powers context at odds with the approach to constitutional interpretation that one takes elsewhere. For example, one should not embrace the strict textualism that Rostow favored regarding the war powers without being willing to apply it consistently to other questions of constitutional meaning. Consistent embrace of an overall methodology means that the reading of the particular constitutional clause — such as the "declare war" clause — reflects rule of law concerns, rather than a particular policy vision. It also allows the citizen to decide if she finds that methodology normatively attractive. To me, for example, the Rostow approach is flawed, not because it is internally inconsistent but because I see no good reason to privilege a strict reading of text when that reading leads to a result inconsistent with original purpose.

Ely's and Dellinger's views, in contrast, do not suffer from this weakness. Whereas Rostow privileges text over original understanding, Ely and Dellinger make what I find to be a more appealing attempt to make sense of both original meaning and text in a situation in which these two determinants of constitutional interpretation do not perfectly align, in which the contours of original meaning are very unclear, and in which the other determinants of constitutional meaning (such as tradition and judicial precedent) shed little light. Because they are sensitive to the full range of constitutional determinants in a way that I find appropriate, both Ely's view and Dellinger's are attractive to me as ways to think about constitutional commitments in the war powers area. They are satisfactory in the way that a judge's interpretive methodology is satisfactory. Neither is clearly right, but that is because this is not a topic that admits of clearly right answers.

So, how would one choose between the two in trying to decide when congressional authorization is necessary and what constitutes congressional authorization? I should say at the outset that policy views about a particular controversy are not an appropriate basis for choosing between the two views. This is not simply because I believe that because of commitment to the rule of law, principled decision making should govern constitutional interpretation outside the courts; it is also because an outcome-driven approach to constitutional interpretation can also quickly backfire. There is a tendency to assume that the political right is more warlike than the left, but history teaches that neither the right nor the left is consistently more activist or more opposed to military action than those on the other end of the political spectrum. If one were to list the major military conflicts and potential conflicts of the past century or so — starting with the Spanish-American War and running through the First World War, the Second World War, Korea, Vietnam, Grenada, Panama, Iraq, Somalia, Haiti, Bosnia, Rwanda, Kosovo, Afghanistan, and Iraq — there is no clear right-left split on the appropriateness of military action by the United States. Sometimes the left is more strongly in favor of military action; sometimes, the right is. Any attempt of a party or faction to adopt a constitutional vision of the proper role of the president and Congress in order to advance a particular policy end in a particular controversy is thus shortsighted.

If history shows, however, that right and left do not take consistent views on the question of how aggressive the nation's military policy should be, it also shows that the executive and Congress do take fairly consistent views. With the exception of the Spanish-American War — when Grover Cleveland and, less clearly, William McKinley were more reluctant to intervene than Congress — the executive has been consistently more warlike than Congress over the past hundred years. I have suggested that this tendency reflects the different reputational consequences of war for members of Congress and for the president. The founders were aware of this. As Madison wrote in his "Helvidius" letter: "In no part of the constitution is more wisdom to be found than in the clause which confides the question of war or peace to the legislature, and not to the executive department. Beside the objection to such a mixture of heterogeneous powers: the trust and the temptation would be too great for any one man: not such as nature may offer as the prodigy of many centuries, but such as may be expected in the ordinary successions of magistracy. . . . It is in war, finally, that laurels are to be gathered, and it is the executive brow they are to encircle. The strongest passions, and most dangerous weaknesses of the human breast; ambition, avarice, vanity, the honorable or venial love of fame, are all in conspiracy against the desire and duty of peace."[28] Presidents will get the lion's share of the credit for a successful war and the lion's share of the blame for the tragic consequences of inaction. As a determinant of a president's historical reputation, the number of years in which the nation was at war during his presidency is exceeded in importance only by the length of his tenure and whether the president was assassinated. While presidents will get most of the blame for losing a war, the nation's overall record in war — with the exception of Vietnam, we have either prevailed or, as in the War of 1812, more or less tied — means that presidents have an incentive to lead the nation into war. Members of Congress do not have a similar reputational reason to favor conflict.

When we are filling in gaps in the constitutional structure — and when we determine what constitutes congressional authorization or when authorization is not necessary, that is what we are doing — this is precisely the type of large structural concern that should weigh heavily. In choosing between Ely's and Dellinger's models, we should think about whether it makes most sense to interpret the Constitution in a way that accords the president greater freedom of action or in a way that restrains him by interpreting the Constitution so as to give Congress a greater role. Looking at the past, I don't think there is an easy answer to this question.

In this area of indeterminacy, a dialogic model of constitutional interpretation has particular force. Partisans of a strong presidency — à la Dellinger — have a solidly grounded position, and it affords an appropriate basis for executive action. But critics of that view — à la Ely — also have a soundly grounded position, and it too affords an appropriate basis for governmental action; it is the language by which champions of Congress can challenge executive action and seek to rein in the executive.

Ultimately, the discourse may lead to an evolutionary development of our constitutional traditions. One view or the other may so consistently prevail that an answer is provided in an area in which the original understanding and text (and separation-of-powers doctrine and judicial precedent) do not lead to a clear answer.

Or, as is more likely, the dispute will continue. And this points up a significant difference between constitution making inside the courts and constitution making outside the courts. Within the courts, it is more likely that one view will prevail. There is a clear arbitrator. Constitution making outside the courts is more free-form, more unsettled, since it does not have one decision maker at the apex analogous to the Supreme Court.

At the same time, there can be a real thickness to the constitutional discourse among political actors, in the same way that judicial decision making is the product of a thick discourse. Political actors can and should look at precisely the same types of concerns that motivate courts: the text, founders' vision, history, institutional concerns. The war powers area offers a model for thinking about constitution making outside the courts, and it suggests that constitution making outside the courts is properly not that different from constitution making inside the courts.

NOTES

1   For a good discussion, see John Hart Ely, *War and Responsibility: Constitutional Lessons of Vietnam and Its Aftermath* (1993), 15–23.
2   See Remarks of President George Bush Before the Texas State Republican Convention, Federal News Service, 20 June 1992, available in LEXIS, News Library, Script File; George Bush, Remarks at Dedication Ceremony of the Social Sciences Complex at Princeton University in Princeton, New Jersey, 27 *Weekly Compilation of Presidential Documents* 589, 590 (10 May 1991); George Bush, Statement on Signing the Resolution Authorizing the Use of Military Force Against Iraq, 27 *Weekly Compilation of Presidential Documents* 48 (14 January 1991).
3   Authorization for Use of Military Force against Iraq Resolution, Pub. L. No. 102-1, 105 Stat. 3, 3–4 (1991).
4   See Mike Allen and Juliet Eilperin, "Bush Aides Say Iraq War Needs No Hill Vote; Some See Such Support as Politically Helpful," *Washington Post*, 26 August 2002, § A, p. 1.
5   See The Federalist No. 25, at 161 (Alexander Hamilton) (Jacob E. Cooke ed., 1961).

6 See William Michael Treanor, "Fame, the Founding, and the Power to Declare War," 82 *Cornell Law Review* 695, 724 (1997).

7 See Deployment of United States Armed Forces into Haiti, 18 *Opinions of Office of Legal Counsel* 173 (1994).

8 See Authorization for Continuing Hostilities in Kosovo, 2000 OLC Lexis 16.

9 See Ely, *War and Responsibility*, 116–18.

10 See Authority to Use United States Military Force in Somalia, 16 *Opinions of the Office of Legal Counsel* (1992); Deployment of United States Armed Forces into Haiti, 18 *Opinions of the Office of Legal Counsel* 173 (1994); Proposed Deployment of United States Armed Forces into Bosnia, 1995 OLC Lexis 41 (1995).

11 See Deployment of United States Armed Forces into Haiti, 18 *Opinions of the Office of Legal Counsel* 173, 173 (1994).

12 See Authority to Use United States Military Force in Somalia, 16 *Opinions of the Office of Legal Counsel* 11 (1992).

13 See War Powers Resolution sec. 2(c).

14 Edward S. Corwin, *The President: Office and Powers, 1787–1984* (Randall W. Bland et al. eds., 5th ed. 1984), 201.

15 See Treanor, "Fame, the Founding, and the Power to Declare War."

16 Ely, *War and Responsibility*, 3.

17 *Id*. at 66–67.

18 See Deployment of United States Armed Forces into Haiti, 18 *Opinions of the Office of Legal Counsel* 173, 179 (1994).

19 See Eugene V. Rostow, "Great Cases Make Bad Law: The War Powers Act," 50 *Texas Law Review* 833 (1972); Eugene V. Rostow, "'Once More unto the Breach': The War Powers Resolution Revisited," 21 *Valparaiso University Law Review* 1 (1986). See also John Yoo, "The Continuation of Politics by Other Means," 84 *California Law Review* 167, 244 (1996).

20 2 *The Debates in the Several State Conventions* 528 (Jonathan Elliot ed., 1907).

21 See 2 *The Records of the Federal Convention of 1787*, at 318–19 (Max Farrand ed., rev. ed. 1986).

22 I recognize that my views here are controversial. John Yoo, for example, has argued that a reading according to Rostow is consistent with the original understanding. For reasons outlined in my article, "Fame, the Founding, and the Power to Declare War," I disagree. Proof on the matter is beyond the scope of this essay, and I refer my readers to my earlier work.

23 Farrand at 318.

24 When I refer to Dellinger's view here, I mean his view as an assistant attorney general, rather than the view embodied in his earlier scholarly writings. See Walter Dellinger, "War and Responsibility," 50 *University of Miami Law Review* 107 (1995).

25 See Proposed Deployment of United States Armed Forces into Bosnia, 1995 OLC Lexis 41 (1995).

26 See Deployment of United States Armed Forces into Haiti, 18 *Opinions of Office of Legal Counsel* 173, 189 (1994).

27 See Authorization for Continuing Hostilities in Kosovo, 2000 OLC Lexis 16.

28 James Madison, "Helvidius" Number 4, in *The Papers of James Madison* 106, 108–9 (Robert Rutland et al. eds. 1985).

Between Civil Libertarianism and Executive Unilateralism: An Institutional Process Approach to Rights during Wartime

Samuel Issacharoff and Richard H. Pildes

Times of heightened risk to the physical safety of their citizens inevitably cause democracies to recalibrate their institutions and processes, and to re-interpret existing legal norms, with greater emphasis on security, and less on individual liberty, than in "normal" times. This has been true for France during its experience with Middle Eastern terrorism in the 1980s;[1] for Germany during its encounter with the domestic terrorism of the Baader-Meinhof gang in the 1970s[2]; for Great Britain during the sustained violent conflict in Northern Ireland;[3] for Italy in its conflicts with law-and-order terrorist bombings in the 1970s; for Spain during the 1980s;[4] for India in its struggles to maintain order in the midst of the largest and one of the most heterogeneous democracies in the world; and for Israel during its long-running struggle with terrorism. It is now true for the United States, as the government (national and state) modifies the legal framework designed for normal times to adjust to the radical new security threat posed by militant Islamic fundamentalism reflected in the events of September 11, 2001. These changes may be effective or counterproductive, necessary or excessive. But that change will take place is certain, based on the experience of all modern democracies confronted with security threats of this type and magnitude.

Yet in the political culture today, at least in the United States, acknowl-edgment of this reality is clouded by the polarized assertions of two factions.

On one side are executive unilateralists. Reasoning from the correct starting point that the security domain necessitates a greater degree of the distinct qualities possessed by the executive branch — "speed, secrecy, flexibility, and efficiency that no other governmental institution can match"[5] — these advocates conclude that unilateral executive discretion, not subject to oversight from other institutions, is required. On the other side are what might be called civil libertarian idealists. Advocates of this view sometimes deny that shifts in the institutional frameworks and substantive rules of the trade-offs between liberty and security do indeed regularly take place during times of serious security threats; at other times, they recognize that these shifts have occurred in the past but refuse to accept any induction from experience that would legitimate them in the future.

The American constitutional system has the longest experience with these issues. The United States has not, before now, been subject to the kind of security threats, or the risk of external wars with domestic consequences, that have characterized many European democracies; yet with military governments imposed for over a decade in parts of the country, a civil war that slaughtered 600,000 citizens, foreign saboteurs, and risk of military attack, the United States has hardly been immune from the struggle to accommodate liberal values in extreme political circumstances.

This chapter begins by chronicling the American experience with these issues, to gain perspective on how they have been addressed by the constitutional regime that historically has most prized individual liberty. That experience reveals that the judicial approach in this area has been, on the whole, more complex, and oriented toward different questions, than either executive unilateralists or civil libertarian idealists recognize. Contrary to the modern civil libertarian stance, the American courts have only rarely addressed the issues through the framework of individual constitutional rights. Yet contrary to the executive unilateralist position, courts have also been reluctant to find that the executive has unfettered discretion to make trade-offs between liberty and security. Instead, the courts have developed a process-based, institutionally oriented (as opposed to rights-oriented) framework for examining the legality of governmental action in extreme security contexts. Through this process-based approach, American courts have sought to shift the responsibility of these difficult decisions away from themselves and toward the joint action of the most democratic branches of the government.

We then shift from past to present. Intriguingly, the few judicial decisions to date which address the new legal structures emerging in the United States embody the same framework for analysis that American courts have used in earlier eras of exigent circumstances. Despite the flourishing since the 1960s of a rights-based mode of discourse among political philosophers and abstractly oriented constitutional theorists, the American courts continue to employ a process-based, institutionally focused approach. That approach permits deviations from the ordinary legal structures and rules, but it rarely endorses the position that the executive can make these deviations through unilateral decision.

By revealing this process-based approach to the American judicial role during wartime, this chapter aims to suggest (but not answer) several large theoretical questions. One is comparative. The American courts work in a system of separated and divided executive and legislative powers. When the American courts emphasize the importance of institutional endorsement by both political branches of new legal structures for addressing exigent security concerns, they can therefore rely on two institutional actors, with different democratic pedigrees, different incentives, and different interests to which they respond, to provide the political judgment behind policies adopted in the name of security. Separation-of-powers systems can also introduce temporal space between the moments at which each institution acts. Is the deference American courts show to the judgments of "the political branches" appropriate only within a system of separated and divided legislative powers? Or is this deference justified even when courts confront the unified executive-legislative powers of a parliamentary regime, which characterize most European democracies?

A second large question concerns process-based approaches to issues of individual rights and constitutionalism more generally. In the American legal academy, process-based approaches came under withering intellectual critique in the 1980s.[6] Despite the academic criticism, process-based approaches have had an enormous pull on American courts and continue to do so — particularly in times of crisis. In exploring the actual experience of constitutional democracy during crisis, it is therefore important to ask why, despite the theoretical questions about process-based reasoning, such methodologies continue during crises to have such a powerful grip on courts. Does this record suggest a problem in the intellectual critique of such approaches? Or does it suggest a problem in how courts have conceived their task in difficult circumstances?

THE RULE OF LAW AND
BILATERAL CONSTITUTIONAL POWER

Few would contest the essential proposition that a constitutional democracy under military threat must find a "balance to be struck between liberty and security."[7] Nor is there much reticence on either side of the balance for advocates to invoke the "rule of law" as the dispositive high ground in mediating between liberty and security. In seeking to enter this fray, we choose to begin not at the highest levels of abstraction with an effort to reason deductively from such concepts as "the rule of law," "individual rights," or "liberty." Instead we start inductively, with the doctrinal building blocks that are the stock-in-trade of constitutional lawyers.

A review of the positive law indicates that much of the debate over liberty versus security misses the most essential structure of this law. The cases speak to a modest and uncertain role for the courts in addressing issues of national security. In terms of actually defining first-order claims of rights, American courts show great reticence to engage the permissible scope of liberties in direct, first-order terms. Perhaps, as expressed by Chief Justice Rehnquist, "[j]udicial inquiry, with its restrictive rules of evidence, orientation towards resolution of factual disputes in individual cases, and long delays, is ill-suited to determine an issue such as 'military necessity.' "[8]

At the same time, the cases do not quite support the Chief Justice's further claims that "[t]he traditional unwillingness of courts to decide constitutional questions unnecessarily also illustrates in a rough way the Latin maxim *Inter arma silent leges*: In time of war the laws are silent."[9] Rather, the cases show a high level of judicial attentiveness to questions of institutional decision making in general and, more specifically, to the role of the Constitution as a check on unilateralism by the executive. If the framework for judicial decision making is shifted from individual rights to processes of decision making, the American experience offers some rather surprisingly stable observations about legal constraints in times of national emergency.

Before we examine the current disputes over the use of military commissions, or indeed many of the extraordinary powers claimed in the wake of the terrorist attack of September 11, it is useful to revisit some of the more dramatic assertions of military prerogatives within the United States. Here the standout cases are the imposition of martial law within the United States in the states of the former Confederacy after the Civil War, the internment of American citizens of Japanese descent during the Second World War, the decidedly lesser seizure of American steel mills during the Korean War, and enforcement of the terms of the hostage release agreement with Iran.

The Civil War and Reconstruction Governance

Much of the discussion of the wartime role of civil liberties has looked to the two habeas corpus decisions of the post–Civil War years, *Ex Parte Milligan* (1866) and *Ex Parte McCardle* (1868). In each case, the Court examined the power of the executive to order military forces to maintain public order against civilians; each case challenged the use of military tribunals to try and sentence civilians. *Milligan*, decided first, condemned these tribunals. *McCardle*, decided when the war itself was two years more distant, paradoxically avoided the question altogether by concluding that the Court had no jurisdiction to address the issue — a decision whose effect was to permit the use of military tribunals. From these two momentous decisions, which stand in some practical tension with each other, many modern commentators assert that the U.S. Supreme Court developed a rights-based constitutional framework for constraining executive power, even during the most threatening constitutional crisis in our nation's history.[10] But the actual engagement with rights, power, and crisis reflected in these cases is richer, and has a far more profound shaping influence on contemporary law, than these rights-based accounts suggest.

Milligan played out exactly the same struggle between competing frameworks for judicial confrontation that is being faced now. The government argued — much as today — that in times of war, the executive power "must be without limit" and that the Constitution's provisions were "silent amidst arms."[11] But all nine justices on the Court agreed that the use of military commissions to try civilians in places "where the courts are open and the process unobstructed"[12] was beyond the scope of the president's powers. Thus, while the Court acknowledged that "[d]uring the late wicked Rebellion . . . considerations of safety were mingled with the exercise of power," the Court also unanimously agreed that this crisis could not translate into an ongoing suspension of the writ of habeas corpus.[13] But passionate, intense disagreements tore the Court in two about how to understand the relationship between constitutional law, rights, and executive power during crisis.

A bare majority of the Court believed that the right judicial approach was to tackle head-on the issue of individual rights during wartime. Thus in famous, soaring passages that civil libertarians have quoted ever since, this narrow majority concluded that President Lincoln's use of military tribunals violated the individual due process rights of Milligan (who was part of a military branch of the Peace Democrats, a border-state organization in favor of conceding Southern independence and using armed force to free Confederate prisoners). A military trial, rather than a civilian one, had been insisted on by Secretary of War Stanton; Milligan was convicted and sentenced to death. Typical of the Court majority's constitutional proclamations were passages in which the Court denied that the scope of rights varied at all during times of war: "The Constitution of the United States is a law for rulers and people, equally in war and in peace, and covers with the shield of its protection all classes of men, at all times, and under all circumstances. No doctrine, involving more pernicious consequences, was ever invented by the wit of man than that any of its provisions can be suspended during any of the great exigencies of government. Such a doctrine leads directly to anarchy or despotism, but the theory of necessity on which it is based is false."[14] Sweeping declarations of this character are what led commentators — several generations down the road — to proclaim *Milligan* "the palladium of the rights of the individual" and "one of the bulwarks of American liberty."[15]

If the majority opinion were all there were to *Milligan*, it would indeed stand as a striking endorsement — from within the practice of constitutional law — of the civil libertarian position. Moreover, in the context of heated debates in times of perceived threats to security or liberty, there is a strong temptation to read this passage from *Milligan* as if it were a clear and irrevocable holding. But the actual battles inside and outside the Court over the response to the suspension of habeas corpus suggest that there is more to this moment, for at least three reasons.

First, President Lincoln's administration had first suspended the writ of habeas corpus nationwide through unilateral executive action; this action, on the basis of his own purported unilateral authority, was among the most controversial that President Lincoln took during the war.[16] But less than a year later, Congress responded by adopting legislation that expressly authorized the suspension of habeas corpus. President Lincoln always continued to assert that he had the power on his own authority to take such measures, but by the time *Milligan* came to the Court, the justices faced institutional endorsement, from both Congress and president, of the need to suspend habeas corpus. By legislating, Congress had empowered the president, but it had also constrained him to exercising powers only within the boundaries that the legislation had set.

If one accepts the notion of the Court, according to its own sweeping rhetoric, as a stalwart guard against anarchy and despotism, the congressional response should not matter at all. However, the dynamic political process between legislature and executive is precisely what caused four justices, spearheaded by Chief Justice Chase, to go out of their way vehemently to disavow the rights-grounded line of reasoning of the *Milligan* majority. This concurring bloc of justices rejected the constitutional approach of the majority even as they too held the military tribunals illegal. But this group wanted nothing to do with framing the case as a clash between executive power and the rights of individuals. Instead, for them the issue should turn on the relationship between Congress and the president. The fatal flaw of Lincoln's administration, in this view, was that the president had exercised power beyond the domain in which *Congress* had authorized him to act. Confronting the question in terms of the rights of individuals was, in the view of these justices, disastrous; for doing so left no room for contingencies in other exigent times in which there might be good reason for more intrusive restraints on individual rights — as long as both Congress and the president agreed that such intrusions were justified. In the situation at hand, the civilian courts had integrity and remained loyal to the government. "But it might have been otherwise. In times of rebellion and civil war it may often happen, indeed, that judges and marshals will be in active sympathy with the rebels, and the courts their most efficient allies."

In this view, rights-oriented constitutional decisions freeze into place, much more rigidly than is desirable, the institutional options that ought to be available to the government. For as the four process-oriented justices saw it, "when the nation is involved in war . . . it is within the power of Congress to determine [when exceptional measures, such as military tribunals, are justified]." In essence, in this view, Milligan sought relief against unconstrained executive action — against a president who was trying to wield emergency powers beyond the boundaries that Congress had authorized.

The enormous failing of the majority approach was to transform this challenge to executive authority into a challenge to legislative authority; indeed, the majority approach, by constitutionalizing the issues around matters of individual rights, transformed the case into a challenge to the power of the entire national government, even when acting in concert, to invoke emergency powers (such as suspension of habeas corpus) and recalibrate the rights of individuals during wartime. This, Chief Justice Chase and those who joined him concluded, was an absolutist, nonpragmatic vision of constitutional law that ought to be strenuously resisted.

Thus, where five members of the Court spoke in terms of unchanging individual rights, the other four members rejected this approach and spoke only in terms of institutional powers. The contrast could not be more striking. Rather than ringing declarations of rights, themes of political institutions and democratic politics course through the concurrence's insistent approach:

> Congress is but the agent of the nation, and does not the security of individuals against the abuse of this, as of every other power, depend on the intelligence and virtue of the people, on their zeal for public and private liberty, upon official responsibility secured by law, and upon the frequency of elections, rather than upon doubtful constructions of legislative powers?
>
> We have confined ourselves to the question of power. It is for Congress to determine the question of expediency. And Congress did determine it. That body did not see fit to authorize trials by military commission in Indiana, but by the strongest implication prohibited them. With that prohibition we are satisfied, and should have remained silent if the answers to the question [from the majority of the Court] had been put on that ground, without denial of the existence of a power which we believe to be constitutional and important to the public safety — a denial which . . . seems to draw in question the power of Congress.[17]

The constitutional inquiry therefore started and finished with what authority Congress had given to President Lincoln. The concurrence, in a perhaps strained, pro-liberty reading of the statute suspending habeas corpus, concluded that Congress had prohibited military trials of civilians where the regular courts were open (even though the same persons could be arrested and detained without further process until a grand jury could meet).

Milligan, therefore, despite its unanimous rejection of military trials for civilians, is not even on its own, internal terms a "palladium of the rights of the individual." It can be described as *a play* for that vision of constitutional law, led by five members of the Court, but it was a play just as forcefully and immediately countered by the institutional process–oriented view of the rest of this profoundly divided Court. Of course it may be countered that whatever the concurrence may have declared, the holding of the Court is represented by the majority opinion. But this is only the first reason why the Civil War cases do not represent any sort of unvarnished rights-oriented, libertarian view of national powers during wartime. As with any first declaration of constitutional principle, particularly one that barely obtained a majority of the Court, the question remains whether this was only a first cut at the issue or rather a stable and reasoned rendition of constitutional principle.

This uncertainty leads us to the second reason to question the stability of the claimed rights resolution in *Milligan*. Public reaction to *Milligan* was vehement and outraged toward the Court — and the Court clearly got this message. The outrage was not because of the result (that military trial had been illegal, a result that itself seems to have been widely accepted), but precisely because of the framework within which the Court majority had addressed the issue. That is, the public in reacting to *Milligan* specifically took sides in the debate that had taken place in the Court; and it seems to have sided with the politics-reinforcing approach of Chief Justice Chase's concurrence, not with the rights-oriented approach of the narrow majority. The debate was no mere academic disagreement among the élite; it was heated and public. As one of the leading studies notes, when the decision in *Milligan* was made public, "the country erupted into the most violent and partisan agitation over a Supreme Court decision since the days of Dred Scott. The views of the majority on the lack of power in Congress to institute military tribunals, which were not necessary to the decision . . . split the nation, or at least its press, into two hotheaded camps."[18] For by turning the case into a direct confrontation between executive power and individual constitutional rights, the majority had suggested that courts, through constitutional law, would play a major role in resolving the looming conflicts between claims of rights and national power as the country entered Reconstruction. The analogy to *Dred Scott*, invoked repeatedly, was resonant because in that case too the Court had invoked individual constitutional rights in a gratuitous way not necessary to the decision, and had done so to constrain the power of the entire national government's political branches, acting in concert, to address central debates about how the government ought to respond to exigent times.

For these reasons, the rights-oriented, abstract, and absolutist majority approach of *Milligan* provoked reactions that turned the decision into a completely partisan event. Those who supported congressional power to shape the aftermath of the Civil War vilified the Court; Southerners and their supporters praised the Court. None of this was necessary, because had the Court taken the pragmatic, institutional-process approach of the concurrence, the decision would have been widely accepted.

The third reason why the majority opinion of *Milligan* must be seen as no more than a feint in the direction of a rights-based constitutional law of wartime is that the Court itself, two years later, very likely responding to the storm that the sweeping language of *Milligan* had caused, essentially changed direction, repudiated the rights-based approach, and embraced the institutional-process vision. In *Ex parte McCardle*, the Court found that it had been legally stripped by Congress of jurisdiction to review the fate of a newspaper editor held by military authorities in Maryland for trial before a military commission for having published incendiary pro-Confederate tracts.[19] The entire controversy in *McCardle* was itself caused by the "needless breath of language in *Milligan*," as a leading historian of these events has concluded.[20] In response to the threat that the broad, rights-based pronouncements of *Milligan* had cast, Congress had quickly enacted (over presidential veto) a statute that took away the Court's jurisdiction in the pending case of *McCardle*; for that litigation raised the possibility that the Court would pass on broad issues concerning the constitutionality of Reconstruction that Congress was then controlling. Thus, the lesson of *Milligan* and its attempt at an aggressive, rights-based set of constraints on Congress during wartime and its aftermath was that exigent circumstances were ultimately going to be controlled by Congress, not the Court: "Far from inducing Congress to act with greater restraint, the effect of the opinion [in *Milligan*] was rather to put party leaders into a more revolutionary frame of mind."[21] The *Milligan* majority's approach, the Court quickly learned, begat the political response that returned to the Court in *McCardle*.

This time around, the Court resolved matters by what can be understood as the institutional-process method for addressing rights during wartime. Unanimously, the Court in a brief decision held that Congress had the power to legislate and deny the Court jurisdiction to review whether the military trial for McCardle was lawful. Thus, the Court did not reach the merits of the issue one way or the other; instead, it held, a valid institutional process, involving legislation by the politically accountable institutions of the government, had determined that the Court was to be closed to these issues. McCardle's "rights" were therefore fully determined by the process by which Congress had acted, and that was the end of the matter. As to whether Congress had acted for legitimate reasons in closing the courthouse doors, the Court wrote simply, "We are not at liberty to inquire into the motives of the legislature."[22] Thus, the brief dalliance with a rights-based approach in war-related cases was over, and it has largely stayed over ever since. Milligan, the individual, was freed from the sentence that his military trial imposed, but not on the basis of reasons the Supreme Court was prepared to endorse a second time.

American scholars have long argued over whether *Milligan* and *McCardle* can be "reconciled." More interesting, though, is to see them as elements in an early struggle between alternative visions of constitutional law during times of crisis that we have described here. *Milligan*, beneath its unanimous result, reflects judges riven between two competing ways of understanding their role during times of crisis. The majority tried to constrain political institutions with a rights-grounded approach and reaped the whirlwind. The concurrence would also have constrained unilateral executive power, but only because such a constraint could be read into the relevant congressional legislation that addressed the same issue. That institutional process–oriented constraint placed responsibility and control of the issues back in the hands of the politically accountable branches — though the courts would still play the significant interpretive role of deciding exactly what Congress had or had not permitted the executive to do.

By the time of *McCardle*, therefore, the Court had overwhelmingly concluded that its role should be institutionally oriented rather than rights-oriented. And the lesson that the Court drew in this era from its engagement with such charged and complex issues seems to have been the lesson it has held to ever since, for judicial oversight in analogous times has similarly been overwhelmingly process- rather than rights-oriented. Indeed, in modern cases raising the most similar issues, such as use of military trials during wartime and its aftermath, the Court has repeated, almost verbatim, the same, process-oriented rationale of *McCardle* and the concurrence in *Milli-*

gan, even when it has held executive action illegal. Thus, in striking down the use after the Second World War of military tribunals instead of civilian courts for individuals not connected with the military, the Court focused on a close textual analysis of the congressional authorization of martial law in the Hawaiian Organic Act. In that interpretive mode, the Court found that Congress had not manifested an intent to grant the executive the "power to obliterate the judicial system of Hawaii."[23] Thus, the military trials were unilateral executive action that was illegal precisely because the president had acted outside the area of congressional-executive agreement.

In other cases during the aftermath of the Civil War, the Court confronted an even more far-reaching challenge to executive power than it did in *Milligan* and *McCardle*. In *Mississippi v. Johnson*,[24] the Court further worked out the institutional-process approach to defining presidential power during military circumstances. At issue in *Johnson* was the constitutionality of Reconstruction-era military command over the states of the former Confederacy, under a provision that was termed "an act for the more efficient government of the rebel States" but is generally referred to as part of the Reconstruction Acts. The case is full of wonderful historical ironies. President Johnson was forced to defend powers assigned to the executive under the Reconstruction Acts, powers that were implemented over a presidential veto, which in turn prompted Johnson's impeachment. Mississippi, for its part, invoked the reserved sovereign powers of a state of the Union as a defense to the imposition of martial law. Having lost the Civil War on the battlefield, and having had its claims of a right to secession thwarted, Mississippi now turned around and argued that the Constitution protected the inherent powers of the states against the federal executive.

Relying on the nineteenth-century distinction between the executive and ministerial functions of the president, the Court found that so long as the president acted pursuant to the powers set out by Congress in the Reconstruction Acts, the Court was without jurisdiction to enjoin the president in the discharge of his non-ministerial functions. The critical issue was the scope of the congressional mandate, which required the president under the Acts "to assign generals to command in the several military districts, and to detail sufficient military force to enable such officers to discharge their duties under the law. [O]ther duties are imposed on the several commanding generals, and these duties must necessarily be performed under the supervision of the President as commander-in-chief. The duty thus imposed on the President is in no just sense ministerial. It is purely executive and political."[25] Accordingly, there could be no "judicial interference with the exercise of Executive discretion."[26] As the Court summarized the matter, "A bill praying for an injunction against the execution of an act of Congress by the incumbent of the presidential office cannot be received, whether it describes him as President or as a citizen of a State."[27]

In sum, even during the moment of greatest constitutional crisis in American history, when the Constitution's claim to define governance for nearly half the country was under direct challenge, courts did engage questions of the limits on executive and military governance. They did not defer uncritically to claims of unilateral executive authority. And while *Milligan* did offer a brief moment when the Court was drawn to an individual-rights approach to the role of constitutional law in times of emergency, the political and public response to that foray almost immediately led the Court to back away—not toward abdicating any role at all in these times of emergency, but toward a different way of implementing that role. The Court continued to assert that there were limits to unilateral executive power, even in these periods. But they were limits of institutional process, not of individual rights. The Court concluded that it would do best by insuring fidelity to the overall constitutional commitment to the dynamic, deliberative judgments reached by the politically accountable branches, the legislature and executive, as to how the trade-off between liberty and security ought to be made during wartime.

Japanese Internment

Our claim thus far is simply that the decisions of the Civil War years manifest a pronounced judicial emphasis on the role of Congress in limiting the danger of executive unilateralism, even in the context of a complete breakdown in constitutional order. We do not mean to wax rhapsodic over the sufficiency of bilateralism as a check against oppression during wartime challenges to domestic security. The risk that an entire nation, and its elected representatives, might succumb to wartime hysteria is ever present. Among the most egregious examples in American history of wanton disregard of important individual interests during wartime is the forced evacuation and relocation of Japanese residents and citizens during the Second

World War. In legal circles, this event is associated with the *Korematsu* decision. The episode is a powerful counterexample to any view that executive and legislative checks and balances, even in a system of separated and divided powers, are adequate to protect against excessive security measures.

The West Coast of the United States was put under military command during this period. Through the military command of General J. L. DeWitt, the forced relocation of the Japanese was imposed. President Roosevelt specifically authorized this policy in the infamous Executive Order No. 9066. In addition, within a month the Congress confirmed and ratified this executive order. The argument made for the military order was that there was no way, short of evacuation, for the military commanders to determine which Japanese residents and citizens were loyal and which not, and the purported evidence of espionage threats among some Japanese on the West Coast was serious enough to justify exclusion of the entire group. The entire federal government effectively concurred. The forced evacuation quickly led to forced detention for several years in relocation centers, with devastating attendant losses of property, livelihood, and much else.

That the evacuation and detention policies were unjustifiable is not one of the seriously disputed issues in American history. The evidence offered for General DeWitt's decision rested on ethnic stereotyping and fear, not fact. The relative political powerlessness of the Japanese on the West Coast does much to explain why they were relocated while the more politically influential Japanese in Hawaii (under a different military command) and Germans on the East Coast were not. But what about the Supreme Court's role in all this? Any judgment on the positive-law experience of the United States must come to terms with this event.

Conventionally, the Court fares no better than the other institutions of the national government. *Korematsu* is excoriated as one of the two or three worst moments in American constitutional history. The decision is thought to offer numerous lessons about the inability of courts during wartime to provide any check on political excesses, particularly those jointly endorsed by the executive and the legislature. But the idea that *Korematsu* and its inherent racialism represent the full story about the judicial encounter with the internment of the Japanese is partly a creation of the narrative that American constitutional law has come to tell about this episode. This conventional account ignores the companion case to *Korematsu*, *Ex Parte Endo*, decided the same day as *Korematsu* itself. As Professor Gudridge describes it in a recent revisionist analysis, *Korematsu* can only be properly understood in the context of *Endo*.[28] For while the Court in *Korematsu* found constitutional the initial evacuation order that required the Japanese to leave the West Coast, in *Endo* it unanimously held, at the very same time, that the detention of the Japanese was illegal.

The Court saw a fundamental distinction between the policies of acts perceived as those of exigency, such as the detention order in *Korematsu* or the imposition of curfew restrictions on Japanese upheld in *Hirabayashi v. United States*,[29] and ongoing detention, which was the subject of *Endo*. Evacuation and restrictions on mobility reflected military judgments (faulty or pernicious as they may have been) of what was necessary for security. Detention, however, reflected political and policy judgments, not military ones. Despite the emphasis that *Korematsu* has received at the expense of *Endo*, the fact is that even during this bleak episode, the Court continued to resist executive branch actions that rested, at most, on political and policy, rather than military, judgments.

Disturbing as it is as a symbol of the policies of the national government, *Korematsu* as an actual legal decision turns out to have had no practical effect at the time it was decided. By the time the Court decided *Korematsu*, forced evacuation had taken place two years earlier; the practical question was whether continued detention was permissible. And on that, *Endo* was decisive; indeed the president, perhaps having been notified that the Court was going to hold the detentions illegal, had already ordered the relocation camps closed the day before *Endo* was decided. On the day that the two decisions were handed down together, the most immediate practical matter at stake was whether the detained Japanese would be released. Under *Endo*, they were. The initial evacuation had long ago taken place; the Court could not undo that reality or its consequences. In immediate practical terms, the Court could only order the end to continued detention. And that is what it did.

But in reviewing *Korematsu* in light of both *Endo* and *Hirabayashi*, an interesting picture emerges of judicial attentiveness to the sweep of executive authority, even if the result may not satisfy all civil liberty concerns. Thus in *Hirabayashi*, the Court specifically relied on the fact that "Congress authorized and implemented such curfew orders,"[30] which left unresolved any claim of unilateral authority vested in the executive: "We have no occasion to consider whether the President, acting alone, could lawfully have made the curfew order in question."[31] Only once assured that Congress and the executive have acted in tandem does the Court assume the quietism claimed by Rehnquist: "Where . . . the conditions call for the exercise of judgment and discretion and for the choice of means by those branches of the Government on which the Constitution has placed the responsibility of warmaking, it is not for any court to sit in review of the wisdom of their action or substitute its judgment for theirs."[32] This then provides the jurisprudential method distinguishing the result in *Endo* from that in *Korematsu*. Insofar as the issue before the Court concerned detention taken pursuant to bilaterally determined exigency, the Court remained on the sidelines: "[W]e are unable to conclude that it was beyond the war power of Congress and the Executive to exclude those of Japanese ancestry from the West Coast war areas at the time they did. . . . We cannot say that the war-making branches of the Government did not have ground for believing that in a critical hour such persons. . . . constituted a menace."[33] By contrast, in *Endo* the Court found the critical element of Congressional participation missing. Thus, *Endo* became an exercise in statutory interpretation, not constitutional law; the question was not judicial boundaries on the executive, but legislative ones:

> The purpose and objective of the Act and of these orders are plain. Their single aim was the protection of the war effort against espionage and sabotage. It is in light of that one objective that the powers conferred by the orders must be construed. . . .
>
>   But we stress the silence of the legislative history and of the Act and the Executive Orders on the power to detain. . . . If there is to be the greatest possible accommodation of the liberties of the citizen with this war measure, any such implied power must be narrowly confined to the precise purpose of the evacuation program.[34]

Throughout the Japanese internment and related cases, the Court self-consciously struggled to preserve a congressional oversight role for the executive, even as it upheld all the executive's actions up until the *Endo* case.[35] Before leaving the topic of the Japanese internment, we must note that *Korematsu* has also had no legal or jurisprudential effect. At least until now, the decision has never been cited to support any government action of which we are aware. The only jurisprudential effect of *Korematsu* has in fact been to encourage more aggressive, not more passive, judicial review of executive and legislative actions during times when national security was implicated. *Korematsu* has constituted "an infernal baseline" in American constitutional law: far from legitimating repressive wartime policies, its only doctrinal role has been as a symbol of what ought to be avoided in political practice and constitutional law.[36] But there is also the cautionary note struck by Justice Jackson in dissent. Jackson argued that it was unrealistic to expect courts to do anything other than rubber-stamp military decisions during times of war. To ask or expect more can be no more than a foolhardy, self-defeating illusion. The danger, according to Jackson, is that once courts are drawn into the process of substantive review of extraordinary powers, their role as constitutional arbiters will be at the very least compromised, if not altogether undermined.

At least for half a century, Jackson was wrong about the lasting effects of *Korematsu*. Nonetheless, his caution pushes to the frontier of where we are willing to go in this chapter. There is a historical and descriptive argument to be had about the role of American constitutional law in forcing bilateral review of claimed states of emergency. On that score, we are fairly confident that the courts have, in practice, neither abdicated a role entirely nor defined their role aggressively; instead, courts have only sought to ensure vigilance over the institutional tendency to concentrate power in the hands of the executive and its military. If Congress has endorsed, or perhaps only acquiesced in, that concentration, the courts have accepted that judgment. If Congress has resisted, the courts have found the executive to have gone beyond even its wartime powers. Beyond that institutionally focused enforcement of checks and balances, however, is the question whether courts could or should attempt substantive oversight when extraordinary powers are invoked through proper channels. Even with the full collaboration of all political branches, critics will say, important rights can nonetheless be violated. But as a descriptive and historical matter, American courts have viewed the net benefits of putting judgment of these freighted questions into the hands of courts as outweighing the net benefits of leaving these questions in the joint hands of the legislature and executive.

Probing the Limits

The focus on bilateral sources of authority for emergency powers has carried American courts through some of the most difficult departures from the ordinary workings of American criminal law. For example in *Ex Parte Quirin*,[37] the most direct precedential authority for the current use of military commissions to try civilians, the Court upheld the use of extraordinary processes to try German saboteurs who had landed on Long Island, shed their uniforms, and entered the murky world of "unlawful combatants." The Court returned to the now familiar inquiry into the constitutional division of powers: "It is unnecessary for present purposes to determine to what extent the President as Commander in Chief has constitutional power to create military commissions without the support of Congressional legislation. For here Congress has authorized trial of offenses against the law of war before such commissions."[38] Thus, the Court in *Quirin* refused to address whether the executive, acting on his own authority, had the power to order the use of military tribunals for those he designated enemy combatants, even though the executive expressly pressed this claim (similarly, the Court declined to address whether Congress could deny this authority to the executive).[39] Instead, the Court upheld President Roosevelt's actions precisely because he was exercising authority that Congress had expressly delegated to him.

Once observed through this prism, many highly problematic cases concerning the tension between emergency powers and ordinary workings of law begin to align themselves in recognizable fashion. The negotiated resolution of the Iran hostage crisis in 1981 offers another example. As part of the negotiation, the United States pledged to release all Iranian assets held in the United States from any legal embargo. This agreement brought the negotiated terms of release into direct conflict with ongoing legal proceedings against Iran, including a prejudgment attachment of assets by Dames & Moore against Iranian bank assets in the United States. In *Dames & Moore v. Regan*,[40] the Court had to decide whether the president was properly empowered to use "blocking orders" against foreign assets as part of his arsenal in negotiating the resolution to the hostage crisis. In now familiar fashion, the Court turned to the scope of congressional authorization under the International Emergency Economic Powers Act to define the ambit of emergency power: "Because the President's action in nullifying the attachments and ordering the transfer of assets was taken pursuant to specific congressional authorization, it is 'supported by the strongest presumptions and the widest latitude of judicial interpretation, and the burden of persuasion would rest heavily upon any who might attack it.'"[41] The Court's conclusion that the congressional statutes did, in fact, authorize the president's actions has been deeply controversial. But the Court did preserve the formal structure of authority in which bilateral endorsement is, in principle, required even in crises.

It should come as no surprise that the Court in *Dames & Moore* relies directly on the *Steel Seizure Case* as its polestar, for our thesis would be considerably weakened were we not able to show the converse of our claim: the Court will step in when the executive acts without congressional authorization or clearly beyond the bounds of authorization. Like *Dames & Moore*, the *Steel Seizure Case* involved emergency powers in derogation of customary civil processes, as opposed to criminal prosecutions. At issue was an order of President Truman seizing domestic steel mills to insure continued production during the Korean War in the face of a threatened nationwide strike. In contrast to the cases in which the Court was able to find that the executive had acted within the scope of an extraordinary grant of power by Congress, President Truman claimed "that his action was necessary to avert a national catastrophe which would inevitably result from a stoppage of steel production, and that in meeting this grave emergency the President was acting within the aggregate of his constitutional powers as the Nation's Chief Executive and the Commander in Chief of the Armed Forces of the United States."[42]

In striking down the seizure of the steel mills, the Court made two separate determinations that are critical as we turn to the current setting. First, the Court found the seizures beyond the president's inherent authority as commander in chief because they were executed outside the theater of battle.[43] More significantly, the Court relied on the absence of a formal declaration of war as indicating a lack of congressional authorization for the claim of exceptional powers: "The President's order does not direct that a congressional policy be executed in a manner prescribed by Congress — it directs that a presidential policy be executed in a manner prescribed by the President."[44] The presidential claim, accordingly, was an unconstitutional arrogation of the "law-making power of Congress to presidential or military supervision or control."[45] In further support of that finding, Congress had expressly considered, and rejected, the authorization of executive power to seize vital industrial plants to secure labor peace when it passed the Taft-Hartley Act in 1947.[46]

As in *Korematsu*, it fell to Justice Jackson to fully expound the normative

theory underlying the Court's concern. In an appeal to transcendent principle, Jackson cautioned:

> The opinions of judges, no less than executives and publicists, often
> suffer the infirmity of confusing the issue of a power's validity with the
> cause it is invoked to promote, of confounding the permanent executive
> office with its temporary occupant. The tendency is strong to emphasize
> transient results upon policies — such as wages or stabilization — and lose
> sight of enduring consequences upon the balanced power structure of
> our Republic.
>
> While the Constitution diffuses power the better to secure liberty, it
> also contemplates that practice will integrate the dispersed powers into a
> workable government. It enjoins upon its branches separateness but in-
> terdependence, autonomy but reciprocity. Presidential powers are not
> fixed but fluctuate, depending upon their disjunction or conjunction
> with those of Congress.[47]

Although Justice Jackson fully anticipated that threats and the exigencies
of national security would necessarily alter the constitutional balance between liberty and security, he saw the Court's role primarily as one of
preserving the separation of political power between the executive and the
legislature: "When the President takes measures incompatible with the expressed or implied will of Congress, his power is at its lowest ebb, for then
he can rely only upon his own constitutional powers minus any constitutional powers of Congress over the matter. Courts can sustain exclusive
Presidential control in such a case only by disabling the Congress from
acting upon the subject. Presidential claim to a power at once so conclusive
and preclusive must be scrutinized with caution, for what is at stake is the
equilibrium established by our constitutional system."[48] After canvassing
the mechanisms by which emergency or state-of-siege powers are assigned
in various European democracies, Jackson concluded with what must be, in
our view, the foundation of the constitutional inquiry:

> This contemporary foreign experience may be inconclusive as to the wis-
> dom of lodging emergency powers somewhere in a modern government.
> But it suggests that emergency powers are consistent with free govern-
> ment only when their control is lodged elsewhere than in the Executive
> who exercises them. That is the safeguard that would be nullified by our
> adoption of the "inherent powers" formula. Nothing in my experience

convinces me that such risks are warranted by any real necessity, although such powers would, of course, be an executive convenience. In the practical working of our Government we already have evolved a technique within the framework of the Constitution by which normal executive powers may be considerably expanded to meet an emergency. Congress may and has granted extraordinary authorities which lie dormant in normal times but may be called into play by the Executive in war or upon proclamation of a national emergency.[49]

Failing such congressional authorization, the invocation of emergency powers to authorize the seizure of the steel mills failed.

The Uncertainty of Unconventional War

Executive Detention of "Enemy Combatants"

The most controversial legal power that the U.S. government has not just asserted but actually deployed at this point in the war on terrorism is probably the power to detain preventively both citizens and noncitizens who the executive concludes are "enemy combatants." The consequence of such a designation is that an individual can be detained under military control for the duration of the circumstances that constitute the "war" or combat. There is no process resembling in any way those governing the circumstances of proof that prevail in an ordinary trial. There is no question of the punishment involved; the justification for confinement is both interrogation for intelligence purposes and incapacitation to prevent future harms. Confinement is for an "indefinite period" under this approach, as the government acknowledges. Thus far, the United States has applied the "enemy combatant" designation to three persons, including one U.S. citizen allegedly taken off the battlefield in Afghanistan, Yaser Hamdi, and one U.S. citizen captured in Chicago, Jose Padilla, who was allegedly associated with al-Qaeda and engaged in "hostile and war-like acts," including efforts to construct and deploy a radioactive "dirty bomb."[50]

What rights does a person, particularly a U.S. citizen or a person having the status of a permanent member of this society (i.e., a legally resident alien), have in this situation? The typically polar positions that we described at the outset are vividly displayed here. Civil libertarians vehemently assert that a U.S. citizen, or for that matter any person in the United States, cannot be confined without the ordinary protections of a criminal trial. They have descried the government's attempt to create a "two-tiered legal system,"[51] in which terrorism cases are segregated institutionally (through military detention), procedurally (through radically distinct, and more minimal, processes of fact finding), substantively (in terms of what the government was required to show, and by what standards of proof), and philosophically (preventive confinement rather than punishment-based confinement). The lens through which these critics view the "enemy combatant" problem is that of the ordinary criminal trial, which these criticisms implicitly or explicitly take to be the model of what the rule of law requires to justify locking up an American citizen. At the same time, the government has asserted a strong version of the unilateral executive position that it views as necessary to respond effectively to terrorism. Thus, the government has argued that a person designated an "enemy combatant" is not entitled to counsel so as to challenge the facts underlying that designation, and that in any event the courts are not empowered to review the executive's factual judgments justifying the designation.[52]

Lower federal courts have now weighed in on these disputes, in the two cases involving U.S. citizens deemed by the president to be "enemy combatants" and hence detainable without a criminal trial. These courts have taken precisely the path that the predecessor courts we have described took in determining how to adjust the rule-of-law model from ordinary times to the context of a serious threat to domestic security. The *Padilla*[53] litigation both highlights the analytic structure employed by earlier decisions and confirms that there is sufficient "bite" to this approach to actually check executive unilateralism. Most revealingly, both the district and circuit courts employed the same analytic structure to test the degree of joint executive-congressional endorsement of the clearly extraordinary measures at issue when an American citizen is seized in the United States and held incommunicado. The trial court in *Padilla* began its analysis by strongly rejecting the civil libertarian view that only ordinary criminal trial processes could justify confining an American citizen for indefinite duration. At the same time, Judge Michael Mukasey refused at several points to endorse executive unilateralism. Nor did Judge Mukasey take on the first-order role of defining, through constitutional law, the "rights" of American citizens in this context. Instead, the court played the process-based, institutionally focused role that American courts have consistently played in addressing similar issues. Thus, the court defined the boundaries of governmental powers and individual protections by insisting on a bilateral, executive-congressional partnership; once it established that such a partnership was reflected in the process by which the category of "enemy combatant" was created and applied, the court largely deferred to the first-order judgments of other institutional actors. Moreover, Judge Mukasey did so by directly invoking the "democratic process" focus of earlier cases such as the *Steel Seizure* decision.

The steps by which the court navigated its way through the difficult issues reveal this institutional focus so characteristic of American courts during exigent circumstances. The most profound questions centered on whether a citizen could be confined indefinitely, without trial, based on a presidential designation of "enemy combatant" status. Intimately bound up with that question was the bearing of an Act of Congress, 18 U.S.C. Sec. 4001, that bars the detention of American citizens "except pursuant to an Act of Congress."[54]

The government argued that the position of executive unilateralism was so embedded in the constitutional text and structure that the Act of Congress could not stop the president from using his powers as commander in chief during wartime to determine that individuals were "enemy combatants." That is, the government argued that Congress could not constitutionally legislate to deny the president this power. Judge Mukasey echoed earlier Supreme Court decisions in stating that what military measures might be necessary in these circumstances was well beyond the realm of the kinds of questions courts ought to address. Nonetheless, the court also refused to endorse unilateral executive authority; thus, it rejected the claim that Congress could not bar the president from detaining classes of citizens, including enemy combatants during wartime. Instead, the court found that the Act of Congress precluding citizen detention without congressional authorization was fully applicable to Padilla's case.

Judge Mukasey then went on to hold that executive detention of "enemy combatants" was nonetheless lawful. He did so because the court found that Congress had itself legislated in a way to endorse the president's power to order these detentions. A week after September 11, 2001, Congress had legislated broadly to give the president the authority to "use all necessary and appropriate force against those . . . organizations, or persons he determines planned, authorized, committed, or aided the terrorist attacks that occurred on September 11, 2001 . . . in order to prevent any future acts of international terrorism against the United States."[55] Only as a result of finding that this specific Act of Congress provided the indispensable element of congressional authorization did the court conclude that the president had the legal power to detain enemy combatants (if the facts supported his designation). Thus, on the central question at stake, Judge Mukasey upheld the president's power, but not on the unilateral basis that the president asserted. The court held that the prior legislation barring all detentions except pursuant to an Act of Congress continued to constrain the president's powers, but that the requirements of that earlier Act had been met because Congress itself had legislated to bring about bilateral endorsement of presidential power to detain "enemy combatants" in the wake of September 11.

Having resolved the general issue about the potential scope of presidential power, Judge Mukasey turned to the more narrow question of who could decide, and through what processes, whether the specific facts supported the conclusion that any particular individual was indeed an "enemy combatant." Here too the court resolved the issues by focusing more on institutional allocation of authority than directly on "individual rights." Judge Mukasey rejected the view that specific constitutional rights associated with the trial process had any application to an alleged enemy combatant, who was neither being tried nor punished for past acts but simply detained. This was consistent with his earlier rejection of the view that only the familiar criminal trial model could be used to justify confinement of a citizen. Once again, though, the court was not willing to go all the way to unilateral executive control of the decision to detain; once again, it relied on the authority of other institutions, rather than the judge's own first-order judgments, about what process was required to justify detention.

Thus, Judge Mukasey did find that Padilla was entitled to consult with a lawyer. But he did not hold that this right rested on any constitutional foundation. Instead, the court relied on congressional statutes that regulated the habeas corpus process and the court's own remedial powers. Judge Mukasey concluded that Padilla's "right to present facts [through counsel] is rooted firmly in the statutes that provide the basis for his petition." That is, Padilla would get access to counsel, contrary to the claims of unilateral executive proponents, but he would not do so because of constitutional rights, contrary to the strong civil libertarian position. By grounding this right in congressional legislation, the court enabled an ongoing political process to play a significant role in resolving the difficult questions about the boundaries of executive power during emergencies. Had Judge Mukasey instead found the right to counsel to be constitutionally grounded, that would have made the courts, rather than Congress and the president, the central actor in resolving these issues.

Yet despite this overwhelmingly institutional and process-based approach, the court was not prepared to relinquish all substantive assessment of the government's action. For the final question was how much factual evidence the government had to marshal to support the president's designation of a citizen as an "enemy combatant" and how, if at all, the courts would review that designation. On this highly individualized judgment, the court carved out one arena of substantive judgment for itself. Not surprisingly, on this issue each side pressed the polar positions characteristic of these struggles. Padilla argued that "he is entitled to a trial on the issue of whether he is an unlawful combatant or not." The government argued that the court should not review the president's determination at all. Here too Judge Mukasey rejected both poles. Instead he concluded — on a question with admittedly little prior authority either way — that the president's determination would be judicially reviewed, but only under a minimal requirement that there be "some evidence" to support the "enemy combatant" designation.

This minimal standard of judicial oversight retains a substantive domain for the courts, although a relatively small one, in a predominantly procedural approach to judicial review. And even though the context was novel, the court offered a remarkable articulation of the general judicial stance toward analogous questions throughout American history. The limited judicial role entailed in the minimal, "some evidence" standard resulted not, in Judge Mukasey's judgment, from the inability of judges to decide "whether facts have been established by competent evidence"; indeed, Judge Mukasey said that if there was any task — viewed in isolation — that judges were trained to perform, it was that very one. But the very point of the institutional focus brought by American courts to these issues is that the right judicial role is not a question that ought to be considered in isolation. Instead, the question had to be viewed from the perspective of which institutions do and ought to have the authority to make these decisions. Given the stakes involved in wartime judgments, and the ultimate accountability of political branches for whether domestic security is achieved, the court concluded that the right institutional allocation of authority argued for some judicial oversight of the executive, but only the minimal oversight reflected in the "some evidence" standard.

For both the executive unilateralists and the civil libertarians, the district court opinion in *Padilla* unexpectedly deviated from first-order constitutional questions to apparently secondary issues of statutory interpretation. Yet the apparent focus on questions of statutory construction masks the critical role of courts in policing not rights or executive prerogatives but a set of institutional arrangements by which bilateral sources of authority are necessary to exercise exceptional powers.

This approach was confirmed by the Second Circuit, which overturned the trial court not on the question of institutional authority, but on the seemingly narrower issue of whether the requisite level of congressional authorization was present. Precisely because of the existence of 18 U.S.C. Sec. 4001, the appellate court held that there must be "clear congressional authorization . . . for detentions of American citizens on American soil." That such extraordinary measures were being utilized domestically demanded rigorous application of institutional bilateralism: "These separation of powers concerns are heightened when the Commander-in-Chief's powers are exercised in the domestic sphere." The court went on to find that the general resolution of Congress after September 11 was insufficient to override the express prohibitions of 18 U.S.C. Sec. 4001. Accordingly, despite agreement with the trial court's methodology, the requisite level of congressional authorization was absent. Let us now step back from the specifics of this intriguing decision on the most difficult legal question involving claims of "rights" that has yet confronted the current American courts. The court framed each question it had been asked in the language and structure of institutional analysis that Justice Jackson had lucidly outlined in the *Steel Seizure* case. Rejecting both a rights-based analysis and the assertions of unilateral executive authority, both courts in *Padilla* explicitly invoked Justice Jackson for the conclusion that presidential power to detain even citizens as "enemy combatants" was lawful, precisely because the president was acting with the bilateral endorsement of Congress in exercising this power. Both courts then carved out a minor role for judicial oversight — a role itself justified by congressional enactments — and a far more important role for executive-legislative partnership to determine the boundaries of these powers. This is a view based on the democratic process, which emphasizes that the judicial role in reviewing assertions of power during exigent circumstances should focus on ensuring whether there has been bilateral institutional endorsement for the exercise of such power—rather than a view that the judicial role should be to determine on its own the substantive content and application of "rights" during wartime. This is not a view that might please more abstract academic "rights theorists," be they political philosophers or constitutional theorists. It is, however, the characteristic way in which American courts have approached their role of reviewing exercises of power of the political branches during wartime. In one of the most complex legal settings so far posed by the events following September 11, the detention without trial of those whom the president has designated enemy combatants, it is thus intriguing to see the courts turning to the same general framework for analysis that the courts have drawn on since the Civil War for defining their role in addressing rights claims during times of war.[56] Whatever one thinks of how that framework is applied in specific cases, the endurance of this general structure of analysis is noteworthy.

BILATERALISM AS HEALTHY ILLUSION?

Civil libertarians will not, of course, be content with the historical practice of American courts to channel these disputes into bilateral, executive-legislative decision-making structures. The most direct challenge to that approach will be the same as to all "legal process" approaches to decision making: a challenge grounded in the view that courts ought not avoid dealing with the substantive issues of what rights we have during exigent circumstances by deferring to the judgments of political branches, even if both the executive and the legislative agree. Rights should not, in this view, be hostage to the vagaries of democratic politics, even the consensus politics, when it exists, of both political branches.

Our project is not to engage in these first-order normative debates. Instead, we seek to characterize the positive-law experience of the United States in a way that highlights features of that experience often neglected—as a necessary prelude to serious normative assessment. But even from within the historical interpretation that we offer here, civil libertarians can still raise two further objections. First, even if courts have constructed a doctrinal and rhetorical framework which emphasizes bilateral institutional participation in decision-making tradeoffs of rights and security, how is this framework applied in actual practice? Isn't it an illusion to suggest that Congress has endorsed the executive action — a dangerous illusion, indeed — for it enables courts to defer responsibility for hard decisions to the putative agreement of both political branches? Second, even if the courts take this framework seriously, how much can the political process effectively cabin a determined president or chief executive during wartime? Isn't it a further illusion to believe or suggest that Congress or other political actors *could* stand up to the executive branch during eras of serious security threats? Thus, even if there is bilateral institutional endorsement, isn't the congressional role inevitably a meaningless rubber stamp? And doesn't that turn judicial review, which piggybacks onto the congressional role, also into a meaningless rubber stamp?

The first category of question tests how the institutionally oriented, process-based theory is (and ought to be) applied in fact. Certainly, this framework defers many of the critical questions that will matter in specific cases. Thus, even if congressional participation is doctrinally required, there are further questions of how specific that participation must be and how close in time to the executive action to justify concluding that the required bilateral institutional endorsement is present. On timing, for example, Congress might have legislated close in time to a specific executive action, so that Congress can plausibly be viewed as having acted to endorse that particular action, but the legislation might then stay on the books for years. When the next crisis comes, should the courts accept this much earlier congressional endorsement as effective endorsement of similar executive action in new circumstances? Or should the courts require more contemporaneous authorization — in effect, remanding the problem back to Congress for a current affirmative act on its part? The current debate over military tribunals illustrates this point.[57] When the Supreme Court confronted the constitutionality of these tribunals during the Second World War in the *Quirin* case, Congress had legislated recently to authorize use of such tribunals. Those who argue that such tribunals are also constitutional in the present context point to this same legislation, which has remained in place for many decades, as evidence of continuing legislative endorsement. Yet Congress has not directly debated the issue in many years. Should Congress's silence in intervening years, its failure to repeal the earlier legislation, be treated as tantamount to affirmative legislative endorsement? Should it matter that Congress did expressly confirm and endorse the *Quirin* Court's interpretation of this law in 1950, when Congress recodified these provisions? Or is this 1950 confirmation still insufficient? Should courts shift the burden of inertia and require more contemporary legislative endorsement, if bilateral institutional endorsement is constitutionally required?

Second, and more broadly, such congressional legislation as there is will often be cast at a high level of generality. Only rarely will Congress have focused in an exact way on the precise assertion of executive authority at issue; more typically, Congress will have legislated, if at all, in more general terms, in situations not exactly the same as those in which the executive currently seeks to act. Courts therefore will have a good deal of interpretive latitude to decide whether the congressional legislation is "close enough" to be treated as effective endorsement of the disputed executive action. More corrosively, the argument would run, courts in most cases will have so much interpretive room, given the generalities of legislation, that the legislation itself cannot control or determine the outcome; instead, courts will necessarily be relying on other considerations in making this judgment. Thus, this process-based framework, tied to the judicial demand for bilateral institutional endorsement, provides no meaningful constraint on judicial decision making.

These are the right kinds of questions to ask from within the institutionally oriented, process-based approach to these questions. To evaluate any of these criticisms would require case-by-case analysis of how the Court has applied the requirement of bilateral institutional endorsement to specific issues. That is not our project here, for our aim is only to illuminate the general principles that characterize the predominant American judicial approach during wartime. But there is one intriguing point to note even if some or all of these criticisms turn out to be convincing. For the structure of judicial analysis always preserves the *possibility* of ultimate congressional control. The courts consistently resist any endorsement of the notion that ultimate unilateral authority rests with the executive branch, though the executive typically presses this argument. As a result, even if it is fair to view the courts as quite expansive in their willingness to find congressional action present, this structure of analysis ensures that should Congress disagree at any point, it would have the authority to step in and block a great deal of the executive action that courts have otherwise found constitutional. Indeed, given the extraordinary political salience of war powers issues, it might be more appropriate to conclude in these contexts than in routine ones that Congress's failure to act to stop the executive is actually tantamount to endorsement (or shows, at least, an unwillingness to take responsibility where it is appropriate for courts to lay the responsibility at Congress's feet). If Congress wanted to stop the use of military tribunals, or the executive detention of captured battlefield combatants, the cases leave open the possibility that Congress would be able to override the executive and do so.

If courts incline toward construing broad legislative commands as endorsements of executive action, Congress can unmistakably legislate in a more pointed way that courts will then likely take as an effective bar to that executive action (absent an unusual conclusion that the area is reserved for executive authority alone). Thus, even if one concluded that congressional endorsement in the cases should be seen as a fiction created by the courts, the fiction could still be a healthy one. Through such doctrinal and rhetorical structures of analysis, courts channel the issues back into the bilateral political process and keep open a critical congressional role, should Congress strongly disagree with executive action during crises.

The second question is whether the political process approach does, descriptively, ever provide a check on executive power during times of crisis. While the conventional wisdom seems to be that presidents rarely face resistance during wartime or similar circumstances, particularly on tradeoffs between civil liberties and security, the story is not as simple as that. For one thing, it is a mistake to conceive of the "executive branch" as necessarily a unified entity, even (or especially) in wartime. Often, there are rivalries between different parts of the executive branch, and at times these conflicts become a means by which liberties receive some degree of protection; at other times, specific individuals in powerful executive branch positions marshal their authority and power into means for challenging executive impulses toward unjustified suppression of civil liberties.

The first process is illustrated by the British experience during the Second World War, which is magisterially documented by Brian Simpson.[58] Simpson argues that despite the absence of a written constitution, Great Britain had the best wartime record of preserving civil liberties among the western democracies; this result stemmed from the intense distrust and rivalry between the intelligence services and other components of the government's executive branch. The second process is chronicled in Geof Stone's history of the American experience during the Second World War, when the courts again played a minor role in protecting civil liberties, and yet the First World War experience of state suppression of political dissent was not repeated to nearly the same extent.[59] The attorney general, Francis Biddle, himself steeped in the civil liberties tradition, managed to resist most of President Roosevelt's insistent demands to "indict the seditionists." Indeed, the Justice Department played a major role in ensuring that there were virtually no state prosecutions for disloyalty and that no sedition acts were enacted during this period. Though in hindsight the record of rights protection for dissident speech was not perfect, it was dramatically better than it had been during the First World War, largely as a result of dynamics within the executive branch itself. Once again, this is hardly to say that the results were optimal, nor that conflict and debate within the executive branch will work the same results, or even work at all, in different circumstances. But it is notable that even internal executive branches have at times provided genuine protection for rights during wartime — even in the face of countervailing pressures from the chief executive or other parts of the executive branch. To disparage the process-based approach of the American courts, based on the assumption that a unified executive branch will always fail to internalize civil libertarian values to some extent, is, at least, too simple.

Congress, too, is often assumed to abdicate wholly to the executive in this realm. But if there is sometimes tension, even within the executive branch, one would expect even more of that tension to be manifested through Congress. After all, there are partisan incentives for at least one party to seek to expose or exaggerate executive failings, along with institutional incentives of Congress to resist executive power. The current experience during the "war on terror" suggests precisely this mixed picture; and that picture will surely change, as according to the political-process model it should, depending on whether there are further major terrorist attacks. Congress did overwhelmingly, six weeks after the attacks of September 11, 2001, adopt the USA PATRIOT Act. Some have criticized the Act for its rebalancing of the scales between liberty and security; others have praised Congress for ensuring a continuing oversight role for itself and courts in key areas. Yet since that moment in the immediate aftermath of September 11, Congress has resisted several executive branch initiatives. Congress barred funding for the data-analysis program known as the Total Information Awareness

Program, unless the Defense Department agreed to report to Congress on the effectiveness of the program and its impact on civil liberties. When the government asked Congress for authorization to obtain broader personal information on American citizens, including financial information, the relevant congressional committees refused. When the executive branch, with some congressional support, sought to make permanent the provisions of the PATRIOT Act, Congress again refused. After the legislation was then pared down dramatically to address the problem of "lone-wolf" terrorists, members of Congress succeeded in adding even to that power a sunset provision that will require it to be revisited. And when the executive floated proposals for legislation, known as Patriot II, more expansive than that initially enacted after September 11, the legislation was quickly killed off in Congress. And all this congressional resistance has taken place at a time when Congress and the White House are controlled by the same political party. As Jeffrey Rosen concludes, there has emerged in the U.S. Congress, a year or so after September 11, "a principled, bipartisan libertarian constituency" that is "willing to defend privacy, even in the face of popular fears."[60]

Finally, the political system has itself created institutional structures for attempting to build mechanisms into the executive-congressional relationship for addressing civil liberties and security issues in an informed, deliberative manner. Recently many more Americans have become aware of a longstanding entity, the Office of the Inspector General, within many executive branch agencies, including the Justice Department. That office has already issued two extraordinarily comprehensive — and often quite critical — evaluations of how federal security policies are being administered during the "war on terror." These reports, which have received front-page media coverage, offer many advantages over litigation as an institutional mechanism ensuring executive accountability during wartime, as long as the officials involved act with the requisite independence and diligence. First, they generate detailed information on enforcement more quickly than litigation would have been able to do. Second, because these reports are produced from within the executive branch, the investigators have access to officials throughout the government. Third, these reports appear to have significant credibility, including among those inclined to support executive branch policies, precisely because they are produced by executive branch officials themselves. Finally, because the reports are meant to inform policy, rather than attach sanctions or monetary liabilities to specific individuals, as in litigation, they are not constrained as court decisions are by problems of affixing blame to individuals. As a result, the reports might well contribute more productively to ongoing political debate and assessment of executive branch actions during wartime.

Once again, none of this is to argue that the political process–based approach of the courts is without serious costs, or that it leads to the optimal balance between rights and security. We do mean to enrich discussion of this neglected perspective, though, by suggesting at least two points. The first is that while there has long been a debate about whether the courts fall silent during wartime, it is clear that at least sometimes the political process does not: political deliberation and conflict over rights and security continue in these periods — and probably increasingly so over time. The second point is that one cannot evaluate the judicial channeling of these debates into politics simply by looking at the failures and costs that have resulted from the way the political process has responded in different circumstances. The costs and benefits of the process-based judicial approach must be weighed against the costs and benefits of a full-blown, aggressively rights-oriented alternative that the courts might otherwise pursue. One should not assume that such an alternative is without potential costs of its own. Any serious analysis of the role of courts versus the role of political institutions during wartime must compare alternative approaches against each other, and must realistically recognize both the costs and benefits associated with alternative institutional strategies for addressing the difficult legal issues that arise during wartime.

Systems that separate and divide executive and legislative powers might justify a more process-based, institutionally focused judicial role in addressing questions of what changes in the substance of rights and the institutional structures for protecting them are warranted during times of crises, such as wars. Courts in all systems are placed in a difficult position in being asked to take on such questions; while the courts have the advantage of independence from immediate political circumstance, courts also suffer manifold disadvantages by virtue of their lack of access to full information, lack of systematic appreciation of the interlocking consequences of individual actions, and lack of direct responsibility for the consequences that their decisions might have. Though critics of the limited judicial role in the area of national security often frame the problem as a character failing — courts need to have more "courage" — this long-standing judicial practice, across many generations, suggests deeper structural and institutional reasons that consistently lead judges to define their role in specific, limited ways.

In the American system, courts have drawn on the distinct attributes of a separated-powers system to carve out a well-defined but underappreciated role during times of crisis. The American courts have neither endorsed unilateral executive authority during wartime nor taken it as their role to define directly the substantive content of rights. Instead, the courts have tied their own role to that of the more political branches; where both legislature and executive endorse a particular tradeoff of liberty and security, the courts have accepted that judgment. Where the executive has acted in the face of legislative policies or without legislative approval, the courts have invalidated executive action, even during wartime, or scrutinized it more closely. That deep historical pattern is reemerging today as we begin to see the judicial response to issues like the power to define "enemy combatants" or the role of intelligence gathering and prosecutorial actors in pursuing "foreign agents," or in debates over the proper role for military tribunals. Bilateral institutional action might provide a special kind of check on the institutional excess that is always a concern during times of crisis. American courts have long acted on the view that it does. Approaches that focus on abstract disputes over the meaning of various "rights" or "the rule of law" miss the central feature of actual American constitutional practice in the national security domain — the judicial emphasis on second-order issues of appropriate institutions and processes, through which courts seek mainly to ensure that the right institutional process supports the tradeoff between liberty and security at issue. Whether that jurisprudential approach is the right one for courts that operate in parliamentary systems of unified executive and legislative powers is a question to be left for another day.

NOTES

1 For terrorist trials, France changed the nature of its fact-finding bodies; it eliminated the participation of a majority of lay individuals and substituted a panel of judges (all but one of whom were anonymous) as the fact finders in these terrorism trials. Philip B. Heymann, *Terrorism and America: A Commonsense Strategy for a Democratic Society* (1998), 121.

2 Germany centralized the prosecution and adjudication functions in terrorism cases, and provided special protections for those involved in these roles. *Id.* at 121.

3 The changes in the legal framework applied in Northern Ireland are far too extensive to list here, but among the most noteworthy was the creation of special terrorism courts, known as Diplock Courts, for trying specific offenses such as bombings, weapons offenses, and murders. These courts were presided over by a single judge without the jury normally required. The British also resorted to more aggressive use of surveillance techniques, greater use of confessions, and similar changes in the legal approach to "normal" crime. *Id.* at 122–25.

4 Among other policy changes, Spain authorized its intelligence agents to assassinate terrorists living abroad. *Id.* at 115.

5 Harold Hongju Koh, *The National Security Constitution* (1990), 119. Lest this quote be misconstrued, we point out that Professor Koh is critical of the extent to which both courts and Congress defer to executive branch initiative in areas of national security.

6 See, for example, Laurence H. Tribe, "The Puzzling Persistence of Process-Based Constitutional Theories," 59 *Yale Law Journal* 1063 (1980); Richard Davies Parker, "The Past of Constitutional Theory — and Its Future," 42 *Ohio State Law Review* 223 (1981). For a critique of this critique, see Michael Klarman, "The Puzzling Resistance to Political Process Theory," 77 *Virginia Law Review* 747 (1991).

7 David Cole, "Enemy Aliens," 54 *Stanford Law Review* 953, 955 (2002).

8 William H. Rehnquist, *All the Laws but One* (1998), 205.

9 *Id.* at 202. For criticism from another Chief Justice of Chief Justice Rehnquist's suggestion that law is silent during times of war, see the discussion of the Israeli Supreme Court's decisions in Aharon Barak, "Foreword: A Judge on Judging: The Role of a Supreme Court in a Democracy," 116 *Harvard Law Review* 16 (2002).

10 This view seems to have originated with Charles Warren's classic history of the Supreme Court, published in 1923. Charles Warren, *The Supreme Court in United States History* (1923), 3:149, 153.

11 The facts in these and the following paragraphs are taken from Charles Fairman, *Reconstruction and Reunion, 1864–88* (1971), 182–253.

12 *Id.* at 120–21.

13 Ex Parte Milligan, 71 U.S. (4 Wall.) 2, 109 (1866).

14 71 U.S. 209.

15 Warren, *The Supreme Court in United States History*, 3:149, 154.

16 The facts surrounding the suspension of habeas corpus are drawn from the central work to address these issues, Mark E. Neely Jr., *The Fate of Liberty: Abraham Lincoln and Civil Liberties* (1991), 51–75.

17 71 U.S. at 139, 141.

18 Clinton Rossiter, *The Supreme Court and the Commander in Chief* (2nd ed. 1976), 30–31.

19 Ex Parte McCardle, 74 U.S. (7 Wall.) 506 (1868).

20 Fairman, *Reconstruction and Reunion*, 237.

21 *Id.*

22 74 U.S. at 514.

23 Duncan v. Kahanamoku, 327 U.S. 304 (1946).

24 71 U.S. 475 (1866).

25 *Id.* at 499.

26 *Id.*

27 *Id.* at 501.

28 Patrick Gudridge, "Remember *Endo*?," 116 *Harvard Law Review* 1633 (2003).

29 320 U.S. 81 (1943).

30 *Id.* at 91.

31 *Id.* at 92.

32 *Id.* at 93.

33 *Korematsu*, 323 U.S. at 217–18.

34 *Endo*, 323 U.S. at 300–302.

35 For internal evidence of this self-conscious effort, consider Irons's account of Chief Justice Stone's comments at Court conferences on the cases: "Convinced that the Court must not compromise the exercise of the military's wartime powers over the civilian population, [Stone] was equally determined to affirm the primacy of Congress in setting limits on military authority." Peter H. Irons, *Justice at War* (1983), 325.

36 See, for example, Sternberg v. Carhart, 530 U.S. 914, 953 (2000) (Scalia, J., dissenting) (invoking *Korematsu* and *Dred Scott* to attack Court's ruling on abortion rights).

37 317 U.S. 1 (1942).

38 *Id.* at 39.

39 317 U.S. at 47.

40 453 U.S. 654 (1981).

41 *Id.* at 656 (citing Youngstown Sheet & Tube Co. v. Sawyer, 343 U.S. 579, 637 (1952) (Jackson, J., concurring)).

42 Youngstown Sheet & Tube Co. v. Sawyer, 343 U.S. 579, 582 (1952).

43 *Id.* at 587.

44 *Id.* at 588.

45 *Id.*

46 *Id.* at 586.

47 *Id.* at 634 (Jackson, J., concurring).

48 *Id.* at 637–38.

49 *Id.* at 652.

50 The third designated enemy combatant at the time this book went to press was a Qatari citizen named Ali Marri. See "Enemy Combatant Designation Challenged in Court," *Washington Post*, 10 July 2003, § A, p. 11.

51 Charles Lane, "In Terror War, 2nd Track for Suspects; Those Designated 'Combatants' Lose Legal Protections," *Washington Post*, 1 December 2002, § A, p. 1.

52 The government's fallback position was that any such review must be limited to determining only whether "some evidence" supports the executive's determination—the position the court adopted.

53 Padilla v. Bush, 233 F.Supp. 2d 564, 607 (S.D.N.Y. 2002), affirmed in part and reversed in part, and remanded, by Padilla v. Rumsfeld, 2003 U.S. App. LEXIS 25616 (2d Cir. N.Y., 18 December 2003).

54 18 U.S.C. Sec. 4001 (a).

55 Authorization for Use of Military Force, Pub. Law No. 107-40, Sec. 2(a), 115 Stat. 224, 224 (2001).

56 The other case involving military detention of an American citizen, Hamdi, also operates within this framework, though more ambiguously. In upholding these detention practices, while still endorsing some degree of judicial review over executive determinations of enemy combatant status, the Fourth Circuit relied heavily on its judgment that Congress had endorsed these detentions. The court wrote: "It is difficult if not impossible to understand how Congress could make appropriations for the detention of persons 'similar to prisoners of war' without also authorizing their detention in the first instance." Hamdi v. Rumsfeld, 316 F. 3d 450, 467–68 (4th Cir. 2003). At the same time, however, that court also strongly emphasized, in a case involving battlefield capture, that the powers of the executive branch fall "under the war powers of Art. II." *Id.* at 473. That emphasis on Art. II suggests the possibility of an inherent executive authority, which might conceivably obtain even absent congressional endorsement. But the court did not need to resolve these ultimate questions of authority, given its conclusion that Congress had indeed endorsed the detentions.

57 We are indebted to Jack Goldsmith for this example.

58 Brian Simpson, *In the Highest Degree Odious: Detention without Trial in Wartime Britain* (1992).

59 Geoffrey R. Stone, "Free Speech in World War II: 'When Are You Going to Indict the Seditionists?'" (chapter in forthcoming book).

60 Jeffrey Rosen, "Why Congress Is Brave and the Courts Aren't," *New Republic*, 26 May 2003, 19.

Realizing Constitutional and International Norms in the Wake of September 11

Peter J. Spiro

As September 11 looms a little smaller in the imagination, there is the possibility of a less alarmist perspective on its significance. In the immediate wake of the attacks, there was well-founded anxiety that the enormity of the episode and the war talk that followed would result in the significant curtailment of civil liberties, and particularly the rights of aliens. The historical precedents pointed in that direction, and some proposals, offered seriously, would indeed have constituted a serious setback to individual rights. But the more extreme fears have not been realized. Although elements of the government's response to 9/11 have been rights-restrictive, the overall resiliency of rights protections has perhaps been more remarkable.

This chapter explores three possible explanations for why the early predictions of rights reversals have not come about. First, perhaps the attacks, however dramatic, did not in fact constitute so serious a threat as to warrant—as a matter of policy—the severe curtailment of rights. A second explanation highlights a largely extrajudicial dynamic in which the restriction of civil liberties was defeated as inconsistent with constitutional norms. Finally, the international community and international law appear to have played a significant role in restraining the government from a more serious assault on civil liberties. Geopolitical dominance and the magnitude of the security threat notwithstanding, the United States, like it or not, is being brought into the ambit of international norms.

The Rights Scorecard

September 11 generated a new security discourse. It also provoked a parallel campaign to protect individual rights in the face of anti-terrorism efforts. The civil liberties community has condemned the government's response to 9/11 as a major assault on individual rights.[1]

Vigilance is warranted. The anti-terrorist security agenda has rights implications at every turn. The potential threat has been grave, especially with respect to the rights of aliens. The most significant legislative response to the attacks, the USA PATRIOT Act, expands domestic law enforcement authority in important respects. Three individuals (two of them U.S. citizens) have been apprehended in the United States and detained without charge as "enemy combatants," denied access to counsel and any form of legal process. The rounding up and incommunicado detention of several hundred aliens on minor immigration or criminal charges has posed significant liberty concerns.[2] The president has authorized military tribunals for noncitizens, initially with almost no provision for procedural protection of the accused, and this option has not been formally rejected. Congress has enacted legislation allowing for the detention of aliens certified as terrorists, and significantly expanding the definition of terrorism for immigration purposes.[3] Thousands of others have been subjected to special registration requirements imposed only on young male aliens of Middle Eastern nationality.

On the other hand, the damage to civil rights has been mitigated, and may ultimately prove minimal. The PATRIOT legislation is unexceptional in many respects, for example in its updating of surveillance authority to reflect such new technologies as voice mail. More controversial provisions are subject to a four-year sunset, if they are not repealed or amended before then (which recent legislative developments have suggested is a possibility), and the act does not single out noncitizens for differential treatment in most respects. Detention of aliens certified as terrorists is limited to seven days; at that point the attorney general must commence removal proceedings or lodge criminal charges, failing which the alien must be released.[4] The detention of aliens for other causes has been undertaken on the basis of existing authority, and few detainees from the initial roundup remain in custody. Immigration authorities have made little use of the expanded definition of terrorist activity. Although the military tribunals remain an option, especially for those in detention at Guantánamo Bay, it is possible that in the end no military tribunals will be deployed. Whatever civil liberties concerns persist, the picture is a far cry from such historical anti-alien episodes as the Palmer raids and the internment of Japanese, precedents often invoked in the early days after September 11.

There Are Wars and There Are "Wars"

The factual context has plainly facilitated the government's relative restraint. If this had been real war, in the sense of massed armies hurling themselves against each other in a clear conflict of peoples, the setback to civil liberties would have been far more serious. In this sense, the Japanese internment presented a false precedent. So long as the attacks were limited to those on September 11, and insofar as the attacks did not evidence a conflict between Americans and some other society, the situation did not demand the significant curtailment of individual freedoms.[5] In other words, this wasn't "war," and the less-than-extreme enforcement response simply reflected that. To the extent that rights have been suppressed, it has been in the same peripheral way that rights have been suppressed as part of the "war" on drugs and on crime generally. The adversary here is more like a shadowy criminal syndicate than an ethnic, religious, or national community; although all the terrorists may be Muslims, it has been clear from the start that few Muslims are terrorists. The reversal to individual freedoms would have been pronounced if we faced continuing casualties, conscription, ration books, and a clearly defined "enemy." Assuming its relevance to anti-terrorism responses, the conflict in Iraq supports the point. Even though it involved military operations, in historical perspective the invasion hardly rose to the level of conflicts having significant constitutional consequences.[6]

This take on the facts — characterizing the response as "war" in the metaphoric sense only — is necessary to an account in which rights reversals have been limited. But it doesn't suffice to explain the restraint. It seems clear that the executive branch would have adopted far more intrusive measures in the wake of September 11 had it been able to act unilaterally. Initial legislative proposals from the administration would have authorized the attorney general to remove any alien certified as a terrorist, with no review of either the certification or the removal. A follow-on legislative vehicle, dubbed "Patriot II," would have further expanded surveillance authority, allowed for the collection of genetic information from suspected terrorists, and provided for the termination of U.S. citizenship on the grounds of support for terrorist organizations, among other provisions. The roundup detentions after 9/11 and the executive order authorizing the establishment of military tribunals, both undertaken without legislative participation (or indeed any advance notice), also evidence the administration's tendency to consider civil liberties an afterthought. In the end, the attacks may not have required a war footing, but given its druthers the administration would have assumed one.

CONSTITUTIONAL FRONTLINES

The executive branch has ultimately been constrained by domestic and international actors working to vindicate domestic constitutional and international norms. In the domestic political sphere, various constitutionally relevant entities have resisted the curtailment of civil liberties. Most notably, Congress refused to accept executive branch entreaties for significantly expanded enforcement powers. The USA PATRIOT Act adopted only a limited subset of original administration demands; it is hard to describe it as anything other than watered down. Patriot II has proved a non-starter after a leaked draft drew fierce criticism. Congress has used committee hearings to highlight questionable executive branch practices undertaken on existing authority, such as the roundup detentions. Some of this resistance from the legislative branch has been framed in constitutional terms; that is, Congress has denied demands for expanded enforcement powers on the grounds that the expansion would violate constitutional norms, as conceived by the legislative branch. Congressional resistance has been echoed among élite opinion makers, including editorialists at such major papers as the *New York Times* and the *Washington Post*, as well as among legal and other academics. More than 150 state and local jurisdictions have passed resolutions condemning the PATRIOT Act. Most of this opposition has come from the left, but significant elements on the right have also denounced moves to broaden enforcement capacities.

This interbranch and public interplay has been of constitutional consequence. The episode has evidenced and defined constitutional norms, and the result has been characterized in large part by their successful enforcement. As is now accepted by most constitutional theorists, the courts are not essential to interpreting constitutional standards; the Constitution lives outside judicial decisions.[7] Events following 9/11 present an example of this extrajudicial constitutional dynamic. (As a general matter, episodes implicating foreign relations, where the courts have often demurred under the "political question" and other jurisdictional doctrines, are particularly useful in demonstrating the efficacy and evolution of constitutional norms beyond the courts.)[8] September 11 was of course unprecedented in many respects; never had the homeland suffered such an attack, nor confronted the specter of a faceless, insidious adversary. That left the constitutional parameters of the response unclear, at least in the immediate wake of the attacks; if one conceives of the episode as a new "case," its resolution was not foreordained, at least not on the margins. Subsequent developments made clear that the threat was not a mortal one. That clarification narrowed the constitutional playing field; wholesale suspension of civil liberties was never a real danger in, say, a Civil War sense. But the constitutional constancy of some proposed responses was not so easily dismissed.

Among those closer questions were ones involving the treatment of aliens in immigration proceedings. Constitutional constraints set by the Supreme Court have been minimal. Under the plenary power doctrine, the Court has ceded almost all its standard powers of review in the immigration domain to the political branches, in decisions studded with references to the peculiar competencies of the executive and legislative branches in matters involving national security and foreign relations.[9] An apparent retreat from plenary power premises (most notably in the Court's decisions in the *Nguyen* and *Zadvydas* cases in 2001)[10] has at least been interrupted with *Demore v. Kim*,[11] and all the while the Court has been careful to carve out cases involving core national security concerns.[12] Against that doctrinal backdrop, it takes no great leap to see the Court upholding virtually any immigration measure adopted in the aftermath of September 11. Even so extreme a proposal as that initially sketched by the administration, under which permanent resident aliens could have been deported without review if certified as terrorists, would likely have been upheld by the Court, another in the long line of cases in which perceived threats to national security trump any claim of individual right. Taken as the only law applicable to the problem, court-made doctrine posed an improbable barrier to the curtailment of alien rights. In the end, however, no such judicial barrier was necessary to stave off the basic challenge.

This is not to diminish the value of judicial review, at least not to protect against arbitrary action in particular cases. The courts can police the boundaries of constitutional rectitude more precisely than can the political branches, and there will be many issues at the margins where the courts will expand the scope of individual rights. Nor is this to defend the plenary power doctrine, an artifact of another era. Plenary power and the enormity of attacks notwithstanding, some lower federal courts have shown surprising fortitude in constraining, or attempting to constrain, various elements of the anti-terrorist response.[13] But this judicial activity has been second order, pointing again to the possibility that the Constitution can be sustained by institutions other than the courts, and that aliens, even though deprived of a direct voice in the polity, can find their rights largely vindicated by action of the political branches, or at least vindicated more than the courts would require. As a matter of domestic constitutional function, events following 9/11 tested the system and showed it (mostly) to work.

Others would disagree. There has been a steady drumbeat, mostly heard from progressive elements, that the response to September 11 has cut to the core of constitutional rights. The extreme nature of these characterizations may owe more to political strategy than to a desire to provide accurate description. It seems hard to deny, to the extent that we have witnessed civil liberties reversals in the wake of September 11, even significant ones, that they have been much less severe than initially feared. Isolating possible agents of restraint thus becomes a useful undertaking. Second, the mere fact of such characterizations, and of mobilized advocacy against rights-infringing responses, is itself constitutionally consequential, especially when set in historical relief.[14] Such constitutionally grounded opposition to anti-terrorism measures reflects a constitutional discourse in which security concerns no longer represent a constitutional trump. There have surely been abuses of individual rights in the wake of September 11. But important players in the constitutional dynamic have mounted a vigorous and for the most part successful defense of constitutional liberties, as framed in pre-attack terms.

So the protection of basic civil liberties here can be seen through a domestic lens, in the dynamic interplay of domestic constitutional actors. It was understood by the Congress and other constitutional actors that the situation did not warrant severe curtailment of civil liberties, and those actors were able successfully to bury executive branch initiatives that would have been destructive of rights. This defense was framed in constitutional terms, and executed with little assistance from the courts. September 11 thus sustains the concept of an extrajudicial Constitution, tested under the pressures of a security crisis.

INTERNATIONAL LAW, INTERNATIONAL WILL, AND INTERNATIONAL POWER

But this domestic focus cannot fully explain the result. International actors and international law have also been consequential to the resolution of rights-related issues. Indeed, it is this aspect of the legal implications of 9/11 that may in historical relief emerge as most significant. If international law proves irresistible in this core security context, then it is likely to prove irresistible in other contexts as well. The observation is consistent with other trends concerning the relationship of U.S. law and policy to international law and decision making. Notwithstanding the bluster of an administration whose culture is deeply antagonistic to international institutions, the United States is coming to find itself in a position where the costs of noncompliance with international law outweigh the benefits of asserting full sovereign discretion.

Most telling here is the treatment of noncitizen detainees outside the immigration process. Early on, the Bush administration formally authorized the establishment of military tribunals to prosecute noncitizens for terrorism and related activity. The order itself allowed for significant departures from standard criminal due process protections, even as diluted under military justice.[15]

No tribunal has yet been constituted under the order. The administration notably rejected the option in initiating prosecution of the alleged twentieth hijacker, Zacarias Moussaoui, under normal procedures in federal district court. Though extreme circumstances in the Moussaoui case may yet find the government changing course, there has been no suggestion of deploying tribunals against other aliens present in the United States. There remains the possibility that tribunals will be constituted to prosecute some of the al-Qaeda and Taliban detainees at Guantánamo Bay; as of this writing, the Bush administration had identified six Guantánamo detainees as eligible for trial before military commissions. The tribunals would operate with procedures not dramatically removed from those used in military justice. In the end, however, the tribunals may not be deployed at all.

Given an unencumbered choice here, prosecutors would likely have launched the Moussaoui case before a tribunal and have already put them to work in Guantánamo. The question then is what is acting as the agent of restraint. As above, some of these agents are domestic. Some members of Congress have criticized the tribunal innovation, especially the administration's failure to consult with Congress, much less secure its approval, before issuing the order. To a greater degree, editorialists have scorned the initial authorization of the tribunal option. But the domestic response has been more variable than with respect to the administration's demands for broadened enforcement powers. Congress has made no institutional pronouncement against the tribunals, and it would not likely obstruct their use against the Guantánamo prisoners. A significant mainstream academic component, including most notably the law professors Laurence Tribe[16] and Ruth Wedgwood,[17] has lent its qualified support to the tribunal concept,[18] and the use of tribunals would draw credible doctrinal support from the *Ex Parte Quirin* decision.[19] The American public strongly supports the tribunal option; few Americans would take to the streets in response to tribunal prosecutions of al-Qaeda and Taliban detainees. Even the editorialists have conditionally accepted some use of the tribunals, assuming the adoption of procedural rules significantly constraining of tribunal prosecutions.[20] If, then, we looked at the question as a matter of purely domestic norms, we would expect the government to make at least some use of the tribunals.[21]

And yet the tribunals may not be constituted, and the posture of the international community may provide the explanation. International opposition to the tribunals (and to the terms of the Guantánamo detention generally) has been intense. European public opinion and the major international human rights groups have been particularly vocal in condemning the tribunal option.[22] Much of this opposition has been framed in terms of international law; that is, the conduct of the United States is condemned not just as bad policy, but as illegal.[23]

In the past, international sentiment that the United States was acting inconsistently with international law did not make such opposition conse-quential (the mining of Nicaraguan harbors by the United States and its related withdrawal from the limited compulsory jurisdiction of the Interna-tional Court of Justice providing a notable example from recent history). In contrast to domestic lawmaking, the existence of effective international norms still must be confirmed case by case. Where alleged lawbreakers face few costs for noncompliance, one can question whether in fact they are breaking the law. The widespread noncompliance with various formal inter-national norms during the cold war explains in part why international law suffered so long in the American legal community from a perception that it was not "law" at all. That mentality persists, not the least among major players in the Bush administration. The administration has rhetorically made good on its unilateralist campaign pledges, and on some issues — such as the Second Amendment attack on a proposed international small arms control regime — it has aggressively followed through with action. In the face of this normative hostility, the Bush administration's practice supplies a controlled environment in which to apply an interest-based test to U.S. compliance with international law.

Bringing the Hegemon to Heel

In some areas the United States will be able to resist the imposition of international norms. But there are others in which eventual submission appears inevitable. The issue of military tribunals may be one where the United States, notwithstanding an open contempt for international opin-ion, may have to buckle under. There are three possible mechanisms for imposing international norms on the United States in this context: first, where other states have terrorist suspects in custody and make conditional their rendition to the United States; second, where other states make forms of important cooperation conditional on American disposition of the sus-pects; and third, where the reputational costs of proceeding pose other significant costs to American interests.

In the first case an international capacity to dictate is most obvious but also infrequently available. He who has the bodies can call the shots. The Europeans are resorting with increasing frequency to this device with regard to the death penalty, especially since the European Court of Human Rights ruled in 1989 in the Soering case that it was a violation of the European Human Rights Convention to extradite an individual to the United States if he might face not only a death sentence but (as is invariably the case) an extended stay on death row before execution.[24] Since *Soering*, extraditions in capital cases have been made conditional on agreement by the United States not to pursue the death penalty. The same is occurring in cases arising since 9/11, with the twist that extraditions are likely to include the additional condition that those extradited not face prosecution in military tribunals. Spain announced this policy with respect to suspected al-Qaeda operatives in its custody. The United States has no choice but to accept the European position, assuming an interest in rendition. Of course, the mechanism is available only when the foreign country has custody of terrorism suspects wanted by the United States.

Second, European and other governments are in a position to condition their cooperation on terrorism in such areas as intelligence sharing on a decision by the United States to abjure the tribunals. The immediate U.S. response to 9/11 may have been essentially unilateral, with only token international forces participating in the military operations in Afghanistan. But it is clear that effective preemptive action against terrorist organizations must be multilateral. Too much groundwork for terrorist attacks can be laid outside the target country's borders (as was true with 9/11 itself, for which significant planning was undertaken in Germany). In this respect, the United States needs something from other governments. If those governments care enough about military tribunals and related issues, they are in a position to extract behavioral changes from the United States. The added value of the tribunals may be a higher confidence of conviction as an incident of procedures that are more flexible than in an ordinary federal criminal prosecution. But that added value may not outweigh the downside of qualified European cooperation in the fight against terrorism.

Hence the apparent decision by the United States to refrain from bringing British national detainees in Guantánamo before military tribunals. In July 2003 the Bush administration identified six detainees, two of them British, as eligible for tribunal proceedings. The prospect provoked broad-based condemnation in the United Kingdom and created a serious political headache for Prime Minister Tony Blair, already embattled for his support of the U.S. invasion of Iraq. British authorities objected to the possible prosecutions, extracting specific assurances from the Bush administration regarding the use of the death penalty and leaving open the possibility that plans for the prosecutions would be quietly abandoned. British arguments against the tribunal were draped in the mantle of human rights and international law. The leverage here was clear: if the United States proceeded with the tribunal prosecutions, it risked the support of a loyal partner in the fight against terrorism, too steep a cost for the marginal returns of flexible tribunal procedures. And in stepping back from its contemplated tribunal prosecution of the British detainees, the United States further compromised the tribunals as an option in other cases, insofar as other states work to win similar concessions for their detainee nationals.

Finally, there is the less easily measured fallout from condemnation of the tribunal option by transnational public nongovernmental organizations (NGOs). To the extent that this opposition is fierce, it can translate into the foreign governmental policies highlighted above; governments facing transnational opposition to cooperation with the United States are obviously less likely to undertake it. But there is a more direct impact on the perceived international legitimacy of U.S. prosecution of suspected terrorists. On the one hand, the immediate American interest is to put terrorists behind bars, and the tribunal option facilitates that objective. On the other, the implications of perceived illegitimacy could be serious.[25] The credibility of future anti-terrorist strategies and responses would be undermined. Terrorists imprisoned by the commissions might be more easily glorified, possibly contributing to the destabilization of friendly Arab regimes whose hold on power may already be tenuous. In this legitimacy game, the position of key NGOs is critical.[26] With such groups as Amnesty International, Human Rights First, and the International Commission of Jurists opposing tribunal prosecutions as inconsistent with international human rights, the administration would start on the defensive were it to take the tribunal route. The marginal gain in exploiting relaxed tribunal procedures might not be worth the hit taken in other quarters.

This international positioning already helps to explain the relatively exacting procedural rules imposed on the tribunals in regulations following the initial sketchlike executive order. If the government does not in the end deploy the tribunals, the international community will have likely tipped

the balance against them. International views will not always be determina-
tive, in somewhat the same way that nonjudicial perceptions of constitutional norms will not always be effectively enforced. An example of this in
the 9/11 context involves the application of the Geneva prisoners-of-war
convention to the Guantánamo detainees. Although there appears some
basic consensus that POW status should itself be determined by some judicial or quasi-judicial entity, the administration unilaterally declared the
convention inapplicable to both al-Qaeda and Taliban detainees, without
a significant international backlash. The administration arguments were
stronger here, however, than with respect to the tribunals, and the consequences of the decision (relating mostly to conditions of confinement)
were less significant. The invasion of Iraq similarly demonstrates the capacity of the United States to defy the conceptions of other actors on questions
of international legality. But neither example disproves the salience of international law to decision making by the U.S. government. It is highly unlikely, for example, that in the face of international rejection of the grounds
for invasion the United States will undertake "preemptive" action against
other states. That the costs of illegitimacy can be borne in some situations
will not make them bearable in others. As in the domestic law context,
imperfect enforcement of legal norms does not undermine their ultimate
status as legal norms.

Playing Out the Triumph of International Law

One must also qualify this account with the rather obvious caution that the
episode is still unfolding and that its ending could deviate from the storyline
here suggested. After having been derailed in the immediate wake of the
post-attack detentions, the tribunal option has not been abandoned, and incremental steps have been taken to operationalize it. If it were deployed
selectively against senior al-Qaeda operatives (with respect to whose prosecution a strong argument for secret proceedings might be made), European and other governments might quietly go along. This development,
however, would not be inconsistent with the insinuation of international
norms; it would, rather, be reflective of the substance of those norms.

Perhaps the more significant remaining test would be posed by what is emerging, either by default or by design, as the Bush administration's alternative to prosecution (whether by military tribunal or through the ordinary instruments of criminal justice) or release, namely, the possibility of indefinite detention without charge. This option is now being openly vetted, with an accompanying legal justification that the laws of war permit detention until the cessation of hostilities, hostilities here comprising the long-haul fight against terrorism. International concern regarding the detentions has accelerated on the time line, at the same time that domestic actors are unlikely to mobilize on the issue.[27]

International pressure is beginning to show affirmative results. The United States has agreed to release three juveniles whose detention had been highlighted by rights groups. At least eight friendly states, including the United Kingdom, Russia, Pakistan, and Spain, have lodged diplomatic protests regarding the continued detention of their nationals at Guantánamo, prompting a cabinet-level fracas within the administration. Opposition from other international quarters will intensify. It is not implausible that sustained international pressure — and associated costs — will result in the release or prosecution of substantial numbers of the Guantánamo contingent in the near future. If so, it would further demonstrate how events in the aftermath of September 11 have both reflected and advanced the efficacy of international norms.

The events of September 11 were exceptional, but there are some broader lessons here for less exceptional situations. On the domestic side, 9/11 evidences that rights can be largely vindicated outside the judicial process. But that possibility has already been established in other contexts. So it may be a new international dynamic that proves the more interesting development. If international actors are able to cabin the discretion of the United States in this core security context, they will surely be in a position to do so elsewhere. Other developments are pointing in the same direction. Where 9/11 might at first have been feared an obstacle to the advancement of international law and institutions, it may emerge an accelerant. Parallel developments are found in the consular convention cases and with respect to the continued application of the death penalty by some states in the United States. As other battles are engaged in the realms of international environmental law, criminal law, and humanitarian law, and on other human rights issues, 9/11 may point to a multilateralist future, whether by choice or not, for the United States as for everyone else.

NOTES

Thanks to participants in roundtables at the Program in Law and Public Affairs at Princeton University and Georgetown University Law Center for helpful comments. Events described in this chapter are current as of August 2003.

1 See, for example, American Civil Liberties Union, *Insatiable Appetite: The Government's Demand for New and Unnecessary Powers after September 11* (2002); Lawyers Committee for Human Rights, *A Year of Loss: Reexamining Civil Liberties since September 11* (2002); Migration Policy Institute, *America's Challenge: Domestic Security, Civil Liberties, and National Unity after September 11* (2003).

2 See generally David Cole, "Enemy Aliens," 54 *Stanford Law Review* 953, 960–65 (2002).

3 See Uniting and Strengthening America by Providing Appropriate Tools Required to Intercept and Obstruct Terrorism Act of 2001, §§ 411–12, Pub. L. No. 107-56, 115 Stat. 272 (2001).

4 See USA PATRIOT Act, § 412(a). As of July 2002, the attorney general had not resorted to the seven-day detention power in any cases. See Questions Submitted by the House Judiciary Committee to the Attorney General on USA Patriot Act Implementation, at 17, appended to Letter from Assistant Attorney General Daniel J. Bryant to Representative F. James Sensenbrenner Jr. (26 July 2002), available at http://www.fas.org/irp/news/2002/10/doj101702.pdf.

5 Jack Goldsmith and Cass Sunstein make a similar argument in contrasting reactions to the use of military tribunals in the Second World War (leading up to the Supreme Court's decision in *Ex Parte Quirin*) and in the wake of September 11. See Jack Goldsmith and Cass R. Sunstein, "Military Tribunals and Legal Culture: What a Difference Sixty Years Make," 19 *Constitutional Commentary* 261, 280–81 (2002).

6 Cf. Peter J. Spiro, "War Powers and the Sirens of Formalism," 68 *NYU Law Review* 1338 (1993) (setting forth a constitutional typology of military hostilities, with most conflicts not qualifying as "war" for constitutional purposes).

7 See, for example, Cass R. Sunstein, *The Partial Constitution* (1993) (arguing that the aspirations of the Constitution can be ascertained not only from judicial interpretation but also from broad public deliberation); Mark Tushnet, *Taking the Constitution Away From the Courts* (1999) (framing a populist view of constitutional law); Lawrence Gene Sager, "Fair Measure: The Legal Status of Under-

enforced Constitutional Norms," 91 *Harvard Law Review* 1212 (1978) (asserting full validity of constitutional norms even in the face of judicial underenforcement); see also William E. Forbath, "Caste, Class, and Equal Citizenship," 98 *Michigan Law Review* 1 (1999) (describing scholarship focused on constitutional development outside the courts).

8 See Peter J. Spiro, "Treaties, Executive Agreements, and Constitutional Method," 79 *Texas Law Review* 961 (2001).

9 On the plenary power doctrine see generally, for example, Gerald L. Neuman, *Strangers to the Constitution: Immigrants, Borders, and Fundamental Law* (1996), 118–38; Louis H. Henkin, "The Constitution and United States Sovereignty: A Century of Chinese Exclusion and Its Progeny," 100 *Harvard Law Review* 853 (1987). For a nonacademic treatment, see Jeffrey Rosen, "Holding Pattern," *New Republic*, 10 December 2001, 16 ("Over the last 50 years the Supreme Court has imposed few constitutional constraints on the ability of Congress and the president to detain, exclude, and deport aliens in ways that would be grossly unconstitutional if applied to citizens").

10 See Nguyen v. INS, 533 U.S. 53 (2001) (while upholding gender discriminatory provision in naturalization provision, applying ordinary domestic equal protection framework); Zadvydas v. Davis, 533 U.S. 678 (2001) (finding that government lacks statutory authority to detain removable aliens on indefinite basis, on grounds that indefinite detention would raise "serious constitutional doubts"); see generally Peter J. Spiro, "Explaining the End of Plenary Power," 16 *Georgetown Immigration Law Journal* 339 (2001).

11 538 U.S. 510 (2003) (affirming constitutionality of mandatory detention of alien pending removal hearing; "In the exercise of its broad power over naturalization and immigration, Congress regularly makes rules that would be unacceptable if applied to citizens").

12 Most notably in the *Zadvydas* decision, which bracketed the application of its constraints on detention in terrorism cases. See Zadvydas, 533 U.S. at 696 ("Neither do we consider terrorism or other special circumstances where special arguments might be made for forms of preventive detention and for heightened deference to the judgments of the political branches with respect to matters of national security").

13 The circuit courts have split on whether deportation hearings can be conducted in secrecy, paving the way for consideration of the issue by the Supreme Court. Compare North Jersey Media Group v. Ashcroft, 308 F.3d 198 (3d Cir. 2002) (finding press and public to have no First Amendment right to open deportation hearings), cert. denied 538 U.S. 1056 (2003), with Detroit Free Press v. Ashcroft, 303 F.3d 681 (6th Cir. 2002) (finding that closed removal hearings violate First Amendment). On the detentions and secret proceedings, see generally

Cole, "Enemy Aliens," 960–65. More significant civil liberties decisions are likely to emerge in the context of citizens detained without charge as "enemy belligerents," as the plenary power over aliens will not pose a threshold barrier in those cases. The most significant decision to date upheld the government's power so to hold a citizen captured on the battlefield. See Hamdi v. Rumsfeld, 316 F.3d 450 (4th Cir. 2003). That decision would not by itself support the detention as an enemy belligerent of Jose Padilla, who was apprehended at O'Hare Airport in Chicago, nor of the Qatari national Ali Saleh Al-Marri, who was pulled out of the civilian justice system as an alleged al-Qaeda "sleeper"; as an interim opinion of the same court had observed, in the absence of "meaningful judicial review, any American citizen alleged to be an enemy combatant could be detained indefinitely without charges or counsel on the government's say-so" in such cases. See Hamdi v. Rumsfeld, 296 F.3d 278 (4th Cir. 2002). A district court judge in the Padilla case has ordered the government to allow him access to counsel. See Padilla v. Rumsfeld, 243 F. Supp. 2d 42 (S.D.N.Y. 2003). The Padilla and Al-Marri cases represent the only uses of the enemy belligerent designation outside the theater of military operations. One might doubt whether the government will use this approach in future cases, even if Hamdi's and Padilla's detentions withstand court challenges, given apparent judicial reticence and criticism from other quarters. See, for example, "Dangerous Detentions," *Los Angeles Times*, 25 July 2003, 16 (editorial); Henry Weinstein, "ABA Opposes Bush 'Enemy Combatants' Policy," *Los Angeles Times*, 11 February 2003, 18.

14 See Goldsmith and Sunstein, "Military Tribunals and Legal Culture" (describing complete lack of opposition to trial by military commission of Nazi saboteurs during the Second World War).

15 See, for example, Harold Honju Koh, "The Case against Military Commissions," 96 *American Journal of International Law* 337 (2002).

16 See Laurence H. Tribe, "Trial by Fury; Why Congress Must Curb Bush's Military Courts," *New Republic*, 10 December 2001, 18 (while criticizing the administration's failure to consult Congress on tribunals as well as elements of the framework for the tribunals, asserting "the core of the executive order [authorizing the tribunals], its gratuitous branches pruned, is consistent with the Constitution").

17 See Ruth Wedgwood, "The Rules of War Can't Protect Al Qaeda," *New York Times*, 31 December 2001; Ruth Wedgwood, "The Case for Military Tribunals," *Wall Street Journal*, 3 December 2001, § A, p. 18. Wedgwood was consulted by Defense Department lawyers with respect to the formulation of procedural rules adopted for the tribunals.

18 See Tribe, "Trial by Fury"; Wedgwood, "The Rules of War Can't Protect Al Qaeda"; Wedgwood, "The Case for Military Tribunals"; Kenneth Anderson,

"What to Do with Bin Laden and Al Qaeda Terrorists? A Qualified Defense of Military Commissions and United States Policy on Detainees at Guantánamo Bay Naval Base," 25 *Harvard Journal of Law and Public Policy* 591 (2002); Curtis Bradley and Jack Goldsmith, "The Constitutional Validity of Military Commissions," 5 *Green Bag* 2d 249 (2002) (asserting tribunal's constitutionality). Other academics have strongly condemned the tribunals. See, for example, Laura A. Dickerson, "Using Legal Process to Fight Terrorism: Detentions, Military Commissions, International Tribunals, and the Rule of Law," 75 *Southern California Law Review* 1407 (2002); George Fletcher, "War and the Constitution: Bush's Military Tribunals Haven't Got a Legal Leg to Stand on," *American Prospect*, 1 January 2002, 26; David Cole, "National Security State," *Nation*, 17 December 2001, 4.

19 317 U.S. 1 (1942) (upholding trial of Nazi saboteurs by military commission).

20 Including, for instance, so liberal a columnist as Anthony Lewis. See Anthony Lewis, "Wake Up, America," *New York Times*, 30 November 2001, § A, p. 27 ("I do not doubt that leaders of Al Qaeda could properly be tried by a military tribunal" under procedures more narrowly drafted than those in Bush's initial executive order). See also, for example, "Standards for Detainees," *Washington Post*, 6 July 2003, § B, p. 6 (editorial accepting use of tribunals for al-Qaeda operatives). Intense opposition from the professional bar is also premised on the notion that the tribunals would be acceptable were certain features of the existing scheme abandoned, such as the possible monitoring of attorney-client communications. See Neil Lewis, "Rules Set Up for Terror Tribunals May Deter Some Defense Lawyers," *New York Times*, 13 July 2003, § 1, p. 1.

21 On this score, I think Goldsmith and Sunstein exaggerate the magnitude of domestic opposition to the tribunals. No doubt they have been more skeptically received than the military commissions of *Ex Parte Quirin* were, as they amply demonstrate, but there has been significant support, however qualified, from unexpected mainstream quarters.

22 On European public opinion relating to the treatment of the Guantánamo detainees, see "A Transatlantic Rift," *Economist*, 19 January 2002 (reporting that in Europe, "the prisoners' fate dominates airwaves and parliaments").

23 See, for example, Amnesty International, "Memorandum to the US Government on the Rights of People in U.S. Custody in Afghanistan and Guantánamo Bay" (April 2002); Richard Goldstone, "Prosecuting Al Qaeda: September 11 and Its Aftermath," Crimes of War Project, 7 December 2001, available at www.crimesofwar.org/expert/al; "A Matter of Trust: Military Tribunals Are Not the Answer for Guantánamo Bay," *Financial Times*, 14 July 2003, 16 (editorial condemning tribunal procedures as a "denial of both US and international standards of justice").

24 See Soering v. United Kingdom, 161 Eur. Ct. H.R. (ser. A) (1989).

25 See, for example, Cole, "Enemy Aliens," 958; Dickerson, "Using Legal Process to Fight Terrorism," 1465.

26 For a case study of the consequentiality of NGOs in international lawmaking, see Anne Marie Clark, *Diplomacy of Conscience: Amnesty International and Changing Human Rights Norms* (2001).

27 American courts are unlikely to find jurisdiction over constitutional challenges to the Guantánamo detentions, on the grounds that U.S. government conduct on Guantánamo is not subject to ordinary constitutional constraint. See Al Odah v. United States, 321 F.3d 1134 (D.C. Cir. 2003) (rejecting challenge to Guantánamo detentions on this jurisdictional basis). Congress has shown little interest in the issue, nor have other domestic actors. See, for example, John Mintz, "Delegations Praise Detainees' Treatment," *Washington Post*, 26 January 2002, § A, p. 15. There is evidence, however, of an emerging American editorial consensus condemning the continued detention without some form of process. See, for example, "Forsaken at Guantánamo," *New York Times*, 12 March 2003, § A, p. 24; "Impasse at Guantánamo," *Chicago Tribune*, 17 May 2003, 24; "No Justice at Guantánamo," *Boston Globe*, 30 March 2003, § D, p. 10.

Part IV

THE WAR ON TERRORISM
AND THE END OF HUMAN RIGHTS

David Luban

In the immediate aftermath of September 11, President Bush stated that the perpetrators of the deed would be brought to justice. Soon afterward, the president announced that the United States would engage in a war on terrorism. The first of these statements adopts the familiar language of criminal law and criminal justice. It treats the September 11 attacks as horrific crimes — mass murders — and the government's mission as apprehending and punishing the surviving planners and conspirators for their roles in the crimes. The war on terrorism is a different proposition, however, and a different model of governmental action — not law but war. Most obviously, it dramatically broadens the scope of action, because now terrorists who had nothing to do with September 11, even indirectly, have been declared enemies. But that is only the beginning.

THE HYBRID WAR-LAW APPROACH

The model of war offers much freer rein than that of law, and therein lies its appeal in the wake of 9/11. First, in war but not in law it is permissible to use lethal force on enemy troops regardless of their degree of personal involvement with the adversary. The conscripted cook is as legitimate a target as the enemy general. Second, in war but not in law "collateral damage," that is, foreseen but unintended killing of noncombatants, is permissible. (Police cannot blow up an apartment building full of people because a murderer is inside, but an air force can bomb the building if it contains a military target.) Third, the requirements of evidence and proof are drastically weaker in war than in criminal justice. Soldiers do not need proof beyond a reasonable doubt, or even proof by a preponderance of evidence, that someone is an enemy soldier before firing on him or capturing and imprisoning him. They don't need proof at all, merely plausible intelligence. Thus, the U.S. military remains regretful but unapologetic about its attack on the Afghani town of Uruzgan in January 2002, in which twenty-one innocent civilians were killed, based on faulty intelligence that they were al-Qaeda fighters.[1] Fourth, in war one can attack an enemy without concern over whether he has done anything. Legitimate targets are those who in the course of combat *might* harm us, not those who *have* harmed us. No doubt there are other significant differences as well. But the basic point should be clear: given Washington's mandate to eliminate the danger of future 9/11s, so far as humanly possible, the model of war offers important advantages over the model of law.

There are disadvantages as well. Most obviously, in war but not in law, fighting back is a *legitimate* response of the enemy. Second, because fighting back is legitimate, in war the enemy soldier deserves special regard once he is rendered harmless through injury or surrender. It is impermissible to punish him for his role in fighting the war. Nor can he be "unpleasant[ly]" interrogated after he is captured. The Third Geneva Convention follows the Hague Convention in requiring POWs to tell their captors their name, rank, and serial number. Beyond that, it provides: "Prisoners of war who refuse to answer [questions] may not be threatened, insulted, or exposed to unpleasant or disadvantageous treatment of any kind."[2] And when the war concludes, the enemy soldier must be repatriated. Third, when nations fight a war, other nations may legitimately opt for neutrality.

Here, however, Washington has different ideas, designed to eliminate these tactical disadvantages in the traditional war model. Washington regards international terrorism not only as a military adversary but also as a criminal activity and criminal conspiracy. In the law model, criminals don't get to shoot back, and their acts of violence subject them to legitimate punishment. That is what we see in Washington's prosecution of the war on terrorism. Captured terrorists may be tried before military or civilian tribunals, and shooting back at Americans, including American troops, is a federal crime (the statute under which John Walker Lindh was indicted punishes anyone who "outside the United States attempts to kill, or engages in a conspiracy to kill, a national of the United States" or "engages in physical violence with intent to cause serious bodily injury to a national of the United States; or with the result that serious bodily injury is caused to a national of the United States").[3] Furthermore, the United States may rightly demand that other countries not be neutral about murder and terrorism. Unlike in the war model, we as a nation may insist that those who are not with us in fighting murder and terror are against us, because by not joining our operations they are providing a haven for terrorists or their bank accounts. By selectively combining elements of the war model and elements of the law model, Washington is able to maximize its own ability to mobilize lethal force against terrorists while eliminating most traditional rights of a military adversary, as well as the rights of innocent bystanders caught in the crossfire.

A LIMBO OF RIGHTLESSNESS

The legal status of al-Qaeda suspects imprisoned at the Guantánamo Bay Naval Base in Cuba is emblematic of this hybrid war-law approach to the threat of terrorism. In line with the war model, the detainees lack the usual rights of criminal suspects—the presumption of innocence, the right to a hearing to determine guilt, the opportunity to prove that the authorities have grabbed the wrong man. But in line with the law model, they are considered unlawful combatants, because they are not uniformed forces, and therefore they lack the rights of prisoners of war.[4] Initially, the American government declared that the Guantánamo Bay prisoners have no rights under the Geneva Conventions. In the face of international protests, Washington quickly backpedaled and announced that the Guantánamo Bay prisoners would indeed be treated in most respects as decently as POWs— but it also made clear that the prisoners have no right to such treatment. One conspicuous way in which they will *not* be treated as decently as POWs is that they need not be given hearings to determine whether they are actually al-Qaeda or Taliban fighters or simply innocent bystanders swept up by mistake, although in 2004 the Bush administration, facing Supreme Court review, decided to institute a system of hearings for some detainees. Neither criminal suspects nor POWs, neither fish nor fowl, they inhabit a limbo of rightlessness. Secretary of Defense Rumsfeld's statement that the United States may continue to detain them even if they are acquitted by a military tribunal dramatizes the point.

To see how extraordinary their status is, consider an analogy. Suppose that Washington declares a war on organized crime. Troops are dispatched to Sicily, and a number of Mafiosi are seized, brought to Guantánamo Bay, and imprisoned without a hearing for the indefinite future, maybe the rest of their lives. They are accused of no crimes, because their capture is based not on what they have done but on what they might do. After all, to become "made guys" they took oaths of obedience to commit criminal acts if so ordered. Seizing them accords with the war model: they are enemy foot soldiers. But they are foot soldiers out of uniform; they lack a "fixed distinctive emblem," in the words of the Hague Convention (unless wraparound sunglasses count as a fixed distinctive emblem). That makes them unlawful combatants, so they lack the rights of POWs. They may object that it is only a unilateral declaration by the American president that has turned them into combatants in the first place — he called it a war, they didn't — and that since they do not regard themselves as literal foot soldiers it never occurred to them to wear a fixed distinctive emblem. They have a point. It seems too easy for the president to divest anyone in the world of rights and liberty simply by announcing that the United States is at war with him and then declaring him an unlawful combatant if he resists. But, in the hybrid war-law model, he protests in vain.

Consider another example. In January 2002 U.S. forces in Bosnia seized five Algerians and a Yemeni suspected of al-Qaeda connections and took them to Guantánamo Bay. The six had been jailed in Bosnia, but a Bosnian court released them for lack of evidence, and the Bosnian Human Rights Chamber issued an injunction that four of them be allowed to remain in the country pending further legal proceedings. The Human Rights Chamber, ironically, was created under U.S. auspices in the Dayton peace accords, and it was designed specifically to protect against this sort of treatment. Ruth Wedgwood, a well-known international law scholar and a member of the Council on Foreign Relations, defended the Bosnian seizure in war-model terms. "I think we would simply argue this was a matter of self-defense. One of the fundamental rules of military law is that you have a right ultimately to act in self-defense. And if these folks were actively plotting to blow up the

U.S. embassy, they should be considered combatants and captured as combatants in a war."[5] Notice that Professor Wedgwood argues in terms of what the men seized in Bosnia were *planning to do*, not what they *did*; notice as well that the finding by the Bosnian court of insufficient evidence does not matter. These are characteristics of the war model.

In addition, two American citizens alleged to be al-Qaeda operatives (Jose Padilla, also known as Abdullah al Muhajir, and Yasser Esam Hamdi) have been held ever since in American military prisons, with no crimes charged and no hearing. The president has described Padilla as "a bad man" who aimed to build a nuclear "dirty" bomb and use it against America; and the Justice Department has classified both men as "enemy combatants" who may be held indefinitely.[6] Yet as Gary Solis, an expert on military law, points out, "Until now, as used by the attorney general, the term 'enemy combatant' appeared nowhere in U.S. criminal law, international law or in the law of war."[7] The phrase comes from the Supreme Court case *Ex Parte Quirin* (1942), but all the Court says in its opinion is that "an enemy combatant who without uniform comes secretly through the lines for the purpose of waging war by destruction of life or property" would "not . . . be entitled to the status of prisoner of war, but . . . be [an] offender[] against the law of war subject to trial and punishment by military tribunals."[8] For the Court, in other words, the status of a person as a non-uniformed enemy combatant makes him a criminal rather than a warrior, and determines *where* he is tried (in a military, rather than a civilian, tribunal) but not *whether* he is tried. *Ex Parte Quirin* presupposes that criminals are entitled to hearings: without a hearing how can suspects prove that the government made a mistake? *Quirin* embeds the concept of "enemy combatant" firmly in the law model. In the war model, by contrast, POWs may be detained without a hearing until hostilities are over. But POWs were captured either in uniform or in battle, and only their undoubted identity as enemy soldiers justifies such open-ended custody. Apparently, Hamdi and Padilla will get the worst of both models: open-ended custody with no trial, like POWs, but no certainty beyond the U.S. government's say-so that they really are "bad men." This is the hybrid war-law model. It combines the *Quirin* category of "enemy combatant without uniform," used in the law model to justify a military trial, with the war model's practice of indefinite confinement and no trial at all.

THE CASE FOR THE HYBRID APPROACH

Is there any justification for the hybrid war-law model, which so drastically diminishes the rights of the enemy-accused? An argument can be offered along the following lines. In ordinary cases of war among states, enemy soldiers may well be morally and politically innocent. Many are conscripts, and those who aren't do not necessarily endorse the state policies they are fighting to defend. But enemy soldiers in the war on terrorism are, by definition, those who have embarked on a path of terrorism. They are neither morally nor politically innocent. Their sworn aim — "Death to America!" — is to create more 9/11s. In this respect, they are much more akin to criminal conspirators than to conscript soldiers. Terrorists will fight as soldiers when they must, and metamorphose into mass murderers when they can.

Furthermore, suicide terrorists pose a special, unique danger. Ordinary criminals do not target innocent bystanders. They may be willing to kill them if necessary, but bystanders enjoy at least some measure of security because they are not primary targets. Not so with terrorists, who aim to kill as many innocent people as possible. Likewise, innocent bystanders are protected from ordinary criminals by whatever deterrent force the threat of punishment and the risk of getting killed in the act of committing a crime offer. For a suicide bomber, neither of these threats is a deterrent at all — after all, for the suicide bomber one of the hallmarks of a *successful* operation is that he winds up dead at day's end. Given the unique and heightened danger that suicide terrorists pose, a stronger response that grants potential terrorists fewer rights may be justified. Add to this the danger that terrorists may come to possess weapons of mass destruction, including nuclear devices in suitcases. Under circumstances of such dire menace, it is appropriate to treat them as though they embodied the most dangerous aspects of both warriors and criminals. That is the basis of the hybrid war-law model.

THE CASE AGAINST EXPEDIENCY

The argument against the hybrid war-law model is equally clear. The United States has simply chosen the bits of the law model and the bits of the war model that are most convenient for American interests, and ignored the rest. The model abolishes the rights of potential enemies (and their innocent shields) by fiat—not for reasons of moral or legal principle, but solely because the United States does not want them to have rights. The more rights they have, the more risk they pose. But Americans' urgent desire to minimize their risks doesn't make other people's rights disappear. Calling our policy a war on terrorism obscures this point.

The theoretical basis of the objection is that the law model and the war model each come as a package, with a kind of intellectual integrity. The law model grows out of relationships within states, while the war model arises from relationships between states. The law model imputes a ground-level community of values to those subject to the law—paradigmatically citizens of a state, but also visitors and foreigners who choose to engage in conduct that affects a state. Only because law imputes shared basic values to the community can a state condemn the conduct of criminals and inflict punishment on them. Criminals deserve condemnation and punishment because their conduct violates norms that we are entitled to count on their sharing. But for the same reason—the imputed community of values—those subject to the law ordinarily enjoy a presumption of innocence and an expectation of safety. The government cannot simply grab and confine them without making sure they have broken the law, nor can it condemn them without due process before ensuring that it has the right person, nor can it knowingly place bystanders in mortal peril in the course of fighting crime. They are our fellows, and the community should protect them just as it protects us. The same imputed community of values that justifies condemnation and punishment creates rights to due care and due process.

War is different. War is the ultimate acknowledgment that human beings do not live in a single community with shared norms. If their norms conflict enough, communities pose a physical danger to each other, and nothing can safeguard a community against its enemies except force of arms. That makes enemy soldiers legitimate targets; but it makes our soldiers legitimate targets as well, and once the enemy no longer poses a danger, he should be immune from punishment, because if he has fought cleanly he has violated no norms that we are entitled to presume he honors. Our norms are, after all, *our* norms, not his.

Because the law model and the war model come as conceptual packages, it is unprincipled to wrench them apart and recombine them simply because it is in America's interest to do so. To declare that Americans can fight enemies with the latitude of warriors, and yet if the enemies fight back they are not warriors but criminals, amounts to a kind of heads-I-win-tails-you-lose international morality according to which whatever it takes to reduce American risk, no matter what the cost to others, turns out to be justified. This, in brief, is the criticism of the hybrid war-law model.

To be sure, the law model could be made to incorporate the war model merely by rewriting a handful of statutes. Congress could enact laws permitting the imprisonment or execution of persons who pose a significant threat of terrorism whether or not they have already done anything wrong. The standard of evidence could be set low and the requirement of a hearing eliminated. Finally, Congress could authorize the use of lethal force against terrorists regardless of the danger to innocent bystanders, and it could immunize officials from lawsuits or prosecution by victims of collateral damage. Such statutes would violate the Constitution, but the Constitution could be amended to incorporate anti-terrorist exceptions to the Fourth, Fifth, and Sixth Amendments. In the end, we would have a system of law that captures all the essential features of the war model.

It would, however, be a system that imprisons people for their intentions rather than their actions, and that offers to the innocent very few protections against mistaken detention or inadvertent death through collateral damage. Gone would be the principles that people should never be punished for their thoughts, only for their deeds, and that innocent people must be protected rather than injured by their own government. In that sense, at least, repackaging war as law seems merely cosmetic, because it replaces the ideal of law as a protector of human rights with the more problematic goal of protecting some innocent people by sacrificing others. The hypothetical legislation described above would incorporate war into law only by making law look more like war. It no longer resembles law as Americans generally understand it.

The Threat to International Human Rights

In the war on terrorism, what becomes of international human rights? It seems beyond dispute that the war model poses a threat to international human rights, because honoring human rights during war to the same extent as in peacetime is neither practically possible nor theoretically required. Combatants are legitimate targets; noncombatants maimed by accident or mistake are regarded as collateral damage rather than victims of atrocities; in cases of mistaken identity people get killed or confined without a hearing because combat conditions preclude due process. Admittedly, the laws of war specify minimum human rights, but these are far less robust than rights in peacetime — and the hybrid war-law model reduces this schedule of rights even further by classifying the enemy as an unlawful combatant.

One striking example of the erosion of human rights in the fight against terror is the tolerance of torture. It should be recalled that in 1995 a plot by al-Qaeda to bomb eleven American airliners was thwarted by information tortured out of a Pakistani suspect by the Philippine police — an eerie real-life version of the familiar philosophical thought experiment.[9] The *Washington Post* reports that since September 11 the United States has engaged in the summary transfer of dozens of terrorism suspects to countries where they will be interrogated under torture.[10] In the words of one American official, "We don't kick the [expletive] out of them. We send them to other countries so they can kick the [expletive] out of them."[11] But it isn't just the United States that has proven willing to tolerate torture for security reasons. In December 2002 the Swedish government snatched a suspected Islamic extremist to whom it had previously granted political asylum and the same day had him transferred to Egypt, where Amnesty International reports that he has been tortured to the point where he walks only with difficulty. Returning him to Egypt violates European human rights law; apparently, the reason for returning him the same day as his arrest was simply to prevent his wife from taking timely legal action.[12] Sweden is not, to say the least, a traditionally hard-line offender on human rights issues. None of this international transportation is lawful — indeed, it violates international treaty obligations under the Torture Convention that in the United States has constitutional status as "supreme Law of the Land" — but that may not matter under the war model, in which even constitutional rights may be abrogated.[13] As one American official put it, "There was a before 9/11, and there was an after 9/11. After 9/11 the gloves come off."[14] In the words of another official, "If you don't violate someone's human rights some of the time, you probably aren't doing your job."[15]

It is natural to suggest that this suspension of human rights is an exceptional emergency measure to deal with an unprecedented threat. This naturally raises the question of how long human rights will remain suspended. When will the war be over?

In answering the question the chief problem is that the war on terrorism is not like any other kind of war. The enemy, terrorism, is not a territorial state or nation or government. There is no opposite number to negotiate with. There is no one on the other side to call a truce or declare a ceasefire, no one among the enemy authorized to surrender. In traditional wars among states the war aim is, as Clausewitz argued, to impose one state's political will on another's. The *aim* of the war is not to kill the enemy — killing the enemy is the *means* used to achieve the real end, which is to force capitulation. In the war on terrorism, no capitulation is possible. That means that the real aim of the war is, quite simply, to kill or capture all of the terrorists — to keep on killing and killing, capturing and capturing, until they are all gone.

Of course, no one expects that terrorism will ever disappear completely. Everyone understands that new anti-American extremists, new terrorists, will always arise and always be available for recruitment and deployment. Everyone understands that even if al-Qaeda is destroyed or decapitated, other groups, with other leaders, will arise in its place. It follows, then, that the war on terrorism will be a permanent war, at least until the United States decides to abandon it. The war has no natural resting point, no moment of victory or finality. It requires a mission of killing and capturing, in territories all over the globe, that will go on in perpetuity. It follows as well that the suspension of human rights implicit in the hybrid war-law model is not temporary but permanent.

Perhaps with this fear in mind, Congress in authorizing President Bush's military campaign has limited its targets to those responsible for September 11. But the war on terrorism has taken on a life of its own that makes the congressional authorization little more than a pointless formality. (In any case, the White House position is that while the congressional resolution was welcome, the president did not need it to act.) Because of the threat of nuclear or biological terror, the American leadership launched a war on Iraq regardless of whether Iraq was implicated in September 11; and the president's yoking of Iraq, Iran, and North Korea into a single "axis of evil" because all three nations back terror suggests that the war on terrorism might eventually encompass these nations as well. Russia invokes the American war on terrorism to justify its attacks on Chechen rebels, as does China to deflect criticisms of its campaign against Uighur separatists. So too,

Prime Minister Sharon of Israel repeatedly links military actions against Palestinian insurgents to the American war on terrorism. "War on terrorism" is not the code name of a discreet, neatly boxed American operation — it has become a model of politics, a worldview with its own distinctive premises and consequences. As I have argued, it includes a new model of state action, the hybrid war-law model, which depresses human rights from their peacetime standard to the wartime standard, and indeed even further. So long as it continues, the war on terrorism means the end of human rights, at least for those near enough to be touched by the fire of battle.

NOTES

1 John Ward Anderson, "Afghans Falsely Held by U.S. Tried to Explain; Fighters Recount Unanswered Pleas, Beatings — and an Apology on Their Release," *Washington Post*, 26 March 2002, § A, p. 14. See also Susan B. Glasser, "Afghans Live and Die with U.S. Mistakes: Villagers Tell of Over 100 Casualties," *Washington Post*, 20 February 2002, § A, p. 1.

2 Geneva Convention (III) Relative to the Treatment of Prisoners of War, 6 U.S.T. 3317, signed on 12 August 1949, at Geneva, Article 17.

3 Count One of the Lindh indictment charges him with violating 18 U.S.C. § 2332(b)(2), "Whoever outside the United States attempts to kill, or engages in a conspiracy to kill, a national of the United States shall in the case of a conspiracy by two or more persons to commit a killing that is a murder as defined in section 1111(a) of this title, if one or more of such persons do any overt act to effect the object of the conspiracy, be fined under this title or imprisoned for any term of years or for life, or both so fined and so imprisoned." See United States v. Lindh, 212 F. Supp. 541, 547 (E.D. Va. 2002). Subsection (b)(1) imposes a sentence of twenty years (for attempts). Subsection (c) likewise criminalizes "engag[ing] in physical violence with intent to cause serious bodily injury to a national of the United States; or with the result that serious bodily injury is caused to a national of the United States."

4 Lawful combatants are defined in the Hague Convention (IV) Respecting the Laws and Customs of War on Land, Annex to the Convention, 1 Bevans 631, signed on 18 October 1907 at The Hague, Article 1. The definition requires that combatants "have a fixed distinctive emblem recognizable at a distance." Protocol I Additional to the Geneva Conventions of 1949, 1125 U.N.T.S. 3, adopted on 8 June 1977 at Geneva, Article 44(3), makes an important change in the

Hague Convention, expanding the definition of combatants to include non-uniformed irregulars. However, the United States has not agreed to Protocol I.

5 Interview with Melissa Block, "All Things Considered," 18 January 2002.

6 Both have challenged their detention in federal court, and both have lost. Padilla v. Rumsfeld, 256 F.Supp. 218 (S.D.N.Y. 2003); Hamdi v. Rumsfeld, 337 F.3d 335 (4th Cir. 2003).

7 Gary Solis, "Even a 'Bad Man' Has Rights," *Washington Post*, 25 June 2002, § A, p. 19.

8 Ex parte Quirin, 317 U.S. 1, 31 (1942).

9 Doug Struck et al., "Borderless Network of Terror: Bin Laden Followers Reach across Globe," *Washington Post*, 23 September 2001, § A, p. 1. "'For weeks, agents hit him with a chair and a long piece of wood, forced water into his mouth, and crushed lighted cigarettes into his private parts,' wrote journalists Marites Vitug and Glenda Gloria in 'Under the Crescent Moon,' an acclaimed book on Abu Sayyaf. 'His ribs were almost totally broken and his captors were surprised he survived.'"

10 Rajiv Chandrasakaran and Peter Finn, "U.S. behind Secret Transfer of Terror Suspects," *Washington Post*, 11 March 2002, § A, pp. 1, 15.

11 Dana Priest and Barton Gelman, "U.S. Decries Abuse but Defends Interrogations; 'Stress and Duress' Tactics Used on Terrorism Suspects Held in Secret Overseas Facilities," *Washington Post*, 26 December 2002, § A, p. 1. The same article, however, details American interrogation techniques that are very harsh: prisoners "are held in awkward, painful positions and deprived of sleep with a 24-hour bombardment of lights."

12 Peter Finn, "Europeans Tossing Terror Suspects out the Door," *Washington Post*, 29 January 2002, § A, p. 1; Anthony Shadid, "Fighting Terror/Atmosphere in Europe, Military Campaign / Asylum Bids; in Shift, Sweden Extradites Militants to Egypt," *Boston Globe*, 31 December 2001. On the violation of European human rights law, see Chahal v. United Kingdom, (1997) 23 E.H.R.R. 413.

13 Article 3(1) of the Torture Convention provides, "No State Party shall expel, return ('*refouler*') or extradite a person to another State where there are substantial grounds for believing that he would be in danger of being subjected to torture." Article 2(2) cautions, "No exceptional circumstances whatsoever, whether a state of war or a threat of war, internal political instability or any other public emergency, may be invoked as a justification of torture." But no parallel caution is incorporated into the rule against *refoulement* in Article 3(1), and a lawyer might well argue that its absence implies that the rule may be abrogated during war or similar public emergency. Convention against Torture and Other Cruel, Inhuman or Degrading Treatment or Punishment, 1465 U.N.T.S. 85.

Ratified by the United States, 2 October 1994, entered into force for the United States 20 November 1994. Article VI of the U.S. Constitution provides that treaties are the "supreme Law of the Land."

14 Priest and Gellman, "U.S. Decries Abuse but Defends Interrogations."

15 *Id.*

War, Crisis, and the Constitution

Sotirios A. Barber and James E. Fleming

War is special with us constitutional democrats. It repels us in a way that helps to define us. Reflection on our experience with war also exposes our view of human nature, the nature of the Constitution and of constitutional obligation, the nature of constitutional maintenance, and the most fundamental aim of constitutional reform.

Like most animal life, we fear life-threatening physical violence. Yet with us, unlike with some other members of the kingdom and even the species, fear of such violence tends to be our greatest fear, or so our philosophic forebears believed. Hobbes invited us to join his reflections on the fear of violent death as epistemic of our true sociopolitical selves. These reflections gave birth to our Lockean or secular bourgeois way of life, our "constitution" in the cultural sense.[1] The legal part of America's constitution, accordingly, tries to do things that would amaze an ancient Greek or Roman and that outrage some of today's true religious believers. The Constitution subordinates military to civilian authority (implicitly valuing peace over war and comfort over glory); it forbids establishment of religion and religious tests for office (implicitly trusting those who pursue earthly goods over priests, as such); it lets our governments hang horse thieves while forbidding any punishment whatever for those who turn our youth toward false gods and destroy their otherwise immortal souls.

In the same way that Hobbes and Locke presented the social compact as mere means to peace and security, the Constitution was originally presented as a means to bourgeois ends: the union of the many, as distinguished from — better, as opposed to — the distinction of the few; domestic tranquility and the blessings of liberty, as opposed to the honor of disciplined self-sacrifice and the glory of imperial power. Add the amending provisions of Article V to the ends of the Preamble and view both through the window to a constitution-making past (and to a constitution-making future?) that Article VII provides — do these things and you can see the Constitution's instrumentalist dimension. Reflect further and you can see that this instrumentalist dimension dominates the Constitution's legal dimension, especially when the chips are down. Hobbes knew no logic that could convert an instrumental norm to a moral norm — because we consent to save ourselves, we owe nothing to the sovereign who turns on us to destroy us.[2] Jefferson wrote in the Declaration of Independence that a people has the right to abolish and reconstitute any government "as to them shall seem most likely to effect their Safety and Happiness." Madison wrote in *The Federalist* that "the real welfare of the great body of the people is the supreme object to be pursued," and "no form of Government whatever, has any other value, than as it may be fitted for the attainment of this object."[3] For Madison this included more than the articles of confederation and "perpetual Union" to which the states had once consented; it included also the Union and the plan of the Philadelphia Convention.[4]

"[S]upreme object[s]," then, as more compelling with us than supreme laws? Madison cited the people's welfare to disestablish the old articles of union. The people's safety in time of war rationalized the unconstitutional Sedition Act. In time of civil war Lincoln cited the people's welfare to justify overriding constitutional rights, forms, and limits. The people's safety, as perceived, trumped the constitutional rights of Japanese-Americans in the Second World War. Messrs. Bush, Rumsfeld, and Ashcroft cite the people's safety in time of war to justify overriding constitutional forms, rights, and limits today. And, as in candor it would have admitted, the Rehnquist Court sacrificed its own constitutional principles to political and social order in the election of 2000, an episode of the present Kulturkampf, or culture war, to which Justice Scalia referred in dissent in *Romer v. Evans*[5] and *Lawrence v. Texas*.[6] Indeed, *Bush v. Gore*[7] has proved to be something of an augur of what was to come. Mr. Bush, Florida Republicans, and the Rehnquist Court fabricated a constitutional crisis and then the Rehnquist Court averted the crisis by securing Mr. Bush's victory. Then war and crisis without end became Mr. Bush's chief justifications for overriding constitutional limits and consolidating a rightward realignment of American politics.[8]

These events suggest the following mix of normative and behavioral propositions:

1. Constitutional forms, rights, and limits tend to obtain only under more or less ideal conditions, and war (including culture war) isn't one of them.

2. Constitutional forms, rights, and limits give way (and sometimes ought to give way) to substantive constitutional ends, unless they can be conceived as aspects of substantive constitutional ends (free inquiry, reasonable diversity, and broadly representative legislative assemblies as aspects of the pursuit of real rather than merely apparent public goods, for example, or freedom from religious establishment and free exercise as aspects of the moderate religiosity associated with constitutional democracy).

3. Respect for constitutional forms, rights, and limits entails a substantive policy agenda, an agenda informed by the social conditions under which honoring forms, rights, and limits makes sense or would make sense to reasonable actors. These conditions include peace or reasonable prospects for peace, international security, a generally secular reasonableness in domestic politics, racial and ethnic integration, progress in the arts and sciences, and a general economic well-being.

4. Because there are different kinds of war; because both the presence and the imminence of war can be controversial; because what holds for war can reasonably hold for impending war; because war can be used as an excuse to achieve ends not otherwise achievable — for these reasons at least, constitutional forms are no substitute for a population that generally exhibits and respects a more or less common set of virtues and attitudes that support constitutional forms. To that extent, the Constitution really is not meant for people with fundamentally different views.

5. The field of constitutional theory needs theories of constitutional ends, conditions, and virtues, together with theories of how to promote the requisite ends, conditions, and virtues.

In light of these propositions, let us revisit the Supreme Court's action in *Bush v. Gore*. Thayer and Hand warned that courts cannot save a people from ruin.[9] Many have doubted that courts can avert or resolve constitutional crises. But others have disagreed, contending that courts sometimes can resolve divisive national controversies.[10] Scalia, joined by Chief Justice Rehnquist and Justice Thomas, derided this idea in 1992 when the subject was abortion.[11] They had a change of heart in *Bush v. Gore*.

Conservatives generally had a change of heart about judicial statesmanship in the final days of election 2000. They looked to the Court to avert or resolve what they viewed as the constitutional crisis thrown up by the election controversy. Professor John Yoo proposed that the Court should take a page from *Planned Parenthood v. Casey* and resolve the controversy.[12] In a similar vein, the columnist William Safire urged that the Court "did itself proud" and "saved the Republic" from "much tension."[13] In this section, we will explore whether conservatives can justify *Bush* as an act of judicial statesmanship to spare the nation a constitutional crisis.[14]

Make no mistake: We think the 5-4 decision in *Bush* is both unprincipled and bad.[15] Nevertheless, we do want to distinguish these attributes — *unprincipled* and *bad* — and to show how *Bush* might be thought good (or at least not irredeemably bad) while being unprincipled. We'll leave it as a possibility, moreover, without argument here, that being good and unprincipled is better (more good) than being bad and principled. We'll thus leave it as a possibility that *Bush* was a good decision notwithstanding its unprincipled character. This will be small comfort to most of the conservative scholars who have tried in vain to defend *Bush*. For they can't defend *Bush* as we're suggesting without forfeiting their basic view of both the Constitution and the judiciary's proper role.

Forget any and all attempts to square *Bush* with the provisions of Article II, the text, history, and conventional understanding of the equal protection clause, the familiar normative relationships between legislatures, courts, and constitutions, and second-order rules like deference to state courts on matters of state law.[16] These attempts won't work; indeed, some conservatives have admitted they won't work. Conservatives have tried and failed to square *Bush* with the law. Others will follow, and they too will fail, or so we believe and will assume for purposes of this essay. But if rules and more general norms like maxims and principles can't justify *Bush*, maybe constitutional ends, aspirations, or *goods* can. Maybe the Bush five thought that the Court had to ignore the rules, even its own rules, to spare the country and the Constitution harm greater than the harm that comes from a decision exposing both the impotence and the mythical side of "the rule of law."

As we all know, the rule of law is contingent on circumstances that the law can't guarantee; *Korematsu v. United States*[17] demonstrated that. So did the Great Depression, some say. And so, we add, did the actions of the founder of the Old Republican Party, as opposed to the Reaganized party of

Mr. Bush and the Bush five. Lincoln violated the Constitution to save the Union and the Constitution.[18]

Violate the Constitution to save it? No paradox once you realize that as a practical matter at least (and as a theoretical matter too) fidelity to the Constitution always presupposes material conditions that the Constitution can't guarantee. Lincoln felt that he might lose the war unless he displaced Congress's powers to raise armies and navies, authorize spending, and suspend the writ of habeas corpus. Honoring the Constitution to a "T" and losing the war made no sense because losing the war would have destroyed all of the Constitution, and permanently. Conditions had either redefined constitutional fidelity or put it on the side of those who sought the Constitution's violent destruction. Conditions had installed the imperative of prudential statesmanship for the Constitution's sake over that of honoring the Constitution's terms.

Honoring the Constitution to lose the Constitution made no constitutional sense to Lincoln for another reason: he saw the Constitution as means to ends bigger than itself. In his special message to Congress on 4 July 1861, Lincoln said something that the Reaganized GOP has had a hard time appreciating: that the struggle for the Union is "a struggle for maintaining in the world that form and substance of government whose leading object is to elevate the condition of men; to lift artificial weights from all shoulders; to clear the paths of laudable pursuit for all; to afford all an unfettered start and a fair chance in the race of life. Yielding to partial and temporary departures, from necessity, this is the leading object of the Government for whose existence we contend."[19]

Madison made the same kind of point in *The Federalist* 45 when he accused the states' righters of his day of forgetting that the "real welfare of the great body of the people is the supreme object to be pursued; and that no form of government whatever [!] has any other value, than as it may be fitted for the attainment of this value."[20] Madison said more of the same when justifying the unconstitutional provisions for constitutional change that the Philadelphia Convention had proposed in 1787. "Let [the Convention's critics] declare," wrote Madison, "whether it was of most importance to the happiness of the people of America, that the articles of confederation should be disregarded, and an adequate government be provided, and the Union preserved; or that an adequate government should be omitted, and the articles of confederation preserved. Let them declare, whether the preservation of these articles was the end for securing which a reform of the government was to be introduced as the means; or whether the establishment of a government, adequate to the national happiness, was the end at which these articles themselves originally aimed, and to which they ought, as insufficient means, to have been sacrificed."[21]

Formally, these statements by Lincoln and Madison are but instances of a more abstract proposition: our basic law is an instrument of the good. Our best statesmen disregard it when they have to, because the constitutional rules are means to ends that are attractive independently of the means, and it's irrational, as Madison said, to sacrifice ends to means. The circumstances that Lincoln and Madison faced featured a conflict between ends and means such that following the prescribed means would have defeated the very ends for which the means were ordained as law. Following the basic law in these circumstances (either the Articles or the Constitution) would have been anti-constitutional if not unconstitutional. On these occasions constitutions are silent; fully constitutional conduct is impossible. All one can hope for are pro-constitutional actions or, as we prefer, *constitutionalist* actions[22] — actions that either (as in Lincoln's case) restore the conditions for honoring old means or (as in Madison's case) replace means that can't be fixed with better means to the same old *constitutional* ends.[23] To save *Bush* from rank partisanship one must see the case in this instrumentalist light; an unavoidable resort to unauthorized means to secure authorized ends.

We must add, however, that a constitutionalist justification for *Bush* is ludicrous if a situation approximating Lincoln's is taken as a precondition for such arguments. After the Court's intervention in *Bush*, Adam Nagourney and David Barstow detailed in the *New York Times* what many commentators believed during the election controversy: the Republicans would do what they had to do to win Florida — whatever they had to do.[24] That included a resumption of the state legislature's power to name the electors should a count of the ballots have put Gore ahead. The Bush five made clear in their "per curiam" opinion that they read the Constitution as permitting a legislature to reclaim the electoral power at any time.[25] Two competing sets of electors would have left the election to the conscience of the Republicans in Congress, and on any plausible scenario that guaranteed a victory by Bush. The problem with this strategy was of course less legal than political: the political risks included no less than the destruction of the Reaganized

GOP. A party fully prepared to reject the voters' voice for the sake of partisan success must be driven by more than mere partisanship—like an anti-democratic religiosity,[26] an anti-democratic racism,[27] an anti-democratic social Darwinism,[28] or all three combined. The Republicans' thirst for victory thus threatened to destroy the very image of reasonable conservatism so skillfully and assiduously cultivated by their presidential candidate. No one can say what the public's reaction would have been, but action by Republican legislators that would have removed all doubt about their party's extremism could have destroyed the GOP nationally and endangered its allies. These allies included not only the Rehnquist Court, which would have been called upon to approve the actions of the Florida Republicans, but also the Constitution, which can be interpreted to sanction what the Florida Republicans seemed determined to do.[29]

It's far from clear that the *Bush* five could have saved the Republicans from themselves and the Constitution from the Republicans by any action other than the one taken: stopping the count. This action did more than insure Mr. Bush's presidency, though the five doubtlessly saw that as a plus. It also spared the nation a constitutional crisis that the Republicans seemed determined to risk. A victim of that crisis might well have been the public's understanding of itself as part of an entity that can establish, structure, staff, orient, and limit a government by rules instrumental to its well-being. Because that understanding is inseparable from the Court's own reputation as a principled institution, as the joint opinion of Justices O'Connor, Kennedy, and Souter observed in *Planned Parenthood v. Casey*,[30] the Bush five hurt the country to some extent by their unprincipled act. But the damage to Court and country could have been much greater. The Court as an institution is bigger than any five or any nine, and its legitimacy can survive their mistakes, to some extent. But the Court's legitimacy is less able to survive clear *constitutional* mistakes of any consequence, because the Court's legitimacy is predicated on the Constitution's legitimacy. A constitution that would have permitted a group of state legislators to overrule both the voters of Florida and the nation's electorate would doubtless have forfeited much of the community's esteem. And the public's inability to correct that constitutional mistake (the right wing of the Republican Party is more than strong enough nationally to block a constitutional amendment) would surely have damaged the public's own constitutionalist pretensions even more than the decision in *Bush*.

So here we are: Constitution betrayed, but betrayed ostensibly for its own good and not in a way that most Americans couldn't help noticing. "[T]he prejudices of the community [are still] on [the Constitution's] side," a good thing, said Madison.[31] The Court did take what Professor Yoo called an affordable "short-term hit to [its] legitimacy"[32] among the cognoscenti, who had little regard for this Court anyway. But the nation is okay. Happy or at least content with its formal constitution. And that has to count for something. Doesn't it? Who is willing to defend fidelity to the Constitution at the price of chaos? Al Gore wasn't; he went away quietly enough, as everyone expected him to, despite Bush's charge during the controversy that it was Gore who would do anything to win.

A colleague of one of us, Professor Gerard V. Bradley of the Notre Dame Law School, shares our kind of theory of how to justify the actions of the Bush five. He says that even if the five were wrong about the "bloodletting" to come after the count, they acted rightly in trying to stop it before it began.[33] Why not credit them with "an act of political courage[?]" he asks.[34] "[T]hey consciously redirected incoming fire towards the one institution that *everyone* said could take the heat[.] The Court threw itself on Florida's grenade."[35] Heroism enough, to be sure, yet heroism made even "*greater*" because a unanimous court was "unavailable" to the five.[36] Bradley doesn't mention Lincoln, but he might have cited him as another Republican who violated the Constitution to save it and the country. If Lincoln's actions were *constitutionalist*, though not strictly *constitutional*, can the same be said for our heroic five?

Maybe, but not just yet. Consider one more complication. Lincoln violated the Constitution (1) trying to destroy its enemies and (2) in the service of its ends.[37] For Lincoln, securing the conditions of constitutional government meant securing the conditions for the rule of the Constitution's friends, not for the rule of those willing to put the Constitution at risk. On our theory of *Bush*, the five violated the Constitution to save it from harm, if not simply to save it from destruction, as Lincoln did. But Lincoln defeated the grenade throwers and the five didn't even try. (Indeed, Scalia strained, both in his concurring opinion concerning the stay[38] and in the subsequent oral argument,[39] to make sure that the grenades thrown by Bush's lawyer Theodore Olson did not miss their mark.) They avoided what Bradley calls "bleeding" and "institutional meltdown"[40] by giving the grenade throwers what they wouldn't be denied. The party that threatened institutional meltdown won *because* it threatened institutional meltdown. It held the Constitution hostage to its ambitions for the country, and the five paid the ransom. By contrast, Lincoln's actions were constitutionalist if not constitutional because he sought to restore the conditions of constitutional government, conditions favorable to rule by those who would be the last to throw grenades.

Lincoln's actions were constitutionalist also because he acted in the service of constitutional ends, like union and equal opportunity. The *Bush* five can claim to have acted for a constitutional end: domestic tranquility. Had Bush been elected by Congress after Gore prevailed in the Florida recount that would surely have jeopardized domestic tranquility, or so one could reasonably have believed, rendering constitutional means inadequate to constitutional ends, and justifying a constitutionalist act to secure a constitutional end. (Safire could have had this in mind in arguing that the Court "did itself proud" and "saved the Republic" from "much tension" instead of allowing the constitutionally prescribed procedures to take their course at great harm to the country, with the end result that "we would have ended up exactly where we are today: with President-elect Bush.")[41] One problem for constitutional conservatives will be how to abandon a jurisprudence that until now has emphasized institutional norms (like states' rights, deference to the political process, and judicial restraint, to say nothing of separation of powers) and "negative liberties," *not* substantive ends or goods. *Bush* made sensible as a constitutionalist decision is wholly at odds with the negative liberties model of the Constitution long favored by free marketeers and formally adopted by the Rehnquist Court in *DeShaney*.[42] For a constitutionalist justification presupposes a constitution that promotes substantive goods in addition to protecting negative liberties. Constitutional conservatives will have problems justifying a jurisprudence that recognizes one or two constitutional ends — adding domestic tranquility to their negative liberty, in lieu of the framers' positive liberty and the Preamble's promise of liberty's "blessings"[43] — but not other positive goods, like a more perfect union and the general welfare. If theoretical consistency were a force in political events, defending *Bush v. Gore* would move the American right wing away from the constitutionalism of Reagan and back to the constitutionalism of Lincoln.

Though we have few illusions about the political influence of intellectual goods like theoretical consistency, we note (albeit with mixed feelings) the somewhat Lincolnesque opinion of the U.S. Court of Appeals for the Fourth Circuit in *Hamdi v. Rumsfeld*.[44] In the week following the events of September 11, 2001, Congress authorized the president "to use all necessary and appropriate force" against nations, organizations, and persons that planned or aided terrorist acts, *as the president determines*.[45] Pursuant to this act, the United States declared two American citizens "enemy combatants" to be held and interrogated indefinitely without formal charges, legal counsel, or visitors. One such "enemy combatant," Yaser Esam Hamdi, was, in the court's words, "seized in Afghanistan during . . . active military hostilities" that followed the American invasion in early October 2001. Hamdi was brought to the states, declared an "enemy combatant," and held without formal charges, counsel, or visitors in the Navy brig at Norfolk, Virginia.

In affirming the government's power to hold Hamdi in isolation and without formal charges, a unanimous three-judge panel led by Chief Judge J. Harvey Wilkinson emphasized the practical difficulties that courts face in trying to second-guess the decisions of field commanders on distant battlefields. But Wilkinson and his colleagues were not saying that constitutional rights must sometimes yield to the demands of war. They offered "a more profound understanding of our rights" than that implicit in the conventional dichotomy between individual rights and governmental powers. "For the judicial branch to trespass upon the exercise of the warmaking powers," they said, "would be an infringement of the right to self-determination and self-governance at a time when the care of the common defense is most critical. This right of the people is no less a right because it is possessed collectively."[46]

Here the court recognizes a right of the people to act through their government in pursuit of a good, national security, that helps them make sense of the original act of establishing that government and vesting it with warmaking powers. By deferring to those charged with using those powers, the court presents itself as letting the Constitution speak, not silencing it. Thus conceived, the Constitution is first and foremost a charter of ends, goods, or, if you will, benefits. It is more than a charter of negative rights against government. It is also a charter of at least one benefit, national security. And, we would ask, if the Constitution is a charter of the ends that help make sense of some of its granted powers, why not also ends that help make sense of the rest of its powers, ends like the people's welfare and racial justice?[47]

For originalists alarmed by such a prospect, we have cited good authority — Madison in *The Federalist* 40 and 45 — to the effect that justice and the people's welfare, not things like states' rights, are the real ends of government. To concerned civil libertarians, we would ask whether liberties against government are not more secure if conceived not as dichotomous with powers and associated ends, but as elements of them. How, for example, can anyone be sure either that national security is the chief motive of, say, the Iraq War or that the Iraq War has enhanced the nation's security — how can the nation be sure of these things without extensive and robust freedoms to know and criticize the government's actions? How secure can these freedoms be if government has the unreviewable right to detain citizens in isolation simply by declaring them enemy combatants? And of liberals who fear that in present-day America a positive constitutionalism is more likely than not to serve a combination of social Darwinist and imperialist ends, we would ask whether that result is less likely if the Fourth Circuit, described recently as a "bold and muscular" intellectual citadel of the American right — "the shrewdest, most aggressively conservative federal appeals court in the nation" and "the appellate court closest in thinking to the Rehnquist Court"[48] — is left to define the substantive constitution without challenge from the other side. (In this connection, we point to our arguments elsewhere that an honest quest for the substantive constitution, whether conceived in originalist terms or not, clearly favors the American left over the American right.)[49]

Whether the opinion in *Hamdi* is a straw in the wind remains to be seen. In the meantime, however, we see no movement from the negative constitutionalism of *DeShaney* in the writings of Chief Justice Rehnquist. In his book *All the Laws But One: Civil Liberties in Wartime*,[50] Rehnquist approves Lincoln's famous formulation: that if he had not suspended the writ of habeas corpus during the Civil War, that would have meant allowing "all the laws, but one, to go unexecuted, and the government itself to go to pieces, lest that one be violated." More generally, Rehnquist practically embraces the idea — *inter arma silent leges* — that during war the laws (and the Constitution) are silent.

In an essay in the *New York Times*, Adam Cohen ponders the implications of Rehnquist's book for the Bush administration's restrictions on civil liberties in the current war on terrorism.[51] He bemoans that Rehnquist quotes, with approval, not only Lincoln but also Francis Biddle, President Franklin Roosevelt's attorney general, who said: "The Constitution has not greatly

bothered any wartime president." Cohen continues, "[T]he most disturbing aspect of Rehnquist's book is the lack of outrage, or even disappoint-
ment, he evinces when rights are sacrificed."

Rehnquist lacks outrage because although he gets the title of his book
from Lincoln, he does not get his jurisprudence or attitudes from Lincoln.
For Rehnquist, when constitutional forms, rights, and limits are suspended,
indeed the laws are silent and everything is permitted to the executive.
Rehnquist fails to see or to subscribe to Lincoln's positive constitutionalism: he fails to see, as Lincoln saw, that when the Constitution is suspended,
the executive has restorative obligations, affirmative obligations to work
actively toward restoring conditions in which the Constitution can function
as law. These affirmative obligations include the pursuit of domestic policies
that would restore respect for constitutional forms, rights, and limits. As
argued above, Lincoln violated the Constitution to save the Union and the
Constitution, and he did so without paradox because fidelity to the Constitution always presupposes material conditions that the Constitution cannot
guarantee. Again, honoring the Constitution to lose the Constitution made
no constitutional sense to Lincoln for another reason: with Madison, he
saw the Constitution as means to ends bigger than itself. His special message to Congress on 4 July 1861, quoted above, bears quoting again: the
struggle for the Union "is a struggle for maintaining in the world that form
and substance of government whose leading object is to elevate the condition of men; to lift artificial weights from all shoulders; to clear the paths of
laudable pursuit for all; to afford all an unfettered start and a fair chance
in the race of life. Yielding to partial and temporary departures, from necessity, this is the leading object of the Government for whose existence we
contend."

In sum, war is epistemic. It revealed to Hobbes and Locke the nature of
man and the purpose of political life. It reveals to us the nature of the
Constitution and what it means to maintain it. War is conventionally seen as
testing the limits of constitutionalism, the point at which we compromise
or even abandon constitutional forms and rights. But war reminds us of the
Preamble's promise of a good thing: the common defense. This good is
good because it anticipates the peaceful state where we enjoy other pream-
bulary goods like domestic tranquility and the blessings of liberty, justly
distributed and justly secured. Instead of saying that victory in war com-

petes with constitutional forms and rights, we might consider peace a pre-requisite of honoring forms and enjoying rights.

Peace is a provision of power. It is adumbrated by authorizations or "powers" to declare war, raise armies and navies, and so forth. Power and its positive provisions are thus prerequisite to following institutional norms and honoring negative liberties. And the relationship holds for other institutional norms and negative liberties: no market or property, for example, without governmental provisions like a monetary system, laws defining and securing property, civil and criminal courts whose judgments are executed by force if need be, and, in the end, the active cultivation, typically through public schools, of the skills and values on which a culture of property depends. The general point is made in the first *Federalist*: no government, no liberty; they're on the same side.[52] Lincoln repeats the message three score and fourteen years later. See peace (a provision of power like the power to wage war) as prerequisite to forms and liberties and you:

> Restore the Constitution to coherence; Preserve the positive Constitution of the Preamble and the ratification campaign; Carry forward to the present the root idea of the Declaration of Independence and *The Federalist* 1 that constitution making, not fidelity, is at the heart of the constitutionalist persuasion; Expose the positive side of the oath to preserve and defend, for one can do neither without securing peace and what *The Federalist* 45 calls the "welfare of the great body of the people."

War thus reveals the essentially *positive* nature of the Constitution and the overriding *positive duty* of those who take the oath to preserve and defend it. Lincoln is the exemplar of this view: His duty was to restore the conditions for honoring constitutional forms and constitutional rights. Though he sacrificed both to the war effort, they remained normative for him because the war sought to restore the conditions for honoring them. Lincoln also saw the need to perpetuate not just our institutions but the virtues on which they depend—including the virtues of leadership and citizenship on those occasions when fidelity to institutions defeats the very purposes for which they were instituted.

The Constitution's greatest failing is the neglect of these virtues. Along with no clear constitutional commitment to self-consciously educative institutions—like the public schools—we find a constitutional reliance on private incentives in government and in civil society. This reliance leads either to demoting public purposes to derivatives of private ends or denying them altogether. Bereft of public purposes that would engage a liberal public-spiritedness and sense of community, the field is left to anti-liberals who would compromise the secular public-reasonableness of a liberal order. The true heirs of Lincoln must awaken to several facts and act accordingly: the culture war is real, it demands personal risks, and the Constitution is on their side.

NOTES

We presented portions of this essay in meetings of the Georgetown University Law Center/Maryland Discussion Group on Constitutional Law and are grateful to participants in those sessions for valuable discussion. In addition, we received helpful comments from Daniel Farber, Thomas Lee, Linda McClain, Walter F. Murphy, and Mark Tushnet and valuable research assistance from Carrie Tendler.

1 For the notion of a constitution as a way of life, as distinguished from a constitutional text, see Walter F. Murphy, James E. Fleming, Sotirios A. Barber, and Stephen Macedo, *American Constitutional Interpretation* (3d ed. 2003), 1.

2 Thomas Hobbes, *Leviathan* II, chaps. 14, 21 (1651).

3 The Federalist No. 45, at 309 (James Madison) (Jacob E. Cooke ed., 1961).

4 The Federalist Nos. 40, 45 (James Madison).

5 517 U.S. 620, 636 (1996) (Scalia, J., dissenting).

6 123 S. Ct. 2472, 2497 (2003) (Scalia, J., dissenting).

7 531 U.S. 98 (2000).

8 See, for example, Francis X. Clines, "Karl Rove's Campaign Strategy Seems Evident: It's the Terror, Stupid," *New York Times*, 10 May 2003, § A, p. 20; Todd S. Purdum, "Crises, Crises Everywhere, What Is a President to Do?," *New York Times*, 9 February 2003, § 4, p. 1; Carl Hulse, "War Dividend: Looking for Domestic Gains from the Success Abroad," *New York Times*, 13 April 2003, § 4, p. 3.

9 See, for example, James B. Thayer, "The Origin and Scope of the American Doctrine of Constitutional Law," 7 *Harvard Law Review* 129, 156 (1893); Learned Hand, "The Spirit of Liberty," in *The Spirit of Liberty* (Irving Dilliard ed., 3d ed., 1960), 189, 190.

10 In Planned Parenthood v. Casey, 505 U.S. 833 (1992), the joint opinion of Justices O'Connor, Kennedy, and Souter made such claims for the Supreme Court.

11 Scalia, joined by Rehnquist and Thomas, partially dissented in Planned Parent-

hood v. Casey, 505 U.S. 833, 979 (1992), invoking the specter of Dred Scott v. Sandford, 60 U.S. (19 How.) 393 (1857). He argued that the joint opinion in *Casey*, like Taney's majority opinion in *Dred Scott*, displayed the hubris of its authors' belief that the Supreme Court could resolve divisive national controversies with legitimacy.

12 John Yoo, "The Right Moment for Judicial Power," *New York Times*, 25 November 2000, § A, p. 19; David G. Savage and Henry Weinstein, "Supreme Court Ruling: Right or Wrong?," *Los Angeles Times*, 21 December 2000, § A, p. 24 (quoting John Yoo, who draws a parallel between *Bush* and the abortion decisions of the Supreme Court).

13 William Safire, "The Coming Together," *New York Times*, 14 December 2000, § A, p. 39.

14 For the purposes of this essay, we put aside the question of the legitimacy and appropriateness of such prudential judicial statesmanship in a constitutional democracy committed to a constitution of principle.

15 We agree with Ronald Dworkin's arguments that the decision is deeply troubling for those who are committed to a constitution of principle. See Ronald Dworkin, "A Badly Flawed Election," *New York Review of Books*, 11 January 2001, 53. Furthermore, we want to make clear that we do not blush at the mention of arguments that Bush's ascension to power was a coup d'état, see, for example, Bruce Ackerman, "Anatomy of a Constitutional Coup," *London Review of Books*, 8 February 2001, 3, and that the *Bush* five are disgraceful partisans. In fact, one of us has signed, and the other endorses, the law professors' statement that "By Stopping the Vote Count in Florida, the U.S. Supreme Court Used Its Power to Act as Political Partisans, not Judges of a Court of Law," New York Times, 13 January 2001, § A, p. 7. For the stronger claim that the Bush five "committed one of the biggest and most serious crimes this nation has ever seen — pure and simple, the theft of the presidency," see Vincent Bugliosi, "None Dare Call It Treason," *Nation*, 5 February 2001, 11, 14. For an argument that the Senate should not confirm any candidates whom Bush nominates to the Supreme Court, see Bruce Ackerman, "The Court Packs Itself," *American Prospect*, 12 February 2001, 48.

16 The vast literature on the presidential election controversy includes Bruce Ackerman, ed., *Bush v. Gore: The Question of Legitimacy* (2002); Ronald Dworkin, ed., *A Badly Flawed Election: Debating Bush v. Gore* (2002); Howard Gillman, *The Votes That Counted: How the Court Decided the 2000 Presidential Election* (2001); Abner S. Greene, *Understanding the 2000 Election: A Guide to the Legal Battle That Decided the Presidency* (2001); Richard A. Posner, *Breaking the Deadlock: The 2000 Election, the Constitution, and the Courts* (2001); and Cass R. Sunstein and Richard A. Epstein, eds., *The Vote: Bush, Gore, and the Supreme Court* (2001).

17 323 U.S. 214 (1944).

18 For a recent historical examination of Lincoln's constitutional jurisprudence, see Daniel Farber, *Lincoln's Constitution* (2003).

19 *Abraham Lincoln: His Speeches and Writings* (Roy P. Basler ed., 1946), 607.

20 The Federalist No. 45, at 309 (James Madison).

21 The Federalist No. 40, at 260 (James Madison).

22 See Sotirios A. Barber, *On What the Constitution Means* (1984); John E. Finn, *Constitutions in Crisis: Political Violence and the Rule of Law* (1991).

23 We venture a typological hypothesis or distinction here for purposes of discussion. Lincoln is a case of constitutional *maintenance*: restore conditions for honoring old means to old ends. Madison is a case of constitutional *reform*: replace failed means with effective means to old ends.

24 Adam Nagourney and David Barstow, "G.O.P.'s Depth Outdid Gore's Team in Florida," *New York Times*, 22 December 2000, § A, p. 1. See also Bob Herbert, "To Any Lengths," *New York Times*, 11 December 2000, § A, p. 31.

25 Bush v. Gore, 531 U.S. 98, 102–4 (2000).

26 See, for example, the symposium "The End of Democracy? The Judicial Usurpation of Politics," *First Things*, November 1996, 18.

27 See, for example, the complaint filed in NAACP v. Harris (10 January 2001), available at http://www.the-rule-of-law.com.

28 See, for example, Stephen E. Gottlieb, *Morality Imposed: The Rehnquist Court and Liberty in America* (2000) (analyzing the jurisprudence of Rehnquist, Scalia, and Thomas in terms of social Darwinism).

29 We do not believe that the Constitution *rightly* interpreted would sanction what the Florida Republicans seemed determined to do; we mean only that the Constitution *can* be so interpreted.

30 505 U.S. 833, 841 (1992).

31 The Federalist No. 49, at 340 (James Madison).

32 Savage and Weinstein, "Supreme Court Ruling" (quoting John Yoo).

33 Gerard V. Bradley, "Bush v. Gore: A Case in Conservative Judicial Activism?," 16 *World and I*, 1 June 2001, 292.

34 *Id.*

35 *Id.*

36 *Id.* (italics in original).

37 Furthermore, we should bear in mind the distinction between, on the one hand, an executive like Lincoln acting outside the Constitution in order to save it and, on the other, a court doing so. Lincoln not only had broader authority to act but also faced greater accountability for his actions.

38 We refer, in particular, to Scalia's statement concurring in the 5–4 decision to stay the Florida hand count: "The counting of votes that are of questionable

legality does in my view threaten irreparable harm to [Bush], and to the country, by casting a cloud upon what he claims to be the legitimacy of his election." Bush v. Gore, 531 U.S. 1046, 1047 (2000) (Scalia, J., concurring).

39 See Maureen Dowd, "The Bloom Is off the Robe," *New York Times*, 13 December 2000, § A, p. 35 (mocking Scalia's questions of Theodore Olson in the oral argument by saying, "Come on, Ted, do I have to plead your case for Bush as well as hear it?").

40 Bradley, "Bush v. Gore."

41 Safire, "The Coming Together."

42 DeShaney v. Winnebago County Dept. of Social Services, 489 U.S. 189 (1989).

43 See Sotirios A. Barber, *Welfare and the Constitution* (2003); Sotirios A. Barber, "Welfare and the Instrumental Constitution," 42 *American Journal of Jurisprudence* 159 (1997).

44 316 F. 3d 450 (4th Cir. 2003), rehearing and rehearing en banc denied, 337 F. 3d 335 (4th Cir. 2003).

45 Public Law 107-40, 18 September 2001.

46 *Hamdi*, 316 F.3d at 463.

47 Elsewhere, one of us develops a positive benefits conceptions of the Constitution. See Barber, *Welfare and the Constitution*.

48 Deborah Sontag, "The Power of the Fourth," *New York Times Magazine*, 9 March 2003, 40.

49 See Sotirios A. Barber, *The Constitution of Judicial Power* (1993); James E. Fleming, "Constructing the Substantive Constitution," 72 *Texas Law Review* 211 (1993); James E. Fleming, "Securing Deliberative Autonomy," 48 *Stanford Law Review* 1 (1995); James E. Fleming, *Securing Constitutional Democracy* (forthcoming 2005).

50 William H. Rehnquist, *All the Laws but One: Civil Liberties in Wartime* (1998).

51 "Chief Justice Rehnquist's Ominous History of Wartime Freedom," *New York Times*, 22 September 2002, § 4, p. 12. Adam Cohen also published an insightful essay on Rehnquist's more recent book, *Centennial Crisis: The Disputed Election of 1876* (2004). Adam Cohen, "Justice Rehnquist Writes on Hayes v. Tilden, with His Mind on Bush v. Gore," *New York Times*, 21 March 2004, § 4, p. 10. Cohen writes: "[E]ven readers keenly interested in history may have trouble seeing [Rehnquist's book] as anything but an allegory, and apologia, for the Supreme Court's ruling in Bush v. Gore."

52. The Federalist No. 1 (Alexander Hamilton).

Afterword
The Supreme Court's 2004 Decisions

———◆◆◆———

Mark Tushnet

On 28 June 2004, after the contributors to this book had completed their final revisions, the Supreme Court issued its decisions in three cases discussed in several of the chapters. I summarize the Court's opinions here, focusing on issues identified in the book.

Rasul v. Bush involved people detained as "unlawful combatants" at the U.S. military base in Guantánamo, Cuba. They filed suit in a federal court in Washington, alleging that they were being held in violation of the U.S. Constitution, treaties to which the United States was a party, and federal statutes. The issue before the Supreme Court was whether there was *some* federal court in which they could raise their claims. By a vote of 6–3, the Court held that there was — indeed, that they could present their claims to *any* federal trial court. Much of the Court's analysis, in an opinion by Justice John Paul Stevens, dealt with technical issues about the meaning of the federal statutes that the detainees had invoked. The Court concluded that lawsuits could be filed challenging detentions in Guantánamo, an area where, by treaty with Cuba, the United States exercised "complete jurisdiction and control" even though it did not have "ultimate sovereignty."

The procedural posture of the case did not require the Court to decide whether the detainees were being held lawfully or in violation of law. The Court's conclusion was that the federal courts had jurisdiction "to determine the legality of the Executive's potentially indefinite detention of individuals who claim to be wholly innocent of wrongdoing." As a purely technical matter, it remained open, under the Court's opinion, for the lower courts to hold that such detentions, even of "wholly innocent" people, were in fact constitutional. As a footnote indicated, though, allegations by the detainees that they had been held for an extended period "without access to counsel and without being charged with any wrongdoing" even though they had not engaged "in combat or acts of terrorism" did have constitutional implications. This footnote and the tenor of the Court's other decisions issued on the same day do suggest that each detainee had the right to show that he *was* in fact "wholly innocent," and that were he to convince some neutral decision maker (a judge, probably, at least pending the creation of some sort of system within the U.S. military to hear the detainees' cases), he would be entitled to release.

The Court's second case involved Jose Padilla, a U.S. citizen detained as an unlawful combatant primarily for purposes of interrogating him about plots to engage in terrorism in the United States. Two days after Padilla had been transferred from New York to a detention center in South Carolina, Padilla's lawyer filed suit in a federal court in New York, where Padilla had been held. Chief Justice William Rehnquist wrote the Court's opinion for a five-justice majority. Without addressing the merits of Padilla's claims, the Court held that the suit had been filed in the wrong place. Again the decision turned on the wording of the applicable federal statutes, and did not directly address any larger issues.

Justice Stevens's dissent, though, did. He wrote:

> At stake in this case is nothing less than the essence of a free society. Even more important than the method of selecting the people's rulers and their successors is the character of the constraints imposed on the Executive by the rule of law. Unconstrained Executive detention for the purpose of investigating and preventing subversive activity is the hallmark of the Star Chamber. Access to counsel for the purpose of protecting the citizen from official mistakes and mistreatment is the hallmark of due process.
>
> Executive detention of subversive citizens, like detention of enemy soldiers to keep them off the battlefield, may sometimes be justified to prevent persons from launching or becoming missiles of destruction. It may not, however, be justified by the naked interest in using unlawful procedures to extract information. Incommunicado detention for months on end is such a procedure. Whether the information so procured is more or less reliable than that acquired by more extreme forms of

torture is of no consequence. For if this Nation is to remain true to the ideals symbolized by its flag, it must not wield the tools of tyrants even to resist an assault by the forces of tyranny.

In addition, the third of the Court's detention decisions contained language lending support to Padilla's claim that he should be charged with a federal crime or released from detention, in part because the decision was carefully limited to citizen-detainees who were captured in Afghanistan.

That third decision dealt with the detention of Yaser Hamdi, a U.S. citizen who had been turned over to U.S. forces in Afghanistan by soldiers of the Northern Alliance who were assisting U.S. forces in the war against the Taliban. According to a declaration filed in Hamdi's case, the Northern Alliance soldiers told U.S. personnel that Hamdi had surrendered and turned over his rifle along with a group of Taliban fighters. Hamdi never had a chance to contest the allegations in this declaration, though.

The Supreme Court addressed several issues in Hamdi's case. Hamdi claimed that his detention violated a federal statute enacted in 1971 to avoid a repetition of the Japanese internment, during which — as Congress saw it — the military had set up the internment program without Congress's permission. The statute says that "[n]o citizen shall be imprisoned or otherwise detained by the United States except pursuant to an Act of Congress." The government claimed that there *was* an act of Congress authorizing Hamdi's detention, the congressional resolution adopted on 18 September 2001 authorizing the use of military force "against those nations, organizations, or persons" who "planned, authorized, committed or aided the terrorist attacks" of September 11, or "harbored such organizations or persons, in order to prevent any future acts of international terrorism against the United States by such nations, organizations or persons." The government also claimed that the president had inherent authority as commander in chief to detain Hamdi, but a majority of the Court found it unnecessary to decide whether that claim was correct.

Four justices, in an opinion written by Justice Sandra Day O'Connor, held that the use-of-force resolution was a clear enough authorization to satisfy the requirements of the statute enacted in 1971. These justices therefore did not have to address the broad claim of an inherent presidential power to detain enemy combatants. Justice O'Connor's opinion was narrowly written, and it was not entirely clear *what* had been authorized. She emphasized that the resolution authorized detention of a "narrow category" of enemy combatants "who fought against the United States in Afghanistan as part of the Taliban." The opinion noted some uncertainty about the scope of the government's definition of "enemy combatants," but found it unnecessary to resolve the ambiguity. Justice O'Connor described the detention of those taken captive while fighting against U.S. armed forces "for the duration of the particular conflict in which they were captured" as "so fundamental and accepted an incident to war as to be an exercise of the 'necessary and appropriate force' Congress authorized the President to use." Hamdi argued that Congress had not authorized "indefinite or perpetual detention," something that he said was a real possibility given the government's characterization of the "war on terrorism." Justice O'Connor sidestepped that objection by noting that as of 2004, there were still "[a]ctive combat operations against Taliban fighters . . . in Afghanistan."

Justice O'Connor's opinion emphasized, though, that Congress authorized detention to ensure that the captive did not return to the battlefield, and specifically observed that "indefinite detention for purposes of interrogation" was not authorized by the use-of-force resolution — an observation with some implications for Padilla's case. Yet Justice O'Connor's unwillingness to address directly the president's claim that he had inherent authority to detain enemy combatants means that it remains open for the government to seek to justify the detention for purposes of interrogating Jose Padilla, a person seized in the United States, not Afghanistan. Again, the tenor of the various opinions suggests that a majority is prepared to rule against such an assertion of authority, but the decisions, read narrowly, do not require that Padilla be released.

Justice Clarence Thomas agreed that the president had the authority to detain Hamdi, although he stressed the president's inherent powers more than he did the scope of the use of force resolution. Four justices, though, dissented from the treatment of the use of force resolution. Justice David Souter, joined by Justice Ruth Bader Ginsburg, argued that the use of force resolution should not be read to authorize Hamdi's detention. The resolution's focus, according to Justice Souter, was "on the use of military power," authorizing "the use of armies and weapons." But it did not use the word "detention" or anything like it. The background of the 1971 statute, he wrote, indicated Congress's belief that only language much more specific than that contained in the use of force resolution could authorize the detention of U.S. citizens.

Justice Souter briefly addressed the government's claim that the president had the power as commander in chief to detain Hamdi independent of the statute, which, he said, the government "hint[ed]" might be unconstitutional were it read to prohibit detentions that the president thought justified by military considerations. He wrote that any presidential authority would have to exist in the face of a congressional statute purporting to limit the president's power to detain: in that situation, he reminded readers, Justice Robert Jackson's famous opinion in the *Steel Seizure Case* said that the president's power was "at its lowest ebb."

Justice Antonin Scalia also disagreed with Justice O'Connor's analysis, in an opinion that Justice Stevens joined. He argued that the Constitution gave the government two, and only two, choices: suspend the writ of habeas corpus, or charge Hamdi with treason or some other crime. Habeas corpus was designed to address the "very core of liberty secured" by the separation of powers, "freedom from indefinite imprisonment at the will of the Executive." And, he continued, treason prosecutions were the specific procedure, named in the Constitution, for dealing with citizens who were accused of aiding an enemy during wartime. If prosecution was "impracticable," the Constitution allowed Congress to suspend the writ of habeas corpus "for brief periods."

The four justices who would have found Hamdi's detention unauthorized by statute or by the Constitution did not need to deal with Hamdi's additional claims, but Justice O'Connor did. Her opinion went on to discuss whether Hamdi was entitled to due process of law, beyond what he had received, to determine whether his continued detention was justified. (Justices Souter and Ginsburg indicated agreement with this part of Justice O'Connor's opinion simply to get a resolution of the case on terms as close to the ones they preferred as they could.) As a general matter, due process requires hearings at which a person in Hamdi's position has an opportunity to present his case in a meaningful way. But the precise requirements vary with the circumstances.

Justice O'Connor applied a balancing approach, drawn from earlier cases, to determine what those requirements were. She agreed with the government that courts might misjudge the extent to which extensive procedural requirements could interfere with military decision making, and she agreed with Hamdi on the need for some sort of hearing to ensure that "the Executive's asserted justifications for [his] detention have basis in fact and warrant in law." In an attempt to strike a balance, she began with the observation that Hamdi's interest in freedom was "the most elemental of liberty interests," and continued by noting that "history and common sense teach us that an unchecked system of detention carries the potential to become a means for oppression and abuse of others who do not present [an immediate] threat [to national security during an ongoing conflict]." On the other side was the government interest "in ensuring that those who have in fact fought with the enemy during a war do not return to battle against the United States." The courts' role, according to Justice O'Connor, was not as "heavily circumscribed" as the government had claimed. Relying on the *Steel Seizure Case*, she noted that "a state of war is not a blank check for the President when it comes to the rights of the Nation's citizens."

Taking these considerations into account, Justice O'Connor wrote that "a citizen-detainee seeking to challenge his classification as an enemy combatant must receive notice of the factual basis for his classification, and a fair opportunity to rebut the Government's factual assertions before a neutral decisionmaker." But, she continued, hearsay — evidence given by one person that another person recounted some facts — "may need to be accepted as the most reliable available evidence." And the neutral decision maker could use a presumption favoring the government's evidence: if the government provided "credible evidence" that the detainee was an enemy combatant, the detainee could be required "to rebut that evidence with more persuasive evidence." She suggested that the neutral decision maker might be "an appropriately authorized and properly constituted military tribunal," but said that screening processes applied in the field were insufficient. Because no such tribunals existed yet, Hamdi could return to the trial court to attempt to rebut the government's factual presentation. Justice O'Connor cautioned that the judge should "proceed with caution" and engage "in a factfinding process that is both prudent and incremental." Finally, without addressing Hamdi's claim that he should have been given a lawyer much earlier, Justice O'Connor observed that Hamdi now had a lawyer and "the right to access to counsel in connection with" future proceedings.

About the Contributors

Sotirios A. Barber is a professor of government at the University of Notre Dame. His most recent book is *Welfare and the Constitution* (Princeton University Press 2003).

Mark E. Brandon is a professor of law at Vanderbilt University Law School.

James E. Fleming is a professor of law at Fordham University School of Law. He has written many articles in constitutional theory and is working on a book entitled *Securing Constitutional Democracy*.

Mark A. Graber is a professor of government and adjunct professor of law at the University of Maryland.

Samuel Issacharoff is the Harold R. Medina Professor in Procedural Jurisprudence at Columbia University Law School.

David Luban is the Frederick J. Haas Professor of Law and Philosophy at Georgetown University Law Center. He is currently writing on issues of national security, international criminal law, and moral responsibility in complex institutions.

Richard H. Pildes is the An-Bryce Professor of Law and a co-director of the Program on Law and Security at New York University School of Law. He is a co-author of the casebook *The Law of Democracy* (Foundation Press 2d ed. 2002) and the author of numerous articles on the relationship of constitutional law and democracy.

Eric A. Posner is the Kirkland and Ellis Professor of Law at the University of Chicago.

Peter J. Spiro is the dean and Virginia Rusk Professor of International Law at the University of Georgia Law School.

William Michael Treanor is the dean and a professor of law at Fordham University School of Law.

Mark Tushnet is the Carmack Waterhouse Professor of Constitutional Law at Georgetown University Law Center.

Adrian Vermeule is a professor of law at the University of Chicago.

Index

The editor and publishers gratefully acknowledge permission to reprint material in the following chapters of this book, which appeared previously, in different form, in the publications cited:

"War and the American Constitutional Order": 56 *Vanderbilt Law Review* 1815 (2003).

"Emergencies and the Idea of Constitutionalism" and "Defending Korematsu?": 2003 *Wisconsin Law Review* 273.

"Accommodating Emergencies": 56 *Stanford Law Review* 605 (2003).

"Between Civil Libertarianism and Executive Unilateralism": 5 *Theoretical Inquiries in Law* (2003) and 2 *International Journal of Constitutional Law* 296 (2004).

"Realizing Constitutional and International Norms in the Wake of September 11": *The Migrations of Threat: National Security after September 11th*, ed. John Tirman (2003).

"The War on Terrorism and the End of Human Rights": *War after September 11*, ed. Verna V. Gehring (2002), and 22 *Philosophy and Public Policy Quarterly* 9 (2002).

Library of Congress Cataloging-in-Publication Data
The constitution in wartime : beyond alarmism and complacency /
Mark Tushnet, editor.
p. cm. — (Constitutional conflicts)
Includes bibliographical references and index.
ISBN 0-8223-3456-9 (cloth : alk. paper)
ISBN 0-8223-3468-2 (pbk. : alk. paper)
1. War and emergency powers — United States. I. Tushnet, Mark V., 1945– II. Title.
III. Series.
KF5060.C58 2005
342.73'0628 — dc22
2004015809